S0-AWB-157

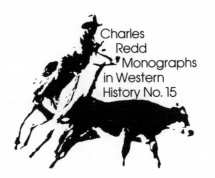

Charles
Redd
Monographs
in Western
History No. 15

Community Development in the American West: Past and Present Nineteenth and Twentieth Century Frontiers

Jessie L. Embry and Howard A. Christy, Editors

Charles Redd Center for Western Studies

Western
Amer.
F
591
C47
no. 15

*The Charles Redd Monographs in Western
History are made possible by a grant from
Charles Redd. This grant served as the basis
for the establishment of the Charles Redd
Center for Western Studies at Brigham Young
University.*

---

*Center editors: Thomas G. Alexander
Howard A. Christy*

ISBN   0-933375-00-X

Copyright 1985
Charles Redd Center for Western Studies
Brigham Young University
Provo, Utah 84602
All rights reserved
Printed in the United States of America

Distributed by Signature Books, Salt Lake City, Utah

4-21-87

Contents

Introduction

When Charles Redd endowed the Charles Redd Center for Western Studies in 1972, he explained, "I would like somehow to get into the hearts and souls of young people the lessons of history, particularly those of Western America. . . . Learning of the successful settlement of this country, we may gain courage to face squarely the challenges and problems of present-day frontiers." Since then the Redd Center has sponsored lecture series and published monographs to help fulfill Redd's edict to learn more about the settlement of the American West.

The West is now facing a new frontier. With the development of new energy sources in the region, towns and cities that were almost in the process of dying are now growing rapidly. By studying the past and the current changes taking place in these communities we can better meet the challenges and problems that Charles Redd described.

The essays in this volume look at the development of communities in the West, past and present. The first two essays deal with current problems in the American West. John L. Sorenson looks at the "West as a Human Problem" and compares the region with less-developed countries where national resources are exploited for another area's development. Stan L. Albrect describes the sociocultural changes that energy development have brought to the West.

The next essays deal with the history of communities in the West. Edward A. Geary and G. Wesley Johnson provide frameworks in which to view the development of towns and cities by using as examples Huntington, a small town in rural Utah, and the spreading metropolis of Phoenix, Arizona. Stanley B. Kimball, Michael S. Raber, and Jessie L. Embry then look at specific communities. Dr. Kimball looks at the economic life of Heber C. Kimball, whose large polygamous family was a community by itself. Dr. Raber and Ms. Embry examine the roles of the Church of Jesus Christ of Latter-day Saints, its leaders, and individual settlers in Utah communities through studies of Spring City and Heber City.

The final two essays examine the roles of business and law in the development of communities in the West. Leonard J. Arrington looks at three Mormon families as a model for the examination of the influence of outside money in the settlement of the Mormon Great Basin. Lastly, Larry R. Gerlach focuses on a lynching in Salt Lake City, Utah as an example of the difficulties of maintaining law and justice in the frontier West.

A number of people have provided editorial and proofreading assistance for this volume. The Charles Redd Center's secretaries, Lori Warren and Jennifer Dean read the preliminary drafts of the papers. Natalie Ethington also read the papers many times and provided valuable assistance and encouragement. Alan Cherry, Rhonda V. Crousey, and Brenda Weber also helped proofread the final page proofs. Their dedication, patience, and friendship made this book possible.

Human Issues in the Development of the American West and Other Less Developed Areas

John L. Sorenson

In 1980 John L. Sorenson, Professor of Anthropology at Brigham Young University, suggested the need for more studies of "The West as a Human Problem" to better understand the changes that are taking place with energy development and environmental concerns in the West. During 1981 and 1982 the Redd Center sponsored a series of lectures dealing with that issue, and Dr. Sorenson gave the keynote address. In this essay, he compares the American West with developing nations where there is a dependence on the export of natural resources and the import of finished goods in which case the real decision-making power is controlled by outside people. Using Utah as a case study, he asks how westerners may understand their position in relation to the process of change and how they might modify it to their best interests.

There was a time, until about a hundred years ago, when concern about what was happening to the American West did not exist. Then uneasiness began to rise to public awareness. By the 1980s it is so fashionable to puzzle over the West's fate that one more look at the issue may seem redundant. Still, there are important things not yet said.

The difficulties began when "the West" was no more than a few miles from the Atlantic coast. Almost from the first, land was seized and exploited by immigrants holding the view that the new country's resources were unlimited and its native possessors of no consequence in deciding how the land should be used. Those attitudes moved westward with the flow of settlers. Each new frontier went through the same two-step process. First, nature was whipped and tamed—transformed to different order from what it had been. For example, passenger pigeons, whose billions had darkened midwestern skies, were utterly exterminated; then the uncountable bison of the Great Plains were slaughtered so that the species barely survived into the twentieth century. Some cynics have charged that the hoped for Garden of Eden had been turned into a wasteland. But others rejoined that 747 airplanes and fields of hybrid corn are inherently superior to mere wild fowl and forests. Even the mountains were subdued. Thus, for example, the Oquirrhs overlooking Salt Lake City have been chewed up and spat out in order to make copper to electrify our lives and provide dividends for stockholders. Is a damaged landscape and fouled air worth the homes and businesses payroll and profits have funded? Depending upon one's cultural and moral orientation, the process of subduing nature has yielded either evil or good, or, more likely, both.

A second constant has been the reflection in society and its symbols of what we have done to nature. The type of personality that gains satisfaction through confronting and overcoming natural (and social) obstacles has been favored throughout American history. The frontiersman, gunfighter, athlete, inventor, go-getter businessman, and robber baron monopolist all have sought similar psychic satisfaction—the feeling of success from mastery over opponents.

The social structure of the country has devoloped in tune with this personality feature. One segment of that structure has provided the "free enterprise," laissez-faire business setting which many people see as the essence of American life. The family farm and single family housing are related manifestations. Science and education are other scenes where individual "success" is encouraged and rewarded; in turn, their growth has depended upon a steady supply of striving individuals. America's heroes illustrate how pervasive is the factor of overcoming the odds. We salute, or envy, both John D. Rockefeller and John Wayne and Henry Ford as well as Henry David Thoreau.

Some Americans turn their admiration for achievement into justification for the concentration of massive wealth and power in a few hands. They tolerate or even enjoy ostentatious displays of wealth and privilege out of respect for what they consider a mainspring—the desire to "get ahead"—which makes so much of our society run.

During the course of westward expansion in the United States, the interplay of psychological, economic, cultural, and ideological factors has produced the widespread view that what now goes under such titles as "economic development" (formerly it was more often called something like "taming the West"), inevitably involved drastic transformation of nature and humanity. However one judges that matter, the sequence is clear: capital accumulated in established urban centers has been invested in lesser-developed areas, then the political and social establishment in the older areas has controlled the pattern of resource exploitation in the new areas, thereby also controlling the economic, social, and political forms of those areas.

Although all of the nation's frontiers have been exploited in this manner, I have chosen to look at Utah as a case study, because, in addition to its being quite representative of the American West, it is my home and data concerning it is easy to obtain.

We shall see Utah shares significant characteristics with many nations worldwide and that what has been learned about those nations and the effects of "development" upon them help define and illuminate problems facing Utah. Among the salient characteristics of the "developing" or "less-developed" nations with which Utah compares are the following:

1. Population weighted heavily on the young side with high fertility and high mortality;

2. Dependence on the export of natural resources and the import of finished goods (with, in most cases, an attendant disadvantageous balance of trade);

3. Decision-making power in the hands of those outside the area ("colonial" or "imperial" dominance);

4. Unsophisticated educational system and low rates of literacy and information flow;

5. Low levels of health and of medical service;

6. Inferior technology and infrastructure, with greater dependence on agriculture and mining as against manufacturing or services;

7. Low individual incomes;

8. Comparatively low rates of participation in the exercise of power and rights by individual citizens;

9. Concentration of wealth in the hands of a few;

10. Traditional rather than modern world view or religion;

11. Tendency for local elites to align their interests with and imitate their counterparts in the dominating centers; and

12. Adoption by acculturation to a social reward system which favors the personal characteristics exhibited by leaders in the external centers, thus replicating a generally materialistic, aggressive system of human relations.

This is not a complete, carefully articulated, or new theory of development. Much of what is said is almost self-evident to students of the subject. My purpose is only to develop a way to think usefully about a particular problem involving mountain America and its development. For that purpose only a general treatment is required.

Note, too, that I am not primarily moralizing about development, although as a participant I cannot ignore the effects it has on my life and that of my neighbors. My major aim, however, is to illuminate what options are open to those of us affected—not to praise or decry.

What is termed the development process may *not* be inevitable. Some nations and peoples seem to have at least temporarily declined to accept it as a course of action for themselves. Burma, several Latin American republics, and various African nations are examples. But most countries have been forcibly modernized, co-opted, or decimated if they held back. The large majority of the world's peoples—at least for the last three hundred years—have found that biological and cultural viability (or even comparative safety) in the world has been achieved only by following the essentials of the development sequence, with increasing mechanization, secularization, and so on. Thus, former variety in the human family has been replaced by increasing sameness (to the dismay of anthropologists). If there ever were any of Rousseau's noble savages, apparently none remain today. Nor do novel social experiments fare better; they too have to accommodate to the general development pattern.

In this century a general world system of nations has come about. Where a century ago significant portions of the earth's population still avoided involvement in that system, such isolation no longer exists, except for small groups in extremely remote areas. Essentially, all nations and people are entrained in a common modernizing, interrelating trend which shows no signs of abating. That trend involves far more than technology and communication; it results in major changes in thinking, feeling, and perceiving.[1]

Nations and regions may be reliably assigned to points on a scale of modernization according to objective criteria established by examining the history of the process. A standard source such as Taylor and Hudson's *World Handbook of Political and Social Indicators* illustrates how some of the factors mentioned above relate to where a nation stands on the scale.[2] For example, those authors show that, based on data for 1966, the four nations with the best infant mortality rate (Sweden, The Netherlands, Iceland, and Norway) were also high on other modernization indices. In contrast, the nations with the highest infant mortality (Saudi Arabia, Libya, Upper Volta, and Gabon), with the recent exception of Saudi Arabia, were very low on the scale of development and modernization. Another example is income distribution. The greatest degree of concentration of income among the elite occurred in Guatemala, Jamaica, Venezuela, and Mexico, while income was most evenly spread in the United Kingdom, Sweden, Israel, and Australia—nations much higher on the modernization scale. Further such comparisons yield a similar pattern, that is, nations suffering the worst human conditions were in most cases at the low end of the total modernization scale.

Of course, all nations are in process of change, so the absolute values marking the extremes of any such scale will change over time. Moreover, individual nations will also be increasing on certain developmental indices at a faster rate than other nations, depending on their history and culture. For example, Japan a century ago might well have had an income distribution not much different from Guatemala or Jamaica in 1966, but over the intervening years, that situation has changed with the modernization of the Japanese people so that the income indicator now is far nearer that seen in Scandinavia. The Japanese have been "catching up," on that measure at least. Such special considerations do not, nevertheless, negate the general value of a worldwide scale of development.

What happens when Utah is placed on such a scale, as though the state were a nation? Take a single index, infant mortality, for example. In 1920 (the earliest year for which we have statistics) Utah was at the 1966 level of the Philippines, Yugoslavia, and El Salvador. (Of course the 1920 rate for those three countries would have been far lower than their 1966 level.) By 1930 Utah's rate had improved, from 71 deaths per 1,000 live births a decade earlier to 57—up to the 1966 level of Nicaragua and Guyana. By 1945 it reached the mortality rate attained by Taiwan and Bulgaria in 1966. The 1960 data show that Utah's infant mortality had improved beyond the figure for the United States to match Denmark and New Zealand, and by 1972 Utah's rate was equal to that for Sweden in 1966, then the highest ranking country in the world on this index.[3] These data show that although a comparatively poor state of infant health prevailed from the first European-American settlement until 1920, Utah made dramatic improvement in the succeeding forty years. Presumably, many of the same factors were then at work in Utah—an increase in hospitals and doctors per capita, mass health education and improved sanitation—which are today lifting Mozambique and Papua New Guinea toward the same levels.

If we were to consider other measures of Utah's movement up the development ladder, the results would differ somewhat according to the factor examined, for any nation (or state) has strong as well as weak points in its profile of development characteristics. "Developed" is, after all, an umbrella concept. It is considered in terms of the statistics used here as simply the set of characteristics exhibited by the nations most often found at the head of the list on the various indices. No single or overall index could possibly convey more than a general impression of the status of a particular country and the unique historical course of its change process. Thus Utah, considered as though it were a developing nation, would rank near the top on education and literacy, but on fertility and average income it behaves more like a less-developed land. But let us look at some specifics in Utah's developmental progression.

Geographical isolation from the mainstream of history is one cause of low development. Pioneer Mormon Utah was physically distant from the key sources of innovative ideas and wealth in the world of the nineteenth century. Besides, the leaders purposely tried to keep "outside" influences from affecting their people. Reduced to a technologically minimal level by the exigencies of the migration across the plains to the mountains, and further robbed of material potency by having to meet entirely new environmental conditions upon their arrival, the Latter-day Saints of the 1850s stood at an extremely simple level by almost any social, political, or economic criterion. While we lack objective indicators for that period, it would be surprising if those pioneers had been living at a level as high as, say, modern Burma. The first Utahns, at mid-century, were forced to concentrate on bare survival.

At the time the railroad arrived in 1869, the territory's economy was predominantly agrarian. Technology was nearly all at a hand-tool level. Nonhuman energy sources were limited to little more than local use of water power for milling and the use of horses and oxen for draft. Prepared roads were effectively absent. Culinary water came from open streams, while schools were few, rudimentary, and intermittent. Commerce did without currency for the most part, and use of printed media of communication was rare.

The sudden arrival in Utah around 1870 of complex technology, substantial capital, imported goods, and political norms from outside the territory caused as much trauma here as in those overt/exotic colonies where British, French, German, or Dutch flags were being raised in the late 1800s. The so-called Utah War was "pacification" similar to the British attempt to subdue the Ashanti of western Africa; both cases were based on cultural misinterpretations rather than on rebellion which was claimed as cause. In Utah, merchants and other would-be "developers" stirred up demands for military and political protection as much in Utah as their counterparts under Dutch rifles in the East Indies or later the gunboats of various European and American navies in China. The reaction of affected peoples tended to follow a psychological sequence of, first, resistance (in most cases futile) to the incoming changes; then a less-than-rational revitalization movement (or "crisis cult"),[4] which tried in terms of wishful ritual to make the new ways miraculously go away; and finally, reluctant accommodation, turned into enthusiasm for the new ways as local leaders climbed on the invaders' bandwagon.[5] While no one at that time used the word "imperialized," Utah was in fact so handled in the Victorian Era about as completely as scores of others of the world's less-developed areas.

The psychology governing social relations between the dominant group and those dominated was also parallel in all these colonial cases, and in accordance with European values of the time. It was seen to be "the white man's burden" to bring enlightenment and civilization to the benighted Mormons as much as to the demoralized American Indians or the native peoples of Africa and the Pacific. Everywhere, civilizing meant christianizing, educating, and clothing the "savages" or "barbarians" while economically exploiting them. Their "beastly customs" had to be exterminated, the dominant group concluded. In the Pacific Islands it was especially sexual looseness, as defined by the Christian missionaries, which it was felt must be controlled. Meanwhile, antislavery societies had their hands full around the world, not just with the U.S. South, and Mormon polygamy was just one more of the targets of the numerous reformers of the time. Schools to bring modernizing education to young Mormons and to succor plural wives who were expected to flee the "harems" were part of the burden that Christian church people dutifully—even enthusiastically—undertook. "The Mormon problem" was not seen to differ in kind from those caused by other subject peoples. In fact, Arrington, Haupt, Bitton, and Bunker have shown that popular and literary propaganda characterized the Mormons as only another sort of "backward race," a kind of white "nigger" of low intelligence, lazy, lascivious, and cunning.[6] Like the others they needed to be saved from themselves by "their betters."

This sketch is not a caricature. It is a fact that Mormons were no more and no less "underdeveloped" (to use today's kinder term) in the eyes of the self-designated civilized people of the European continent and northeastern North America than hundreds of others. Utahns (that is, Mormons) were just as targeted and just as manipulated as the others. Such rationalization was apparently essential for the bearers of the dominant urban, capitalist culture to manage the psychological burdens which their own actions were placing upon themselves.

Expansionist societies of the time were driven by cultural and historical forces they did not understand. So were the groups they came to dominate. Those with power were pressed forward by imperatives in their systems—the strongest one being material. The wealth-getting motives first released and rewarded in northwest Europe from about the fifteenth century both pushed and pulled men to the ambition to "seek their fortune" across the face of the globe. The invention of the corporation as an organizational device was one important feature which facilitated the expansion, for it permitted the accumulation of formidable amounts of usable capital while freeing its users from personal guilt about the consequences of how it was to be used. Increasing technical skill used up unprecedented amounts of "natural resources" which in turn spurred further expansion. Simultaneously, growing literacy and the use of printing speeded up the process of systematically accumulating knowledge, which was growing at a pace never before seen. (Kurt Mendelsohn believes that this accumulation above all constituted "the secret of western domination.")[7] The Protestant ethic and related beliefs and values provided new justification for wealth getting. And finally there was the development of administrative concepts and procedures by which government could take increasingly effective power over citizens. All these elements had matured by the late nineteenth century to the point where small groups of power holders could undertake and maintain dominion almost anywhere on earth they chose.

In Utah, the spread of the railroads, development of the rich Bingham Canyon copper stores by Kennecott, manipulation of the local sugar industry by Atlantic seaboard capitalists, and a host of other interventions by national power interests were all part of this scenario. The role of particular personalities involved in the events made little difference to the end result. Heroes, villains, conspiracies, and political maneuvering little affected the overall sweep of events. As long as the intertwined economic, political, social, and ideological forces which launched the general western European system and propelled it to all continents remained unchallenged, events proceeded toward the exhaustion of that system's logic and vigor.[8]

Events in the twentieth century continued along the same general lines, at least at first. In Utah, local power companies were gobbled up by eastern capitalists and their holding companies. Trainloads of copper, lead, gold, silver, and coal heading east met trainloads of finished goods only obtainable from the developed industrial centers heading west,[9] a classical picture of a colonial economy. Prices and freight rates never favored Utahns, any more than they did other colonials. The core of the local economy was funded from New York, or Chicago, or London, where decisions about the economy were made with little but incidental concern for the welfare of Utahns.

At the onset of World War II the federal government suddenly became a major funder and controller of Utah's economic development. Yet control remained external, so little changed as far as Utah was concerned, except to increase the rate of development. A federal agency built the Geneva steel plant, although effectively the expenditure, greater than the value of all existing manufacturing facilities in Utah, turned out to be on behalf of the U.S. Steel Corporation.[10] (Nobody else would have the capital and marketing capability to run it after the war except the nation's biggest steel corporation.) The various defense installations put into Utah in the last forty years are again the result of decisions made by the industrial-military complex, as President Eisenhower aptly termed it. As much as with the old East India Company, that focus of power is only concerned with completing its own agenda.

Historical examples demonstrate that dominance by the developed centers can be temporarily thwarted. But the costs to a people or nation of resisting the dominant world system have been great, for the result has at least been increased poverty and suffering due to economic and technological lag. Ultimately, nonparticipators have been threatened with losing out in international competition to the point of effective extinction.

Two main factors distinguish the Utah experience. Both are too complex to be easily described in a word, but they essentially involve education in the first case and demographics in the second.

Around 1891 it had become clear to a decisive core of Mormon leaders that survival demanded giving up some Mormon "peculiarity." Many lay Utahns had already reached the same conclusion and acted on it. For example, the 1890 decision to abandon polygamy involved "the apparent promise of Mormon leaders, in return for statehood, to be 'loyal' to American institutions generally."[11] However, it also became necessary to identify institutions within which Utah and its people could actively participate in the life of the nation and thus the developed world. Economic and technological links were among the first to be forged, but education became the most dominant.

Emphasis on educational activity was encouraged in Utah by the fact that the (English) language and cultural/historical background of the Mormons predisposed them to participate in the dominant European intellectual and technical system. Their pioneer experience, moreover, had encouraged a pragmatic bent already valued in the U.S., yet they retained a strong idealism. Still other religious beliefs, for example concern about the value of "intelligence," favored an educational emphasis. In fact, for many years Utahn's have been the most schooled of any developing area.

Although there were some doctrinal and custom-based barriers to full acceptance by Utahns of the values and methods of U.S. secular schooling, sufficient accommodation was made in a short period to minimize those obstacles. By 1926, when the U.S. Bureau of Education made its important *Survey of Education in Utah*, high marks were already being given the state's schools in terms of the national establishment's frankly development oriented philosophy of education as laid out at the outset of the report:

> The history of civilization is largely the record of man's attempt to control his environment and of his successes and failures in obtaining control. Nature has conditioned the character of the fundamental stages of the struggle. But as man has learned more about his environment and about himself, he has increased tremendously his ability to transform and to utilize nature's work for his own purposes. This is education defined in its simplest terms. Man's struggle with his natural environment determines the trend of his education, and successful learning enables him increasingly to modify the influences of nature upon his own progress.[12]

The document makes clear that Utahns had quickly learned how to get ahead in terms of the external system's educational scheme, by picking up on the rhetoric of the nation's development aims.

Within decades thoroughly up-to-date public schools and three major institutions of higher education developed along

Utah's core settlement strip. They involved a costly investment which allowed a major movement of local people into the external system of high skills. Only vastly greater investment could have accomplished anything like it in developing an institutional connection to the outside world in the techological or agricultural sectors. Thus a mechanism was forged rapidly and at low cost by which Utah would make its prime articulation to "the world." No developing nation has succeeded in forging a two-way connection between local and world systems with such immediate efficacy, I believe. Through that connection hundreds of thousands of Utahns— educators, scientists, physicians, lawyers, writers, and artists— have gone forth building more and more firmly that link to the world scene. At the same time, of course, Utah's educational apparatus has become an extension and tool of the external establishment. That is, through that channel a majority of Utahns have become among the most committed of America's believers in the development ideology.

As mentioned, the second unusual feature of the Utah development pattern is demographic. Encouragement by Mormon leaders to have large families, the need for family members as workers in the agrarian system, and heavy immigration combined to produce a population which quickly outran the state's very limited resources of arable land. In little more than two generations from first settlement, a surplus of labor had developed in rural Utah. For another two generations agricultural developments such as water reclamation, commercial canning, and dry farming increased rural productivity enough to absorb some of those, and mining and commerce-based urban growth drew away others. By the 1920s, however, when education was first emphasized in the Intermountain West, growing numbers of Utah's young people could see little other alternative to schooling in nonagricultural, technical fields as the way to economic and cultural opportunity. And more often than not, pursuing that training meant leaving Utah—although many well educated emigrants from the state have maintained strong ties to their places of birth and return when development has allowed to. Another demographically significant aspect is that slow growth in the non-agricultural economic base also meant few newcomers to the state. As result, ethnic and societal homogeneity was essentially maintained.

Whatever the merits of the argument as to what factors characterize the state, it is apparent that Utah's primary mode of adaptation to the sociocultural and economic system which dominates the world has been education. Exporting minerals has been significant in economic terms, but if we ask the question, what has been the prime connection between Utah and the external world by which influence has passed in both directions, the answer is education.

This emphasis is not due just to historical accident or materialistic factors. The whole configuration of the area's culture is involved. Utah's educational activity is a distillation and expression of the whole set of values and social relationships which provide the foundation and justification for that education.[13]

The treatment so far has concentrated on Utah, but other areas in the West have had a broadly parallel history. Ecologically and demographically their situation was similar enough that Mormons could settle in some of those regions more or less successfully on the same basis as in Utah, at least up until the turn of the century. Furthermore, the values categorized as Utahn (and Mormon) are shared widely in neighboring areas by both Mormons and those of other faiths.

In the last few years, new demands have been imposed on Utah and the surrounding states by the holders of power in the developed centers, demands which are in part an outgrowth of the perception that this area is an "empty quarter" (to use Joel Garreau's label).[14] Such a "world view" insists that raw resources continue to be stripped from "unresisting" places like Utah and shipped to outside industrial centers. Other resources of the West—open space, clean air, scenery, and water—are also demanded. A concomitant expectation, looking in from the outside, is that the social and cultural system of this area may be sacrificed if necessary to the "needs of civilization" as conceived in Washington, or Houston, or even Geneva or Tokyo.

If the development process disturbs little Delta or Rock Springs, little more compunction is felt by decision makers than if Indian tribes of inner Brazil are exterminated by the quest for greater GNP or if the people of the Tuamotu archipelago are damaged by French nuclear testing. Like other dependent people, Utahns probably would not, even if they chose to try, be able to resist those externally made dictates very effectively.

What responses are possible by an affected population? Throughout history some peoples have responded to outside influences by resorting to nonrational means. A representative pattern has been the formation of a crisis cult or revitalization movement. For example, frazzled American Indians for a short period in the late 1800s were encouraged by the Ghost Dance cult, which promised to reverse the decimation they had suffered and the loss of integrity in their cultures. Sometimes movements have arisen which have dealt with the confusion of sociocultural change sufficiently to permit a people's survival rather than extinction, as in the classic case of Handsome Lake and the Seneca Indians.[15] For another example, following the advent of the railroad in Utah, the united order movement of the 1870s was instigated by Mormon Church authorities.[16] While it had no chance for enduring success in economic terms, it did serve as a bridge to the new order of things; like other rituals at stressful moments, it at least facilitated reordering the feelings and behavior of the distressed for whom life would never again be as it was. The 1890 Manifesto, which terminated official approval for polygamy among Utah Mormons, resulted in a diffuse crisis cult that finally crystallized organizationally among diehards as a set of fundamentalist sects. Although this kind of movement probably has helped in some cases to maintain psychologically adaptive group life it seems highly questionable that a nonrational response to current problems in the American West could accomplish anything positive. That dead end should surely be avoided in favor of strategically sounder options.

The new thrust of development in the West is journalistically depicted in Garreau's *The Nine Nations of North America*.

He portrays powerful institutions and governments wanting the oil, gas, coal, water, molybdenum, and other substances with which Utah and its neighbors are richly endowed. Then there is the military, which demands other things, especially "empty" land. Since 1975 this area has looked like a Christmas tree from the directions of Denver, Houston, Los Angeles, and Washington, Garreau suggests. How to get the good things off the tree without getting burned is the question, not the safety, let alone the beauty, of the tree. Money has bought some things the developers have wanted, and these developers have allied a portion of the West's population with their aims. Co-opting some of the West's best and brightest to serve as agents of the development forces goes on apace. Meanwhile, governmental/ military power has certainly lain close at hand in the background pushing the process forward.

Still, while the juggernaut of development has so far only been slowed, perhaps some things are changing. At least new adaptive responses to development may now be possible.

No substantial force arose to challenge western civilization's idea of "progress" until about sixty years ago. With World War I, certain questions began to receive widespread attention. "How can such war represent 'progress?'" The retreat of the United States from idealism, manifested in defeat by the congress of the proposal to join the League of Nations, spurred more doubts. The cynicism that infected the 1920s, the sour outcome of the prohibition experiment, the stock market crash of 1929, and the worldwide depression of the 1930s, followed by the advent of Hitler and the first hints of the holocaust, badly shook the belief in progress, at least in some quarters. Optimism could no longer be taken for granted; it had to be cultivated carefully to survive.

Then came World War II, culminated at Hiroshima. How was one to believe in the virtue of unrestrained development, modernization and secularization in the face of possible planetwide destruction? The question was not well answered, yet optimism, nurtured by the peace at war's end surfaced again. The anticolonial, revolutionary movements of the postwar 1940s and 1950s spread the gospel of development to areas which previously had had little reason to expect major benefits from the process. Prosperity in the U.S. and the renascence of Germany and Japan carried along other nations to renewal of a sense of progress.

A new downturn came in the 1960's with turmoil and division in the developed countries and "brushfire" wars elsewhere. The apparent promise had faded from the Cuban revolution, India's euphoria upon independence had turned to dismay over the vast scale of her problems, China's internal changes left it confused, and the Third World's smaller nations found the going harder and harder. Like India and China, they were pressed by growing populations in the face of a development which did not bring rewards they had expected. Even among the major powers, the energy crisis and complicated issues involving inflation made the 1970s still more enigmatic.

In country after country, one response to the loss of optimism has been to question the old assumptions of economic "progress." Built-in waste and obsolescence, the destruction of the environment, and the unsatisfactory outcomes of what had been claimed for solidly desirable development have all fostered a reassessment of goals as among the Greens of western Europe. Proposals have been made to limit population and resource exploitation to stabilize the earth's human burden. These proposals have received support on a considerable scale. Expectations about the future have at least been scaled down. Just possibly the halcyon days of the old man-conquering-nature view have passed.

The question is unanswerable whether a substantial change has yet taken place in the views of the general public in the developed world at large, in the United States, or in Utah. Are Americans prepared to change hero John Wayne for a John Muir or a Henry David Thoreau? Are westerners at all clear on what they do *not* want? Have Utah people considered what they desire Utah to become, other than richer and full of children? Options, resolutions of the questions, costs, and benefits at issue about development here and now seem not clear enough for a new consensus, but some kind of change seems in the air.

Everything said so far can be summarized thus:

1. A philosophical, social, cultural, and political mechanism developed in northwestern Europe for subduing nature, enriching its practitioners and giving them power over those less adept in such matters. And that mechanism has been expanding in surges across the globe for centuries. Its modern version often goes under the label "economic development."

2. Characteristic relationships prevail between the developers and the weaker peoples whose territories get developed. Some benefits flow each way, but costs are less symmetrically distributed. In the long run the weaker groups tend either to follow the ways of the dominators or to suffer demoralization.

3. Responses by people in the less-developed areas are often nonrational, and sometimes thoroughly irrational, resulting in added psychic burdens for them in the long run, in dealing with their changing world.

4. Utah specifically and the American West more generally display many of characteristics of the less-developed areas or developing nations in their relations to the dominant centers of social, economic, political, and military power.

5. Yet Utah's unique accommodation to past development pressures has produced unusual features which deserve attention as we choose a future course of action.

6. Powerful forces are at play pushing a new round of old style development in the Mountain West.

I suggest that Utah and the surrounding area in the West may turn out to be the first developing area in history to have its own capability to understand in advance what further man-against-nature of the classic sort would mean for the area itself. The concentration here of persons and institutions competent in research allows the Intermountain West the chance to do what Indonesia, Bolivia, or Algeria, whose development has been determined by largely external agencies and persons, could not. The unique educational circumstances in this area may have made it possible for us to envision and perhaps shape our future. It will not be easy. Nor can it be delayed without missing the chance. Without doubt using those special local capabilities to accomplish the necessary research about ourselves and those who would affect us will demand a high level of leadership and discipline.

But are we not already studying the issues? Some claim so. Studies are indeed being made of fragmentary issues— produced by "social impact" and "planning" projects—but many of those are red herrings. Few state or local officials or prospective developers are willing to wait for or pay the costs of studies of the scale, scope, and depth necessary to yield the comprehensive understanding necessary for informed decision making by the public.

What is needed is a long-range, widespread, and coordinated series of such studies. They would take a minimum of five years. A ten-year activity would have a better chance of success. But, some might say, by then we could be in such deep trouble that nothing we learned could make a difference. Perhaps, but careful, comprehensive study is a risk that must be taken in order to prevent premature, flawed conclusions. Such studies should examine all aspects of life in Utah and the West under the conditions of development. Piecemeal papers on economics, school attendance, crime, and a few other of the standard categories of the usual "impact assessments" will not be enough. From beauty to beliefs to health, the entire array of life needs careful examination of how things have been and how they are changing. The lessons of development elsewhere also must be considered. What is happening in Alaska and Nigeria and Ecuador under development may be relevant to understanding what could happen here. Local conditions may differ in degree but probably not in kind. Not only negative impacts but positive ones should, of course, be considered. Only the ideologically blind and one-sided would conclude beforehand that all development was bad.

We might end up not learning enough. But we would gain in any case by doing what we can do ourselves—taking our own action ourselves rather than lamenting or welcoming what outsiders say is good for us, or complaining after the fact because *they* failed to have our best interests at heart.

Will such studies be done? I am not optimistic that they will. The educational process which has linked us to the external world might also have robbed our potential researchers of the needed vision and freedom. Our research and educational capacities may be so oriented now to serving the development powers, or we may be so comfortable doing nothing, that not enough of us will accept the challenge. I would like to be wrong on that point.

NOTES

1. Alex Inkeles and David H. Smith, *Becoming Modern: Individual Change in Six Developing Countries* (Cambridge: Harvard University Press, 1974).

2. Charles L. Taylor and Michael C. Hudson, *World Handbook of Political and Social Indicators*, 2d ed. (New Haven: Yale University Press, 1972), 263-65.

3. Ibid., 253-55; Utah Department of Public Health, Bureau of Vital Statistics, *Statistical Summary* (Salt Lake City: Utah Department of Public Health, 1960, 1972).

4. Weston La Barre, "Materials for a History of Crisis Cults: A Bibliographic Essay," *Current Anthropology* 12 (1971):3-44.

5. A. F. C. Wallace, "Revitalization Movements," *American Anthropologist* 58 (1956):264-81.

6. Leonard J. Arrington and John Haupt, "Intolerable Zion: The Image of Mormonism in Nineteenth Century American Literature," *Western Humanities Review* 22 (1968):284-90; Gary L. Bunker and Davis Bitton, *The Mormon Graphic Image, 1834-1914: Cartoons, Caricatures and Illustrations* (Salt Lake City: University of Utah Press, 1983); John L. Sorenson, "The Mormon as 'Nigger,'" Presentation at the Flea Market of Ideas, Brigham Young University, November 1977.

7. Kurt Mendelsohn, *The Secret of Western Domination* (New York: Praeger, 1976).

8. Immanuel Wallerstein, *The Modern World-System: Capitalist Agriculture and the Origins of the European World-Economy in the Sixteenth Century* (New York: Academic Press, 1976); Fred Cottrell, *Energy and Society* (New York: McGraw-Hill, 1955); Richard N. Adams, *Energy and Structure: A Theory of Social Power* (Austin: University of Texas Press, 1975).

9. Chauncy D. Harris, *Salt Lake City: A Regional Capital* (Chicago: University of Chicago Libraries, 1940), vii, 65-83.

10. John L. Sorenson, "Industrialization and Social Change: A Controlled Comparison of Two Utah Communities," (Ph.D. diss., University of California, Los Angeles, 1961), 44.

11. Leonard J. Arrington, "Economic History of a Mormon Valley," *Pacific Northwest Quarterly* 46 (1955):104.

12. U.S. Department of the Interior, Bureau of Education, "Survey of Education in Utah," *Bulletin* 18 (1926):1.

13. Kenneth R. Hardy, "Social Origins of American Scientists and Scholars," *Science* 185 (9 August 1974):497-506.

14. Joel Garreau, *The Nine Nations of North America* (Boston: Houghton-Mifflin, 1981).

15. A. F. C. Wallace, *The Death and Rebirth of the Seneca* (New York: Knopf, 1970).

16. Leonard J. Arrington, Feramorz Y. Fox, and Dean L. May, *Building the City of God: Community and Cooperation Among the Mormons* (Salt Lake City: Deseret Book Co., 1976), 135-294; L. Dwight Israelsen, "An Economic Analysis of the United Order," *Brigham Young University Studies* 18 (1978):536-62.

2

Paradoxes of Western Energy Development: Sociocultural Factors

Stan Albrecht

A number of communities in the West have grown and experienced a great deal of change as a result of continued exploration for and development of new energy resources. In the following essay, Stan L. Albrecht, Professor of Sociology at Brigham Young University, examines changes in population, agriculture, and the locus of power in the West precipitated by such new development. He shows that the populations in a number of counties in the West have grown dramatically over the last ten years. In addition to growth, there has also been a shift in these communities from an agricultural to essentially an energy based economy where decision making is controlled by large companies and the federal government.

Dr. Albrecht goes on, however, to point out that while the "Gillette Syndrome" has been used to describe the increase in crime rates and housing costs that seemed to accompany the energy boom in Wyoming, communities and companies are spending money to help deal with possible problems and to provide good housing, schooling, and health care in the impacted areas. He then describes several frameworks which attempt to explain the effects of growth on the communities. He points out one important factor that has often not been considered in how communities are impacted: how long people have lived in the community. He concludes that studies of social and cultural changes caused by new development are important "if only so that through the information obtained, communities which still have some ability to decide whether or not they want to encourage energy-related growth may be made aware of the consequences."

The Rocky Mountain and Northern Plains states are currently undergoing some of the most important and far-reaching changes that have occurred in these areas since they were settled well over a century ago. To understand these changes and their significance, one must have some awareness of the major driving forces that are behind them. Energy development is clearly the most important of these. However, the impact of energy development has not occurred independently of other changes that are operating not only in the West but in other segments of U.S. society as well. I begin by reviewing some of these important forces of change before concentrating more specifically on some of the social and community impacts of energy development.

Major Forces of Change in the Rural West

There appear to be four major forces of change: population changes, changes in the agricultural sector, changes in the locus of power, and energy development.

Population Changes

Perhaps the most obvious and pervasive change that we can observe is that of population growth. Even prior to the past decade, the warmer areas of the West and Southwest have experienced some population growth as a function of the expanding recreation and retirement industries. However, the most dramatic changes have occurred since 1970. Prior to the 1970s, the vast majority of rural counties in the Rocky Mountain and Northern Plains states had experienced decades of outmigration of the younger members of their populations as agriculture became less profitable and as opportunities for education and economic advancement became more and more concentrated in the urban communities of the region. The result was that the population of rural counties got both smaller and older.

To illustrate this change, Table 1 lists counties in the states of Utah, Colorado, Wyoming, and Montana that are currently being affected or will be affected by some major energy development project, whether this will be a new mine, a coal-burning power plant, a synthetic fuels plant, or other, similar projects. What is interesting about this type of analysis is that over half of these counties actually had smaller populations in 1970 than they did in 1920. And, in some instances, the populations were significantly smaller. However, if we compare their 1980 populations with their 1970 populations, thirty-eight of the forty counties had reversed the pattern of decline and most had surpassed the population they had in 1920. Five of the counties had grown by over 100 percent in the decade and another ten had grown by over 50 percent. Some had experienced annual growth rates of almost 20 percent during their most rapid growth period.

When this historical pattern of slow or negative population growth and cultural homogeneity is combined with the already occurring and projected future growth rate, the critical nature of the potential social consequences becomes more apparent. The magnitude of projected growth varies from area to area. However, in almost all cases the annual percentage growth is sufficiently large that it promises to challenge severely the ability of the affected communities to respond in an efficient and effective manner. In Sweetwater County, Wyoming, for example, the population increased by only a few more than 400 people between 1960 and 1970, but during the next four years it doubled, increasing by almost 18,500. Low projections for the early 1980s are for an increase of as many as 20,000 and high projections indicate a population increase of an additional 50,000. Projected rates of growth to 1985 or 2000 are equally as high and frequently even higher in other Montana, Wyoming, and Utah counties.

TABLE 1

CHANGES IN ENERGY RESOURCE COUNTIES

County	1920	1970	% Change 1920-1970	Direction of Change	1980	% Change 1970-1980	Direction of Change
COLORADO							
Clear Creek.........	2,891	4,819	66.7	+	7,308	51.6	+
Eagle............	3,385	1,498	121.5	+	13,171	75.7	+
Garfield	9,304	14,821	59.3	+	22,514	51.9	+
Gunnison	5,590	7,578	35.6	+	10,689	41.1	+
Lake	6,630	8,282	24.9	+	8,830	6.6	+
Mineral...........	779	786	0.9	+	804	2.3	+
Moffat	5,129	6,525	27.2	+	13,133	101.3	+
Ouray	2,620	1,546	-41.0	-	1,925	24.5	+
Routt	8,948	6,592	-26.3	-	13,404	103.3	+
San Juan	1,700	831	-51.1	-	833	0.2	+
San Miguel.......	5,281	1,949	-63.1	-	3,192	63.8	+
MONTANA							
Big Horn	7,015	10,057	43.4	+	11,096	10.3	+
Carbon..........	15,279	7,080	-53.7	-	8,099	14.4	+
Custer..........	12,194	12,174	-0.2	-	13,109	7.7	+
Lincoln..........	7,797	18,063	131.7	+	17,752	-1.7	-
Musselshell.......	12,030	3,734	-69.0	-	4,428	18.6	+
Rosebud	8,002	6,032	-24.6	-	9,899	64.1	+
Sanders..........	4,903	7,093	44.7	+	8,675	22.3	+
Silver Bow	60,303	41,981	-30.4	-	38,092	-9.3	-

TABLE 1 (cont.)

County	1920	1970	% Change 1920-1970	Direction of Change	1980	% Change 1970-1980	Direction of Change
UTAH							
Carbon	17,798	15,647	-12.1	-	22,179	41.7	+
Duchesne	8,263	7,299	-11.7	-	12,567	72.1	+
Emery	7,042	5,137	-27.1	-	11,451	122.9	+
Grand	1,813	6,688	268.9	+	8,241	23.2	+
Juab	8,605	4,574	-46.8	-	5,530	20.9	+
Millard	9,945	6,988	-29.7	-	8,970	28.4	+
San Juan	3,496	9,606	174.8	+	12,253	27.6	+
Summit	9,527	5,879	-38.3	-	10,198	73.5	+
Uintah	9,035	12,684	40.4	+	20,506	61.7	+
Washington	7,420	13,669	84.2	+	26,065	90.7	+
Wayne	2,067	1,483	-28.3	-	1,911	28.9	+
WYOMING							
Campbell	5,233	12,957	147.6	+	24,367	88.1	+
Carbon	9,525	13,354	40.2	+	21,896	64.0	+
Converse	7,871	5,938	-24.6	-	14,069	136.9	+
Crook	5,524	4,535	-17.9	-	5,308	17.0	+
Fremont	11,820	28,352	139.9	+	40,251	42.0	+
Hot Springs	5,164	4,952	-4.2	-	5,710	15.3	+
Johnson	4,617	5,587	21.0	+	6,700	19.9	+
Lincoln	12,487	8,640	-30.8	-	12,177	40.9	+
Platte	7,421	6,486	-12.6	-	11,975	84.6	+
Sweetwater	13,640	18,391	34.8	+	41,723	126.9	+
Weston	4,631	6,307	36.2	+	6,106	12.7	+

Source: City and County Data Book, U. S. Census, 1920-1980

Not only have the populations of these counties exploded, they have changed in some other very important ways. For example, they have experienced significant increases in their nonagricultural employment with most of this increase occurring in the mining and construction sectors. As a consequence, their populations have become younger. Construction workers, in particular, tend to be young. Many are single, and those who are married tend to have young families. They are obviously far more mobile. Many construction workers remain in a community for a brief period and then move on. This contrasts with the stability of the existing population. For example, more than half the residents of Millard County in Utah have lived there more than forty years. In addition, the newcomers are much more heterogeneous ethnically, religiously, and culturally. The high level of social and cultural homogeneity of the area in the past is reflected in the fact that most rural counties in Utah have had populations that are over 90 percent Latter-day Saint.

Changes in the Agricultural Sector

Three major developments have occurred in the agricultural sector of the rural west (and of American society more generally) that are of particular interest. First, there has been a major change in the size and in the number of farm operations. On a national scale, in 1940 the average farm size was 167 acres, an increase of 14 percent since 1900. In 1960 it had increased by another 67.9 percent. Ten years later it had increased another 30.4 percent. This trend has been accompanied by a significant drop in employment in agriculture. In the Rocky Mountain states the percentage of farm proprietors as a proportion of total employment in the region declined from 8 percent in 1970 to 6 percent in 1977. There was also a decline between 1970 and 1977 in the number of farm workers as a percentage of total employment from about 3 to 2 percent. Nationally, there is a trend toward increasing part-time farming and the combination of farm and off-farm work by proprietors. The percentage of farm operators reporting some days off-farm work increased by about 10 percent between 1974 and 1978. In Colorado, Utah, and New Mexico, more than half of all farm operators worked off the farm by 1978.[1]

A second major change in agriculture is described by Helmberger:

> Today the farmer is surrounded on all sides by large-scale enterprises that have taken over activities once performed by the family farm. He now produces relatively simple raw materials that are picked up at the farm gate by processors or handlers. On the input side especially, activities once performed by farmers have been displaced by large-scale suppliers. Rather than raising horses and mules and the necessary animal feed, the farmer invests in a tractor and buys oil and gasoline from the petroleum industry. He buys fertilizers and insecticides that substitute for his land and the sweat of his brow. . . . In a word, the family farm has been growing in the horizontal dimension at the same time that more and more activities performed in vertical sequence have been spun off to large-scale marketing and supply firms.[2]

In other words, the family farm, even in those areas where it does still exist, is no longer a self-sufficient, independent unit. It is highly integrated into a system of corporations and regulatory agencies.

A third development in agricultural organization that is widely documented is the introduction of advanced technology and specialized knowledge. The introduction of sophisticated equipment, chemicals, and breeding-hybridization have made it possible to increase productivity while reducing labor intensiveness. The addition of specialized knowledge from agricultural economics, agribusiness management, and horticulture are best incorporated into activities of large corporate entities, not traditional family farms. Consequently, agriculture is not only supplied and marketed through corporations, it is also increasingly a corporate activity.

Locus of Power

The interdependencies noted above in the agricultural community have spread to other areas as well and have resulted in "an organizational structure of rural society that is increasingly controlled by forces that are located outside the local community." That is, the increasing centralization of control both within organizations and in networks of organizations means that control leaves rural society. Lynn England has recently reviewed the decision not to locate the giant Kaiparowitz power plant in Kane County in Utah in these terms:

> The . . . decision regarding the location of a giant power generating complex on the Kaiparowitz Plateau was the joint result of the interaction of large organizations, and the decisions made by those organizations, located far from the communities nearest to [the site]. The major governmental organizations, including the Department of the Interior in Washington, D.C.; the major environmental organizations, including the Sierra Club; and the combine of power firms [from Southern California] were the major actors. To some extent, organizations of the states concerned were involved. The people in the local communities that would be most affected took sides, many of them. But their decisions and actions were within the parameters of the decisions made elsewhere. And when the decision was made to drop the project, the supporters of the development were left to assess the consequences for them of the decisions made elsewhere. The fate of the local communities clearly would have been substantially affected whichever way the decision finally was made. [However], that decision was made primarily by organizations remote from the local area, and on the bases of organizational interests with no intrinsic tie and few extrinsic linkages to that local area.[3]

The Forces of Energy Development

The most important change in the West, however, and one which is the driving force behind most of the others—particularly that of population change—is the dramatic increase in energy-related activity. The combined forces of rapidly increasing demand for energy and the desire to achieve greater national self-sufficiency in meeting energy needs has resulted in accelerating pressures to develop natural resources such as coal, uranium, oil, natural gas, oil shale, tar sands, and geothermal power sources. In fact, it is estimated that as many as 250 separate communities in the Northern Plains and Rocky Mountain states will experience significant energy-related growth in the next few years. Many of these rural communities have developed a stability that has grown out of their particular relationship to what is often a rather harsh natural environment and is closely tied to their traditional focus on agricultural and ranching life-styles. However, like many of the surrounding plant and animal communities, they exhibit a fragility that allows them to be easily and dramatically disrupted by the change associated with rapid population growth, the importation of large numbers of workers with different cultural traditions and life-styles, and the need to respond quickly to accelerating demands on the community infrastructure and its public service delivery system.[4]

It is important for us to recognize, however, that despite the importance of energy development in changing the face of the West, the actual and potential impacts associated with this large-scale development of our energy resources was of relatively little concern until the 1970s.[5] In recent years we have observed significant changes for a number of reasons. Most important among these are the following:

First, citizens nationwide are becoming increasingly environmentally aware and concerned. It was only a little more than a decade ago that a broad array of talk shows, teach-ins, symposia, celebrations, and demonstrations began to introduce millions of Americans to their own culpability, as consumers and voters, for the state of the environment.[6] While the initial focus of this increasing environmental concern was directed toward what Dunlap and Catton have called the twin jaws of a very important vice—resource depletion and pollution[7]—additional concern was soon directed toward some of the manifest as well as latent consequences of policy decisions that would lead to the exploitation of huge supplies of abundant energy resources in the western portion of the United States.

Second, siting of power plants and other large energy facilities has become increasingly remote due to increasingly restrictive environmental laws and regulatory siting criteria. Part of the opposition to the construction of the huge Kaiparowitz Power Plant in southern Utah and to other similar projects in that state and elsewhere resulted from the feeling that the less-populated states were the dumping grounds for California waste. Since California power companies could not meet restrictive environmental regulations in their own state without the expenditure of much larger sums for pollution abatement, the move was toward building the plants in other states and then transporting the relatively clean product—electricity—to their own.

And third, there has been an increasing recognition on the part of industry that work force turnover problems that were becoming so common in unattractive energy boomtowns were becoming incredibly costly. This relationship has accelerated industry involvement in socioeconomic impact assessment and monitoring. More will be said about this later.

These changes are sure to have both positive and negative impacts, and reactions will be based on the perspective individuals bring to the problem. For example, local business leaders who stand to gain from an energy development project will react very differently than will retired persons on fixed incomes who will be negatively impacted by dramatic increases in costs of housing and goods and services. Area residents in fact often face a classic paradox: the benefits energy development brings in the form of new employment and income opportunities have been long sought after; however, few seek the changes in local life-styles that accompany such project-induced growth

Some of the early descriptions of western energy boom-towns were not entirely accurate. The "Gillette Syndrome" was a catchy phrase and brought a lot of publicity to Dr. ElDean Kohrs, then Director of the Central Wyoming Mental Health program.[8] Communities like Rock Springs did experience dramatic increases in crime rates and housing costs and were left ugly and despoiled. However, important lessons were learned and the climate is now much different than it was then. Recent visits to energy centers like Wright, Douglas, and Wheatland, Wyoming; Colstrip, Montana; Craig, Colorado; and Price and Vernal, Utah leave the feeling that communities generally are responding much more effectively to the changes that are being imposed upon them.

There are important reasons for this. For one thing, industries have opened their checkbooks to help alleviate the problems associated with rapid growth. Metz notes that this has occurred for several basic reasons: Much mitigation on the part of industry has been directed toward attracting and maintaining a stable, quality work force. Work force problems are extremely costly. For example, it is estimated that $50 million of the $100 million cost overrun at the first three Jim Bridger units in Rock Springs was attributed to high worker turnover—almost 70,000 workers were employed there during construction. On the other hand, the EPA has estimated that approximately $100 million was saved at the Colorado-Ute Yampa project in Craig, Colorado because of worker mitigation measures.[9] Atlantic-Richfield estimates that to recruit and train a single heavy equipment operator for the Black Thunder Mine in Wyoming costs $15,000; if he leaves because he can't find decent housing for his family, the retraining costs and lost productivity hit hard. This lesson has not been lost on industry and has contributed to the construction of several new communities as one means to provide housing and other needs of large work forces. Atlantic-Richfield built Wright, Wyoming; Exxon is building Battlement Mesa, a community eventually expected to house 20,000 to 25,000 people, near its Colony Oil Shale Project in western Colorado; Plateau Resources has been building the uranium town of Ticaboo in Utah; and so on.

Much mitigation work has also been undertaken to facilitate siting by relieving community anxieties. Following the horror stories of Rock Springs and Gillette, many communities in the West developed a "Chicken Little Syndrome;" that is, the fear that what had happened in those blighted communities would happen in their own. Thus, to facilitate community support and involvement, industry has become more actively involved in upfront planning. Some of this hasn't been as up front as would be desirable, but it is still directed toward placating and supporting local communities in their efforts to cope with the changes that are being imposed upon them. A good example is the recent formation of the Overthrust Industrial Association. In the Overthrust Belt around Evanston, Wyoming, some thirty-five concerned companies have joined together to help communities deal with overheated growth. Unfortunately, this association was not formed until 1980, which was five years after the oil boom began. By then, area roads were already crumbled by heavy trucks, housing was critically short, and services were badly overloaded.

Finally, other mitigation efforts are an involuntary response to community and state laws and other political and economic pressures. The Wyoming Industrial Siting Act formalizes a negotiating process whereby industry, in order to be licensed by the industrial siting board, must reach an agreement up front on a mitigation package. That is, specific actions are negotiated and contracted such as an addition to the local high school or a new recreation center. Other states do not yet have such, but in the state of Utah the Department of Community and Economic Development is in the process of formulating what is being called The Utah Approach to socio-economic impact mitigation. The approach calls for the development of state, local, and industry impact teams that will agree on the specific impacts that will be attributable to a given project and will identify the role of the project sponsor in providing funds that will mitigate that impact.

In such areas as housing, transportation, public health and safety, education, and public utilities, a role is being defined for industry and the machinery is being created that will allow impacted communities to avoid or lessen the problems that have, in the past, been associated with energy development. This is a positive sign and will result not necessarily in slowing the forces that are changing the West but in making that change more acceptable and more satisfying both to current residents and to those newcomers who will be moving to the area.

While it would indeed be a mistake to label the changes either "good" or "bad" without further qualifying these terms, there are some interesting features of what is happening that require special attention. These features distinguish contemporary changes from anything experienced since the settlement of this part of the country. They include:

1. The rapidity and scale of population growth surpasses what has occurred before. Communities are now doubling and tripling their populations in only a few years.

2. The pervasiveness of the phenomenon is unique in that hundreds of towns in several states are being affected at the same time.

3. New energy boomtowns are often not being created in a wilderness but are in long-established, stable agricultural communities whose character will shift dramatically as a result of the development.

4. Large-scale construction jobs tend to affect several communities due to modern transportation allowing commuting over long distances.

5. Busts are often built into the booms since many of the projects involve the construction of large power plants requiring large but temporary labor forces.[10]

Some Consequences of Change

During the past decade, there has developed a large and growing literature that has sought to clarify the important social and human consequences of the changes that have been identified above. Much of the research has focused on the problems of providing services to the rapidly increasing population. Other studies have focused on some of the most important social problems associated with rapid growth. Several early studies argued that these communities experience major increases in social problems—among them crime, drug and alcohol abuse, child and spouse abuse, marital conflict, and mental illness.

However, important recent literature argues that many of these problems are not nearly as serious as was initially assumed, or that they can be explained by factors other than rapid, energy-related growth. A good example of this can be found in some recent research I conducted in Price, Utah. While reviewing case records on spouse and child abuse and incest problems, a significant increase in case loads in these areas was observed to occur right in the middle of the most recent coal boom. The initial temptation was to attribute these problems to energy development. However, a more careful investigation revealed that several new case workers had been hired at this time and some had specialties in the areas of spouse and child abuse. Consequently, new programs were developed and highly publicized, and my analysis showed that the increase in case load was a direct result of this change in expertise and emphasis and much less directly related to changes in the community that were occurring as a result of energy development. Analyses in other communities have revealed similar results.

Some Important Community Impacts
of Rapid Industrialization

I would like to compare what is happening in impacted rural communities of the West with the processes of industrialization and modernization that have occurred in other areas of the country in earlier periods of U.S. history. What I want to argue is that observable disruptions and stress are a function of the *process of change* and that understanding this process will assure a much better grasp of what is going on.[11]

The effects of the forces of urbanization and industrialization on the social fabric of communities as well as on the quality of life of individual community residents has long been of concern to social scientists (see, for example, Wirth,[12] Axelrod,[13] and Kasarda and Janowitz[14]). Kasarda and Janowitz note that two models have come to dominate the work of social scientists in this area. They refer to the first as the *linear model* because of the assumption that linear increases in population size and density are the primary factors that influence patterns of social behavior. As they note, this model clearly has its intellectual roots in Toennie's concepts of *gemeinschaft* and *gesellschaft*. "In this view, urbanization and industrialization alter the essential character of society from that based on communal attachments to an associational basis."[15] Urbanization and industrialization are thus assumed to lead to increased population size and density which, in turn, lead to a breakdown in primary group ties, decreasing attachment to community, greater reliance on secondary institutional supports as opposed to family and kin, and so on.[16]

The second model grew out of the work of other early University of Chicago sociologists such as Robert E. Park and Ernest W. Burgess[17] and finds strong empirical support in the research of Axelrod,[18] Bell and Boat,[19] and Adams,[20] among others. This model, called the *systemic model* by Kasarda and Janowitz, recognizes extensive primary group ties and informal networks in the urbanized community that are quite contrary to the notion of *gesellschaft*. "The local community is viewed as a complex system of friendship and kinship networks and formal and informal association ties rooted in family life and on-going socialization processes."[21]

The preponderance of empirical evidence supports the second model. For example, Kasarda and Janowitz found that residents of communities characterized by increased size and density did not exhibit weaker bonds of kinship and friendship. Neither did location in such communities result in the substitution of secondary for primary and informal ties nor did it significantly weaken local community sentiments. However, one finds in the work of Kasarda and Janowitz an explicit focus on a variable that was often ignored in earlier work in this area—length of residence. These researchers found that the best predictor of community attachments and the devel-

opment of social bonds was the amount of time the respondent
has resided in the community.

The importance of this factor is evidenced by another line
of research which clearly indicates that communities characterized by *rapid* population growth and change do frequently
experience increased levels of social pathology, a breakdown
of primary group ties and controls, and other related social
problems. This was illustrated in Shaw and McKay's classic
study of juvenile delinquency in Chicago. In discussing the
rapid growth that occurred in Chicago around the turn of the
century, they note:

> This . . . rapid territorial expansion and geometric in-
> crease in the population of Chicago implies marked
> changes in the areas within the city and a rate of mobility
> quite unknown in stable communities. Likewise, the
> influx of great numbers of people of such widely different
> social and cultural backgrounds implies not only lack of
> homogeneity but also disorganization and reorganiza-
> tion affecting a large proportion of the population.[22]

In describing the social characteristics of those areas of
Chicago that exhibited the highest rates of juvenile delinquency, Shaw and McKay note:

> Certain areas . . . lack the homogeneity and continuity
> of cultural traditions and institutions which are essential
> to social solidarity, neighborhood organization and an
> effective public opinion . . . . The economic insecurity of
> the families, the tendency for the family to escape from
> the area as soon as they prosper sufficiently to do so, all
> combine to render difficult, if not impossible, the devel-
> opment of a stable and effective form of neighborhood
> organization in these sections of the city.[23]

Perhaps the problem is that we are dealing with two rather
different issues. In terms of the classic characteristics of *gesellschaft*, urbanized and industrialized areas may not be particu-

larly different from more rural communities *once they have become stabilized*. That is, individual residents do feel a certain degree of attachment to the community, they do maintain significant informal and primary ties with kin and friends, and so on. At the same time, communities or areas of communities characterized by the rapid social change that *accompanies* urbanization and industrialization do experience at least a temporary breakdown in many of the traditional social support mechanisms that contribute to such things as community stability, individual identification with community, and quality of life. Thus, areas of cities like Chicago that were experiencing rapid social change including growth, changing ethnic character resulting from the influx of European immigrants, southern blacks, and so on, were also characterized by high rates of juvenile delinquency, crime, and other important social pathologies. On the other hand, areas characterized by less social change had the time to stabilize. Individuals reestablished important primary ties with kin and neighbors, came to identify with community, and developed an overall more stable character that, in turn, was reflected in much lower rates of crime and related social problems. Some empirical support for this is found in the work of Shaw and McKay.[24] Areas of Chicago where blacks have resided for the longest period of time have exhibited some stabilization and have experienced decreasing rates of juvenile delinquency. On the other hand, areas experiencing a more recent black influx have continued to exhibit higher delinquency rates.

When one compares the Shaw and McKay analysis of the disruptive consequences of rapid change with a recent discussion of a western community being impacted by energy development, there are some rather startling parallels. As noted by Freudenburg, et al.:

> Over the four or five generations that these towns have been inhabited, the residents have developed a fairly impressive set of informal mechanisms—or "natural systems," if you will—for performing social functions and generally taking care of one another. These mechanisms

tend to be of the sort that sociologists can find nearly everywhere (to name a few noteworthy examples, they are ways of controlling deviance, socializing the young, giving people a sense of place, purpose, and personal worth, and taking care of the communities' weaker members and/or those in need or under stress).

Yet, in the boomtowns:

In what is probably the most characteristic single consequence of the large-scale impact process, these rather finely-tuned (and surprisingly delicately-balanced) arrangements are simply blown apart—scattered to the four winds by the sudden arrival of more new people than can be contained within them. The process requires no plotting, no nastiness—only numbers. The result is that a people who once took care of one another in a naturally-evolving and in fact almost automatic way—for they are often not even aware of doing so—are suddenly left with some very important machinery that's simply inoperative.[25]

These communities clearly are experiencing the processes of industrialization and urbanization in ways that have serious consequences for their ability to maintain their social fabric and a satisfactory quality of life for their residents. The informal mechanisms that supported and sustained area residents in the past are being broken down and while they will be eventually replaced by other mechanisms in the future, the period before that will be one of serious community crisis.

In a summary of the processes of change that have already occurred in many of these communities, Cortese and Jones[26] provide an overview that reminds one again of the movement from *gemeinschaft* to *gesellschaft* as discussed in the traditional community literature:

1. Communities become more culturally *diverse* resulting from the immigration of new people with different backgrounds and traditions. This tends to result in such related

changes as demands for an expanded school curriculum, increased recreational opportunities, a multiplication of religious denominations, and new life-styles.

2. Diversity leads to *less provincialism and isolation*.

3. Community institutions tend to become *more formal and professional* in their orientation. For example, a new police chief with more formal training may be hired, and so on.

4. This leads, in turn, to *greater specialization and bureaucratization* in these community institutions.

5. Institutional growth contributes to the belief that *bigger is better*. Chain operations replace local shops and grocery stores.

6. This trend, in turn, leads to *greater centralization*. The boomtown with its new chain operations now becomes the trade center for an expanding geographic area.

7. The *profit motive* is sometimes strengthened as local property values skyrocket, wages increase, and increased stratification and differentiation occur.

8. Finally, people come to *rely more on formal institutions*. Family problems, once handled at home, are now taken to the local counseling clinic. Neighboring declines as the makeup of local neighborhoods changes, and so on.

In other words, the changes in these communities are very real and they parallel changes that occurred in the industrializing cities of yesteryear. The magnitude of the social problems that are being experienced is indicative of the fact that they are not simply a result of population growth but that a very real multiplier effect is occurring.

It is important to note that a fairly extensive amount of research has been and is being conducted in many of the areas by social scientists as part of the federally mandated social-impact assessment process. However, the vast majority of this work has dealt with logistical considerations such as how many people will be brought into the community and what kinds of facilities and services will be required to meet their needs.[27] While these are important questions, one has to recognize that the impacts on the social systems of these communities can be of far greater magnitude than the impacts on the sewer systems. While the former may be less visible, they are considerably more important. It is also important to note that while changes in service delivery systems can sometimes be made with at least a relative degree of ease and speed—for example, new schools can be built with the expanding tax base—these changes may even exacerbate the problems of impact on the social fabric of the community. As noted by Cortese and Jones, impacts in this latter area

> . . . are not seriously mediated by providing more "adequate" housing, by "professionalizing" the police department, or by building a mental health center. Such solutions are, in fact parts of the *problem*. That is, such innovations add to the process of increasing anonymity, differentiation, centralization, impersonalization, specialization, and orientation of local community units toward extracommunity systems.[28]

In other words, the formal, tax-supported mechanisms that are developed to replace the informal mechanisms in these communities don't seem to do nearly as well as what they replace.

Indeed, many of the social problems associated with large-scale energy development in rural communities of the West are directly or indirectly attributable to the breakdown of what sociologists call "community"; that is, as a direct function of rapid growth and the diversification of the local economy and the composition of the local population, the community loses, at least temporarily, its ability to provide its inhabitants such things as a sense of place, purpose, identity, and personal worth.

Attempts to assess this question have been, of necessity, indirect and have relied on the utilization of indirect measures. It therefore cannot be reliably determined that communities already impacted by rapid growth—due to energy development or otherwise—have experienced increasing occurrences of social problems and personal pathologies reflected in higher crime and delinquency rates, increased frequency of drug and alcohol abuse, and the increased incidence of suicide and family conflict during the early stages of most dramatic change. Moreover, available data does not allow a measure of the direct effect of such things as sense of community on such increases. However, if the lower rates of pathology that occurred in the past can be attributed to the operation of "natural systems" that emerge in communities, then length of residence becomes a critical factor and it is appropriate to anticipate that new residents would have less commitment to, less involvement in, and less of a sense of community than older residents. This, in turn, should result in their expression of less happiness and less satisfaction with life than older residents. It should also result in fewer social constraints on non-normative behavior and fewer informal support mechanisms which traditionally aid people in responding to the problems and difficulties of life.

One recent survey has born this out. When those surveyed were asked to rate their community from "best possible community" to "worst," 50 percent of those living in the area more than five years gave a "best" rating (score of 8, 9, or 10). On the other hand, of those living in the community less than a year, only 29 percent gave a "best" rating. Further, although a clear majority of all residence groups defined their community as "home," this varied from 95 percent of the longtime residents to 78 percent of the newer residents. Similarly, nearly twice as many of over-five-year residents indicated that they were "very interested" in things that go on in their community as compared with those who have lived there under a year. The old-time residents were also much more likely to feel that they had a voice in what goes on in their community and that their views were adequately represented. Forty-nine percent of those living in the community over five years felt adequately represented, while this was true of just 22 percent of the newer residents.

It has been argued that the relatively temporary stay of many contruction workers who move into boomtowns in the West effectively inhibits their interest and involvement in the local community. That is, since this will not be their permanent home, why should they expend a great deal of energy to become involved in community affairs and to make the community a better place to live? Bickert found that commitment to the welfare of the community goes hand-in-hand with long-time residence and a position of higher social status.[29] Similarly, Doran, Duff, and Gilmore found that many newcomers live on the fringe of the community, often in temporary trailer settlements, and never become highly integrated into the community or participate to a high degree in its affairs.[30] My findings generally support these conclusions. Newcomers feel less positively about the community as a place to live, are less likely to consider it home, are less interested in community affairs, and are less likely to feel that they have a voice in the community or that it represents their views.

The systemic model discussed by Kasarda and Janowitz also implies that local friendship, kinship, and associational ties contribute to more positive community sentiments.[31] The same survey described above bore this out also. The data strongly support the link between friendship and kinship bonds and length of residence. For example, when length of residence was compared with percentage of friends who reside in the local community, 77 percent of those living in the community more than five years reported that half or more of their friends resided in the same town. On the other hand, only 27 percent of those residing in the community less than a year said half or more of their friends resided in that same town. The two intermediate length-of-residence categories fell about halfway between these two extremes.

A much smaller percentage of each of the groups reported that half or more of their relatives resided in their community. Nevertheless, the effect of length of residence was strongly positive. For example, while just 6 percent of those in the community for less than a year said that half or more of their relatives lived there, this was true of over five times as many (33 percent) of the longtime residents.

Upon turning to an examination of the survey respondents' participation and involvement in formal organizations and associations in the community, some most interesting differences are apparent. For work organizations, organizations associated with community affairs, and political organizations, there is a direct relationship between level of participation and involvement for the first three length-of-residence categories. That is, those who have been there less than one year and those who have been in the community three to five years participate more than those who have been there one to two years. However, those living in the community more than five years exhibit a lower overall level of participation than any of the other three groups, including the recent newcomers. The obvious factor here is age. Old-timers tend to be significantly older than the other three groups and so their decline in the level of participation in formal associations is predictable.

On the other hand, the newcomers exhibit the *highest* level of participation in educational, church, and civic organizations. This seems to reflect two basic factors. First in terms of educational associations, the newcomers tend to reflect a fairly high level of concern about the quality of local schools and are committed to improving the schools because of the consequences of this for their own children, and second, the newcomers exhibit higher levels of education, income, and occupational status. Therefore, one would expect a high level of participation in certain *types* of organizations and associations. Particularly management-level people who come in to run the power plants and construction operations should begin to show up fairly early as members of boards of civic and related organizations.

However, there is one other very important factor involved here. Each survey respondent was asked to indicate if his or her participation in the above organizations occurred within or outside the local community. A significant percentage of the participation of newcomers—ranging from 75 percent for work organizations to 29 percent for church organizations—occurred *outside* the local community—a finding consistent with the other community sentiment and friendship and kinship tests. Except for work organizations, no more than 8 percent of any of the other three groups reported their participation to be outside the local community.

The above-detailed survey therefore strongly indicates that newcomers to the communities studied do exhibit weaker friendship and kinship bonds and lower levels of participation in formal and informal local organizations and associations, and this lack of "community imbeddedness" does contribute importantly to the social and personal problems that are being experienced in these communities. Many immigrating families are young and have young children. Because of inadequate supplies of local housing, they are often forced to live in unattractive rental accommodations such as fringe trailer court settlements—often without lawns and other amenities. When problems occur (e.g., the birth of a new child, work problems, husband-wife disagreements, etc.), local social support mechanisms tend to be inadequate; family members tend not to live locally, fewer friendship bonds have been established, and so on. The consequences, in many instances, are likely to be increased drinking, more serious marital discord, depression, and even suicide. Such social pathologies are not likely to be seriously affected by the construction of new schools or by the completion of the local sewer system. They are, however, likely to be reduced by the emergence of a sense of community which includes greater friendship and kinship bondedness and increased participation in and commitment to local institutions. Perhaps, more than anything else, longevity will contribute to the development of the latter.

The social science community, in particular, must play a role in the events that are occurring in the West. Lauren Soth, an agricultural economist and syndicated columnist for several midwestern papers, recently observed that "throughout American education and government the seers of economic development and growth—scientists, engineers, production specialists—long have held sway. People who give thought to the social consequences of new technology are listened to politely but ignored in policymaking. In the whirlwind adoption of new farming technology after World War II, the voices of those who talked about the effect on the structure of the farming industry and of the rural society were seldom heard."[32]

Human values, social institutions, like the family, the church, the government, education, and the economy, cultural symbols, norms, roles, social class, and power have been among the most important social science concepts used to understand human social behavior. It requires little imagination to begin to realize the importance of some of these concepts in understanding the important changes that have occurred and are occurring in relationship to the natural environment and the changing rural West. However, to really effectively apply the knowledge at hand may require that westerners change some of the ways they have traditionally thought about their world. As Humphrey and Buttel have recently noted, "assumptions that energy-intensive industrial development is the natural end point of a universal process of social evolution and modernization must be cast aside if [we] are to break out of [our] collective celebration of Western social institutions."[33]

More and more the realization has become clear that "not only are we functionally linked to biophysical processes, as are other forms of life, but we are also socialized into normative ways of acting in relation to that environment. Americans, for example, once believed that factory smoke meant progress, and industry willingly polluted the air in cities such as Chicago and Pittsburgh in the pursuit of economic growth. Later we found that air pollution increased human mortality and levels of chronic disease. This medical knowledge became an important impetus for changing the normative structure of society with regard to air quality in the early phase of the environmental movement in the United States."[34]

There is much that is unknown about the social and human consequences of some of the important changes that are occurring. Westerners do have some obligation, I feel, to continue to ask hard questions and to make sure that an honest consideration of impacts on the human community becomes a part of the decision making equation. They must continue to direct their attention toward the important social and cultural changes that are occurring in the West if only so that through the information obtained, communities which still have some ability to decide whether or not they want to encourage energy-related growth may be made aware of the consequences—both positive and negative—of that choice.[35] The research agenda this provides is both exciting and challenging.

_____

NOTES

1. Gene F. Summers and Virginia Lambert, "Regional Analysis of Community Changes: Energy Impacts in the 1970's," research report prepared for Mountain West Research, Inc., Billings, Montana, 1981.

2. Quoted in Lynn England, "Rural Development and Rural Organization," Department of Sociology, Brigham Young University, Provo, Utah. Typescript.

3. Ibid.

4. Stan L. Albrecht, "Socio-Cultural Factors," in *Mining Ecology*, ed., Mohan K. Wali (London: Academic Press, 1981).

5. William C. Metz, "The Mitigation of Socio-Economic Impacts by Electric Utilities," *Public Utilities Fortnightly*, September 11, 1980, 3-11.

6. Kathleen Courrier, ed., *Life after '80: Environmental Choices We Can Live With* (Andover: Brick House Publ. Co., 1980).

7. Riley E. Dunlap and William R. Catton, Jr., "Environmental Sociology: A Framework for Analysis," in *Progress in Resource Management and Environmental Planning*, vol. 1, ed T. O'Riordan and R. C. D'Arge, (Chicester, England: John Wiley, 1979).

8. E. Kohrs, *Social Consequences of Boom Growth in Wyoming* (Casper: Central Wyoming Counseling Center, 1974).

9. Metz, "Mitigation."

10. Charles F. Cortese and Bernie Jones, "The Sociological Analysis of Boom Towns," *Western Sociological Review* 8 (1977): 76-90.

11. Stan L. Albrecht, "Social Participation, Community Attachment, and Quality of Life in the Rapidly Industrializing Rural Community," paper presented at the Fifth World Congress of Rural Sociology, Mexico City, Mexico, 1980.

12. Louis Wirth, "Urbanism as a Way of Life," *American Journal of Sociology* 44 (July 1938):3-24.

13. Morris Axelrod, "Urban Structure and Social Participation," *American Sociological Review* 21 (February 1956):13-18.

14. John D. Kasarda and Morris Janowitz, "Community Attachment in Mass Society," *American Sociological Review* 39 (June 1974):328-39.

15. Ferdinand Toennies, *Gemeinschaft and Gesellschaft* (Leipzig: Feus's Verlag, 1887).

16. Wirth, "Urbanism."

17. Robert E. Park and Ernest W. Burgess, *Introduction to the Science of Sociology* (Chicago: University of Chicago Press, 1969); and Park and Burgess, *The City* (Chicago: University of Chicago Press, 1967).

18. Axelrod, "Urban Structure."

19. Wendell Bell and Marion D. Boat, "Urban Neighborhoods and Informal Social Relations," *American Journal of Sociology* 62 (January 1957):391-98.

20. Bert N. Adams, *Kinship in an Urban Setting* (Chicago: Markham, 1968).

21. Kasarda and Janowitz, "Community Attachment," 329.

22. Clifford R. Shaw and Henry D. McKay, *Juvenile Delinquency and Urban Areas* (Chicago: University of Chicago Press, 1942), 25.

23. Ibid., 110.

24. Shaw and McKay, *Juvenile Delinquency.*

25. William R. Freudenburg, et al., "Subjective Responses to an Energy Boomtown Situation: A Preliminary Report on Research in Progress in Four Western Colorado Towns," paper presented at the meetings of the American Sociological Association, Chicago, Illinois, 1977.

26. Cortese and Jones, "Boom Towns," 85.

27. Freudenburg, "Subjective Responses."

28. Cortese and Jones, "Boom Towns," 87.

29. C. von E. Bickert, *The Residents of Sweetwater County, Wyoming: A Needs Assessment Survey* (Denver: Denver Research Institute, 1974).

30. S. Doran, M. K. Duff, and J. S. Gilmore, *Socio-Economic Impacts of Proposed Burlington Northern and Chicago Northwestern Rail Line in Campbell-Converse Counties, Wyoming* (Denver: Denver Research Institute, 1974).

31. Kasarda and Janowitz, "Community Attachments."

32. Lauren Soth, "Rural Sociologists Need Audience" *Champaign-Urbana News-Gazette*, September 17, 1981.

33. Craig R. Humphrey and Fred R. Buttel, *Environment, Energy, and Society* (Belmont, Calif.: Wadsworth, 1982):1.

34. Ibid., 3.

35. Cortese and Jones, "Subjective Responses." 87.

3

The Town on the Prickly Pear Flat: Community Development in Castle Valley

Edward A. Geary

The Mormon pioneers initially established communities along the Wasatch Front, but then as more members of the Church arrived in "Zion," the Saints spread north and south along the western edge of the mountains. In the late 1870s, after other areas were filled, the first Mormons moved on to the Colorado Plateau in Eastern Utah. Edward A. Geary, Professor of English at Brigham Young University, explains that these new areas followed the same settlement patterns of earlier Mormon communities. Using the model that Leonard Arrington and Melvin Larkin adopted for Logan, Dr. Geary divides the history of Huntington, one of these final settlements (and his hometown) into developmental periods. The first two stages were a period of pioneering struggle (roughly from 1877 to 1880), followed by the developmental stage (1880 to 1895). The third stage he calls the "flowering period" when the community reached its peak in population and cultural development—which began in about 1895. Finally, Dr. Geary adds to the Arrington-Larkin model what he describes as a long period of decline consisting of two stages. The first stage involved an outmigration of the new crop of children and the second stage was marked by continued population decline as

older residents moved away also. These two stages lasted from
about 1919 to 1970. This trend is reversing itself now as energy
development brings new industry to the Huntington area.

Dr. Geary's study provides an excellent framework for the
study of Mormon communities over time. With this informa-
tion, community planners can understand how they will need
to adapt to the new energy boom in eastern Utah.

In the late 1870s, Mormon territorial expansion moved
east and south from the older towns of the Great Basin to plant
new settlements in the less accessible—and sometimes only
marginally habitable—country of the Colorado Plateau. Several prominent scholars of Mormon history and culture have
come from the communities settled during this period. Lowry
Nelson, for example, whose studies of the Mormon village
have an important place in rural sociology, came from Ferron,
Utah, just a few miles from my own home town of Huntington.
Charles Peterson, who grew up in Snowflake, Arizona, has
made perhaps the boldest claims for the importance of the
town in Mormon history.

It might be argued that we who come from these relatively
late-born towns must have a shallow sense of the past compared to the natives of older Mormon communities, where the
roots run further back to pioneer origins. But Peterson has
suggested that the essential process of the call, the trek, and the
pioneer sacrifices in establishing the community was reenacted
with each settlement.[1] From this point of view, the later towns
have the whole essential history but in a more compressed
form, unfolding through three generations instead of four or
five. In any case, the difference between one hundred and 130 is
not great; all of Mormon country is a place "where nothing is
long ago," as Virginia Sorenson has put it.[2]

Yet, in another sense, any period greater than a single
lifetime is a long time, since gaps of knowledge and experience
can occur. Peterson has spoken of the "timeless" quality of
Snowflake in his youth and his impression that "like the
Roman Empire its past ran back forever," even though he now
realizes that he has lived through fully half of the town's

history. As he expresses the tension in that double conscious-
ness, "By some malevolent magic I have seen a period equal to
eternity."[3] Lowry Nelson explains the motive for his memoir
of Ferron at the turn of the century by saying, "My own
children know very little of the kind of life I lived as a child,
and, inevitably, my grandchildren know nothing of it. Moreover, few others living today [1972] can possibly know firsthand what pioneering was like."[4]

In my own case, growing up in a small town on the
Colorado Plateau has led to a persistent impression that I am
thirty or forty years older than my urban contemporaries, that
I belong to an earlier era. I have tried to deal with various
aspects of that impression in a series of stories and personal
essays. In this essay my intention is to assume a somewhat
more detached position and try to present a more comprehensive picture of a community as it has existed through a cycle of
development, a community which is unique in some respects
but which is also, I think, representative of others established
in the same period.

The community is Huntington, Utah, situated under the
eastern escarpment of the Wasatch Plateau in the wide upland
basin known as Castle Valley. Of all the areas settled in the late
1870s, Castle Valley was the closest to older communities,
located just thirty miles as the crow flies from Sanpete Valley.
In view of this close proximity to what was then one of the
most populous regions in Utah, it might seem odd that Castle
Valley was not settled earlier. However, the Wasatch Plateau
forms a continuous barrier between the two valleys, and the
only passes under 9,000 feet are well to the south through
Salina Canyon or to the north over Soldier Summit, a distance
of nearly one hundred miles either way. During the Indian
unrest of the 1860s, there was little incentive to send settlers
into a region so remote from established towns. In addition,
because of the rain shadow cast by the Wasatch Plateau, Castle
Valley receives considerably less precipitation than Sanpete
Valley, and the land presents a more desertlike appearance.
The soil, too, has a different character, being largely mancos
shale instead of the gravel loam found in the Great Basin, and

there was some question whether crops could be grown in it.

These factors, then—the difficulty of access, the Indian dangers, and questions about the soil and water resources—combined to delay the settlement of Castle Valley until the 1870s. By that time the Indian problem had largely been resolved by removal of the Utes to the reservation in the Uinta Basin. Sanpete Valley, with a population approaching 11,000, had reached the limits that its arable land could support, and an outlet was needed for the young people who were coming of age and seeking homes and land of their own. In 1875 the church leaders discussed the possibility of colonizing "the lands east of Sanpete,"[5] and in that same year the Sanpete cooperative livestock herds began to move into Castle Valley, as did some independent stockmen.

Finally, on September 22, 1877, at a priesthood meeting in Mount Pleasant, seventy-five men were called to settle Castle Valley, with Orange Seely appointed as bishop of all the region east of the mountains.[6] (Orange Seely and his brother Justus Wellington Seely had been among the most enthusiastic promoters of settlement in Castle Valley and the towns of Orangeville and Wellington were named in their honor.) The Seelys led a party over the crest of the Wasatch Plateau and settled on Cottonwood Creek, where the colony soon split into the two communities of Orangeville and Castle Dale. At about the same time, another party came through Salina Canyon and settled on Ferron Creek, and a third party, led by Elias Cox of Fairview, made its way over Soldier Summit and settled on Huntington Creek. The Price River, in the northern part of Castle Valley, was not settled until the following year. Although Orange Seely was the nominal ecclesiastical head of all the colonies, each community had a *de facto* presiding elder from the beginning who was officially made bishop in 1879.[7] When Emery County was created from the eastern portion of Sanpete County in 1880, the county officers were drawn largely from the bishops and other ecclesiastical officers of the various communities, thus continuing the common practice in Mormon communities of blurring the distinctions between civil and ecclesiastical authority.[8]

Not all of those called in 1877 responded favorably, and a second call for settlers was issued a year later.[9] According to the old-timers on our side of the mountains, the call was posted in wardhouses throughout Sanpete Stake. Those who could read it came to Castle Valley; the illiterate remained in Sanpete.[10] Once the settlement process was well underway, the valley grew rapidly, reaching a population of 5,076 by 1890, which was larger than such older counties as Millard, Tooele, and Washington.

The settlement process took place in several distinct stages. Leonard Arrington and Melvin Larkin, in a study published in 1973, identified three stages in the development of a typical Mormon town as indicated in its buildings and institutions. The first stage, they suggest, was marked by "the cooperative laboring on three structures: a short diversion canal . . . the community fort . . . and a makeshift 'meetinghouse' for community worship and recreation." The second stage, following "within two or three years," brought "the construction of longer diversion canals, adobe homes a little larger in size, and a tabernacle—an undertaking of such size and expense that only one was built for each nucleated group of settlements." The third stage saw the completion of the irrigation system, the building of substantial houses of permanent materials, and—in Logan, which Arrington and Larkin used as their model—a temple.[11] In other words (to apply the model to the smaller community which was more common than the few temple cities), this was the period in which the pioneering struggle was over, the major community institutions had been formed, and sufficient resources were available to create the most distinctive monuments the town would have. We might think of this as the flowering period.

Arrington and Larkin identify only the formative or building stages of community development. In most small Mormon towns, these stages were followed by a long period of decline. In the case of Huntington and the other Castle Valley communities, we can divide this period into two fairly distinct stages. In the first stage there is little apparent change from the flowering period. Community institutions retain much of their vitality, and relative isolation helps to preserve a strong sense of community identity, but there is a continual draining off of young people as they come of age because the community has reached the limits of its economic resources. In the second stage of decline the actual population total begins to fall as the birthrate lags behind the rate of out-migration. As the population ages and declines, the institutions which gave cohesiveness to the community noticeably lose their vitality, while at the same time improved transportation and communications break down the community's isolation and its sense of its own distinctiveness, making it increasingly easy, both physically and psychologically, to leave the town for other places where the opportunities are better.

The first stage of development in Huntington began with the thirty-six persons who arrived in the fall of 1877, nearly all of them members of the interrelated Cox-Jones-Avery-Cheney families.[12] There being no Indian danger, they did not build a fort but instead a cluster of dugouts in the banks of the creek near the northeast corner of the present townsite. For the first three years the life of the settlement centered in "the dugout community," as it was called, though there were also several homesteads up and down the creek. When the settlers arrived, they immediately began work on the North Ditch to divert water to the land north of the creek and the Avery Ditch to irrigate the low-lying land south of the creek.[13] In 1878 the community's numbers were augmented by the arrival of the Guymons and Ottesons from Fountain Green and the Leonard family from Rush Valley. In 1879 the related Wakefield and Johnson families came from Fountain Green, along with the Shermans and Browns and several others.[14] On October 7, 1879, the Huntington Ward was organized with Elias Cox as bishop. Church meetings and social gatherings were held in dugouts until the summer of 1880, when a bowery was built near the dugout community.[15] Thus, the three primitive community structures were put in place. We might mention a fourth of nearly equal importance: the first store was opened in a dugout, also by Elias Cox, in 1879.[16]

As might be expected, living conditions were very harsh

during those first years. The new ditches were continually washing out, making it difficult to irrigate the land. The nearest communities in Sanpete Valley were a two-day hike or a week-long wagon journey distant in the summer and virtually inaccessible in the winter. Several men nearly lost their lives in attempting to cross the mountains to visit their families in Sanpete Valley during the winters of 1879 and 1880.[17] To women who had grown accustomed to the relative comfort of Sanpete, the prospect of living in a dugout was not pleasing. Mary Ann Rowbury Brown, who had remained in Fountain Green when her husband, Charles, first came to Huntington in 1879, described her introduction to the new settlement as follows:

> In July of 1880 my husband came for me and what kind of a home do you suppose I came to? There were four dugouts situated along Huntington Creek and my husband had made arrangements with Noah T. Guymon for the use of one of these. Before we arrived some one had locked three pigs in the dugout that we were to occupy. It was night when we landed. I was weary and conditions which confronted me were too much. I broke down and wept.[18]

This unpropitious arrival became a Huntington legend. I recall my grandmother telling the story when I was a boy. According to her version, Sister Brown, who had come from a rather cultivated English background, cried out, "Oh, Charlie, I've lived in many a place, but I never thought I'd live with the pigs!" Mary Ann Brown also recorded that she and her husband planted ten bushels of wheat the first year and harvested a crop of only nine and a half bushels. Hannah Seely probably expressed the feelings of many other women when she reportedly said, on her first view of Castle Valley, "Damn the man who would bring a woman to a place like this!"[19]

The second stage in building the community began in 1880 with the platting of the townsite on Prickly Pear Flat, a low tableland south of the creek. The original plat was one mile square, with sixty-four blocks divided by wide streets. It thus had the form and general dimensions of the prototypical City of Zion, though with the usual modifications of Mormon towns in the West. The blocks were all of one size instead of there being a tier of larger blocks in the center for public buildings; each block was divided into four large lots, to provide for a population of about 250 families rather than the much larger number envisioned for the City of Zion; and the town was designed as a farm village, with barns and corrals on the town lots rather than on the outskirts of town as provided in the City of Zion plat.

These characteristics could be found in dozens of other Mormon towns, but there is one aspect of the Huntington plat that sets it apart. The main street falls exactly on the line dividing Range 8 East from Range 9 East, Salt Lake Base and Meridian. The significance of this lies in the fact that Castle Valley, unlike most earlier Mormon settlements, was settled after the government survey had been completed, and thus under the homestead laws. The homestead laws, with their requirements of residence on the land to secure ownership, tended to encourage a scattered, rural pattern rather than the village pattern which the LDS Church had emphasized. Castle Valley, therefore, presents an interesting test case of the relative appeal of the two different modes of settlement.

The homestead settlement pattern unquestionably had an effect on the development of Huntington. Land distribution was under control of the government rather than the LDS Church, and individual holdings were on the average larger than the land allotments made to individuals in the older Mormon towns—but not as much larger as one might expect. Although many individuals filed for the full 160 acres, they often did so with the intention of dividing the land with relatives. For example, I have in my possession the patent certificate issued to my greatgrandfather, John F. Wakefield, giving him title to 160 acres adjacent to the townsite. But he had never considered that to be all his but had divided it with his brother and brothers-in-law, farming only forty acres himself. In any case, the limiting resource in Castle Valley is not land but water, and the distribution of the water remained in the hands of the LDS Church through the cooperative enterprise of canal building.

The first-stage canals were low diversions cooperatively dug by the concerned landholders. The new townsite, however, was above those canals, and a highline canal was needed to bring water to it and to the extensive South Fields. For this purpose, an organizational meeting for the Huntington Manufacturing and Agricultural Company was held on January 9, 1880, in Bishop Cox's dugout. Construction continued for more than five years before the Field Ditch was completed, though it appears that the Town Ditch was in service by 1884.[20] The extent of cooperative involvement in the project is attested by the fact that the names of more than one hundred men appear in the construction records. The extent of church involvement is indicated not only by the fact that the company was first organized under the direction of the bishop but also by the presence of the Young Men's Mutual Improvement Association records mingled with the canal records.

The first building erected on the new townsite, before any homes, was a large log meetinghouse with dimensions of forty by sixty feet, located at the very center of the town. The meeting house was completed in time for an all-night New Year's Eve party on December 31, 1880.[21] That party, which remained vividly in the memory of the participants throughout their lives, might be considered as a symbolic celebration of the community's permanence. During this second stage of community development, which lasted until about 1895, the townsite was occupied, nearly all of the arable land was brought into production, a certain degree of prosperity was achieved, and community institutions were established that had as their goal the enhancement of the quality of life, rather than bare subsistence, including such institutions as public schools and a seminary, the martial band (organized in 1884), and the Huntington Dramatic Club.

These developments occurred only gradually, of course. While the community life was now focused on the townsite, many families continued to live on their homesteads. As late as 1896 there were still enough people living outside of town to justify schools in the North Fields and the South Fields.[22] However, the majority of families had drawn lots on the town-site, and most of them built permanent homes in town as the years went by, making Huntington almost—though not quite—as much a Mormon village as Parowan or Ephraim. (In Ephraim, in 1925, Lowry Nelson found no families living on farms.[23] In Huntington several families remained on their farms.) A similar gathering into the village occurred in Castle Dale and Orangeville, but in Ferron, for some reason, about half of the community chose to remain on their farms, living in what Andrew Jenson used to call a "scattered condition."[24]

The first houses were very small—usually a one-room log structure about sixteen by eighteen feet, to which a lean-to was later added. A little later, as several sawmills came into production, plank construction became common, soon to be followed by frame construction with adobe lining. This last method produced comfortable, well-insulated dwellings, several of which are still occupied. (Indeed, examples of all three methods of construction can still be found in Huntington.) The furnishings were as spare as the dwellings themselves. My grandfather remembered that the house his father built in 1885 was furnished with "a Charter Oak cook stove, a wooden bedstead, a home made wash bench, a looking glass which hung on the wall, a Woodbury clock, a few chairs including a rocking chair, a cradle, and a wheat bin in one corner."[25]

The superiority of these tiny cabins to the dugouts that had preceded them may be hard for us to imagine, but it was deeply felt by the pioneers. Mary Ann Brown remembered the moving day as one of the great occasions in her life even though she was moving into a one-room cabin: "The sense of exultation we experienced in making the transfer is easier left to imagination than to describe it. . . . The nine years we lived in the dugout really covers the pioneer phase of my life."

Mary Ann went on to describe conditions generally:

We began to have more to do with, for the country in general was building up and it was not so difficult either to raise crops as at first. The cause of poor harvest when we obtained only nine and a half bushels of wheat from ten bushels planted was not due to unproductive soil, but to irrigation conditions. For quite awhile the farmers had difficulty in keeping the water in the canal. It persisted in washing out. They had to learn to control it by experience.[26]

This is a good summary of the developments that had taken place in the first few years of community life, but it is not complete.

Although Huntington was built on the model of the Mormon farming village, its economic welfare has depended on industrial support from almost the very beginning. The money for purchasing the few furnishings, and for the farm equipment that made it possible to bring the land into production, largely came from work on the Rio Grande Western Railway, which was built through the northern part of the valley in 1882. A man with a team could earn five dollars a day, cash, on the grading crew,[27] and others found employment in cutting timber for ties. Moreover, the construction crews provided a good cash market for hay and grain. Without this inflow of cash at a crucial time, it would have been much more difficult to lift the community above the subsistance level. After the railroad was completed, coal mines were opened providing seasonal employment for many Huntington men. Others made a living by peddling eggs, butter, and seasonal produce in the mining camps.

In addition to this economic contribution, the coming of the railroad led to a fundamental division in the valley, as the northern section became industrial in character and attracted a large non-Mormon population, a division which was formalized in 1894 with the creation of Carbon County from the northern part of Emery County.

The railroad also dramatically reduced the isolation of Castle Valley making possible year-round communication with the outside world. These improved conditions did nothing to reduce certain other elements of hardship, such as the epidemic diseases that periodically ravaged the community. In 1886, for example, there was a severe outbreak of diphtheria which took thirteen lives in the single week between Christmas and New Year.[28] In 1888 several people died in an outbreak of typhoid, and in 1896 there was another diphtheria epidemic which brought so many deaths that there was a shortage of lumber for coffins.[29] But these diseases were equally devastating in the cities.

Castle Valley was settled primarily by young families. According to the 1880 census, the average age of landowners in Emery County was twenty-seven, compared to an average age of fifty-two in Sanpete County.[30] However, there were also several older people who might almost be termed professional pioneers. For example, Amos Johnson and his father, George W., had laid out the townsite at Fountain Green in 1859 and had earlier been involved in the settlement of Cedar City and Santaquin.[31] Henning Olsen Ungerman had been among the first Danish immigrants to settle in Spring City. After living there for twenty years, working as a stone and brick mason, he was called to Castle Dale in 1881, where he was involved in constructing most of the houses and public buildings until his death in 1902. For most of these older pioneers, including Charles Pulsipher, Albey Sherman, Elias Cox, Mariah Jane Woodward, and Talitha Avery, Castle Valley was the end of the line, but some went on to help open up yet newer settlements. Talitha Avery, for example, spent her last years in the Teton Valley in Idaho.[32]

A high degree of mobility evidently characterized Mormon settlements at that time. In addition to the many families who came from Sanpete Valley, Huntington attracted in the first five years the Leonards and Gordons from Rush Valley, the Howards and Brashers from Randolph, the McKees from Millard County, Joneses and Neilsons from Heber City, Gardners from Grouse Creek, Marshalls from Long Valley, Granges from Springville, Rowleys and McElprangs from Iron County by way of Bluff, and Gearys from Morgan by way of St. Johns, Arizona, to name just a few.[33] And most of these people had lived in several additional towns as well.

Many of the early settlers were related to one another. I have mentioned the Cox-Jones clan and the six Johnson-

Wakefield-Woodward siblings. The champion kinship group in Castle Valley was doubtless the Nelsons of Ferron, ten brothers and one sister who accumulated a total of ninety-one children.[34] No wonder the population grew so fast!

The young families of 1880 were not so young twenty years later. Whereas in 1880 the average age of heads of families was in the twenties, in 1900 it had risen to forty-three years. A second generation was coming of age in the town, and the town itself had matured along with them. Where the 1880 census had listed just eight different occupations among residents of Emery County, the census of 1900 listed sixty-one occupations, with only 58 percent identifying themselves as farmers or ranchers.[35] The community remained agrarian in focus, however, and even those people in other occupations almost invariably had, as Lowry Nelson recalled, "a small tract of land, if even no more than the acre and a quarter on the village lot. Here a garden and a few fruit trees were the rule, along with a cow, a pig, and a flock of chickens."[36]

I would date the third stage of community development in Huntington from about 1895 or 1896, when after several earlier attempts, construction began in earnest on the brick meetinghouse. J. W. Nixon, who was a counselor to Bishop Peter Johnson at the time, reports that President Francis M. Lyman promised, "If any young man is building a home here now and he will contribute liberally to the construction of this house [the meetinghouse] he will get his own built easier and quicker."[37] Whether this really happened is hard to say, but it is clear that the meetinghouse project ushered in the most active period of building in the town's history, and that at least a part of that activity can be attributed to the brickyard and sawmills developed for the meetinghouse. The period from 1895 to 1910 saw the construction of many two-story brick houses in place of the log and plank cabins, a flour mill which was an important economic asset to the community, schools, business houses, and a social hall. In tangible physical development, it was clearly the golden age of the town. It was a golden age in other respects as well. By then the second generation had entered into community life, strengthening the music and dramatic organizations, and taking the lead in providing improved educational opportunities for the rising third generation.[38]

The town also took on the *look* of a mature community. The trees so carefully nurtured by the first settlers had matured to give the town a grovelike character, with tall rows of lombardy poplars along the streets, wide-spreading shade trees in the yards, and orchards on almost every lot. Between 1900 and 1903 the irrigation system was improved by the construction of a storage reservoir on the Wasatch Plateau to provide more water for late-summer use. Alfalfa seed and honey production had developed into profitable industries to supplement the livestock raising that was the chief source of income for the community.

The physical structure of the community at this period might be envisioned as a series of widening circles. At the center, geographically as well as symbolically, were the two blocks given over to public uses. Here were the new meeting-house, completed in 1899, with a tower added in 1904; the Relief Society Hall, finished in 1906; an elementary school built in 1908; and a high school finished in 1916. Here also were the tithing yard with barn, granary, and bishop's office; a small grovelike park; and an open square for community activities. Surrounding this community core, at first, then tending to move north along Main Street, was the business district, never very large in Huntington, yet with several good-sized stores. The co-op store, built of lumber and adobe in 1892, was expanded into a two-story brick building in 1900. Also in 1900, J. W. Nixon opened a store where he conducted a thriving business for twenty years. In 1908 the Miller Mercantile Company built a brick building for a store and a bank. In addition to these major operations there were drug stores, millinery shops, confectionaries, and hotels. The next wider circle comprised the remainder of the townsite, where nearly every block was occupied with its four farmhouses and outbuildings. At the outer fringe of the townsite were the mill, the public corral, and the cemetery, all encircled by the patchwork of irrigated fields, which in turn were surrounded by the dry valley lands.

These also formed a vital part of the community as they were a segment of the natural grazing drift from the summer range on the Wasatch Plateau to the winter grazing in the San Rafael Desert.

And what of the life that went on in this setting? Though communication with the outside world was much improved from the early days—by a daily stage line in 1884 connecting with the railroad at Price, and by a telephone line in 1896—community life was still characterized by a high degree of self-sufficiency. This was especially true of entertainment. There were large annual community celebrations for the Fourth and the Twenty-fourth of July, for Thanksgiving, Christmas, and New Year. There were frequent dances, including some special events such as the Woodcutter's Dance each fall to reward the young men who hauled loads of wood from the foothills to the houses of the widows and old folks. There seems to have been an especially large amount of attention given to musical and dramatic activities in Huntington. Many of the early settlers had been prominent in these activities in Sanpete Valley, and they brought their talents and interests with them to Castle Valley, where they were carried on by the second generation.

The musical tradition had perhaps its greatest moment in 1895 when the Castle Valley Choir, organized by Thomas L. Hardee, traveled over the mountain to Scofield for an eisteddfod competition with the Welsh Choir there. Scofield at the time—before the great mine disaster of 1900—was a mining town of about the same size as Huntington, and the majority of its population, like that of Huntington, was made up of Mormons with roots in Britain and Scandinavia. (In fact, the community of Cleveland, just east of Huntington, was largely settled by people from Scofield.) But in the legends that have come down in Huntington, Scofield is represented as an immensely worldly place, and the Welsh Choir as haughty in the confidence of their own superiority. When the wagons carrying the Castle Valley Choir arrived in Scofield, the residents on the streets called them "hayseeds," but in the competition, held in the railroad roundhouse, the Castle Valley Choir

was awarded first place. After the formal competition, an
informal program was arranged at which Hannah Johnson
sang an adaptation of an old song that has become legendary
in Huntington:

> I'm as fine a little Danish girl
>   As ever you did see
> And though I live in Huntington
>   I'm as cute as cute can be.
> I'm just sixteen, don't think me green.
>   You'll be mistaken there.
> Fresh from the meadows
>   Yet I have no hayseed in my hair.

As the story goes, "This brought the house down. The people
began shouting 'Castle Valley Hayseeds' and pounded on the
walls of the roundhouse until they fairly shook."[39]

Two years later, in 1898, Brother Hardee took his choir to
Salt Lake City, where they sang in a session of the LDS
Church's General Conference.

Community drama was active in Huntington from the
earliest days until the end of the flowering period, with as many
as ten plays performed in a year. It was a true community
drama in almost every sense of the word, except for the scripts
themselves, which were the usual stock of farces, melodramas,
and temperance plays. Typically, when funds were needed for
some purpose, the bishop would ask the Dramatic Association
to stage an entertainment.

> Since there were few other types of entertainment
> available, and inasmuch as the members of the ward were
> usually instructed that it was their duty to patronize the
> theatre in order to contribute their share to whatever
> project was at hand, audiences were usually large. All
> members of a family would attend, the children compet-
> ing for seats near the stage and adults seeking benches
> near the coal-burning stoves.[40]

Families of the actors received complimentary tickets, as did those who contributed props or other supplies to the production. In addition, the bishop would pick up a block of tickets to be given free to old folks and widows. The remainder were sold, usually at twenty-five cents a ticket, through local merchants, who accepted scrip and barter items as well as cash. For one play, for example, the receipts included $9.50 in co-op coupons and 1,200 pounds of grain.[41]

The earliest productions depended heavily on donated props and costumes. In one early play, Will Green, playing the part of the villain, "strode across the stage in long vigorous steps," and a man in the audience called out, "Hi there, don't tear my pants."[42] Over the years, the Association accumulated a supply of costumes and scenery, and apparently enough acting talent to be quite convincing to the audience. Margaret Young recalled a play performed in the new meetinghouse in about 1901 in which

> Don Woodward threw Nellie Crandall . . . into the ocean. He picked the girl up and completely tossed her off the rear of the stage and down the back stairway onto a feather bed; a stage hand splashed water back upon the stage. The whole scene, with the ocean backdrop, the lighting and the effective acting, was so vividly realistic that the observer, Margaret (age 8), went home and "cried all night."[43]

Another testimonial to effective acting comes from Orangeville, where the talented Alma G. Jewkes, Jr., was often cast in the villain's role. When Jewkes was called on a church mission, the bishop asked all the Primary children to include him in their prayers, but one boy cried out, "I won't pray for him; he kills women." It was not only children who could be caught up by the action, either. When Jewkes was playing one tense scene in Castle Dale, a grown man rose in the audience and shouted, "He's a lyin' son-of-a-bitch!"[44]

Lowry Nelson, looking back at his own childhood with the trained eye of a sociologist, has given an excellent picture of community organization and daily life in Castle Valley during this period. The population, he observes, was

> remarkably homogeneous. There was only one major occupation: that of farming. Practically everyone had a piece of land and a cow or two, one or more horses, and smaller barnyard animals. Of course, some had larger and better farms than others, more livestock, and enjoyed larger returns. Even so, the range between the better-off and the poorest was not great. . . . There were, inevitably, prestige differences, based partly on ecclesiastical considerations, and these were almost always associated with reputations for uprightness in personal life. The bishop of the ward and his counselors were much respected, and often led to a kind of polarization of function. Father, for example, was not only bishop, but for years was president of the co-op store and a member of the town board. He was also a county commissioner for two years, and a member of the state legislature for a year. There is no doubt that he was well respected and enjoyed high prestige, but I recall no feeling whatever that we were in any sense a privileged family. There was really no marked social stratification.
>
>   This is not to say there were no poor people. I visited a family with a boy my age one time that lived in a dugout in a bank along the creek. They had a few boughs over the top of the cave, which could not possibly shed rain, but protected from the sun. . . .
>
>   There were gradations among the people in regard to the puritan work ethic. The range was from the outright, chronic loafer, to the one who was always at work on his farm or with his stock. There were not many true loafers, but a few could nearly always be seen squatting by the Co-op. I always envied them, when I was sent to the store on an errand with instructions to return immediately.[45]

I call this stage of community life the period of flowering because it was the period of greatest vitality, as it seems to me, not because life was especially abundant. Though living conditions were greatly improved from pioneer days, there was still a high degree of economic self-sufficiency. Nelson writes, "I recall one fall after threshing we took a load of oats to the co-op to pay a bill of $70, which amount supplied a family of ten for six months, as far as major items were concerned. For small items, eggs were the usual purchasing power."[46] The diets were very plain, consisting almost entirely of home-grown produce. Butter and eggs were produced abundantly but consumed sparingly because there was always a cash market for them in the Carbon County coal camps. Public utilities were almost nonexistent at the beginning of the period. Water for domestic use had to be carried from the ditch, and during high water periods might be muddy for several weeks at a time. Wash day was an immense project, and this inevitably had an effect on personal hygiene. As Nelson recalls, "Like all our other clothing, underwear, shirts, etc., we wore the socks for a week, until as we said, 'they were able to stand alone.'"[47] Fuel needs were met at first by hauling pinion and juniper from the foothills, but later small coal mines were opened in the canyons. In fact, Huntington had one institution which must be virtually unique: a community coal mine, operated as a cooperative for the townspeople.

The flowering period was also a time of recurring rivalry between Huntington and Castle Dale. Huntington was the largest town in the county, but Castle Dale was the county seat and headquarters of the stake. The conflict came to a head when the stake academy was established in Castle Dale and Huntington was compelled to close its seminary and support the academy.[48] The bitterness engendered by this episode was so strong that forty years later, when Central High School, the successor to the Emery Stake Academy, was closed, the people of Castle Dale refused to send their children to Huntington for high school and insisted on attending South Emery High in more distant Ferron. There was also conflict with Sanpete Valley. The critical watershed lands on the Wasatch Plateau were grazed by Sanpete sheepmen, and overgrazing in the 1890s caused severe damage which was much resented in

Castle Valley, as were the Sanpete attempts to divert water to their side of the divide. These activities led to various protests and petitions, including this letter to the editor from William Howard of Huntington:

> Science has said that running water purifies itself in running seven miles, but during the spring high water and summer rains, the filth from sheep camps comes down from a distance of twenty-five to thirty miles, and when we dip up a bucket of water from our town ditches to drink or cook our food in, and find sheep droppings in it, as we often do, all the science on earth cannot make us believe that it is pure water.[49]

The conditions of daily life grew progressively more comfortable throughout this period, however, with a piped water system installed in 1912, electricity in 1915, and the beginnings of a sewer system in 1918. But, paradoxically, as these improvements were made the community itself was entering a period of decline.

I place the first stage of decline from about 1919 to 1940, and the second from 1940 to 1970. The two world wars provide convenient dividing lines because they both took many young people out of the community who did not return. But there were other factors as well. The decades of the 1920s and 1930s were difficult ones throughout the rural West, with a twenty-year farm depression reaching a peak with the severe drought of 1934. Yet Huntington would have begun to decline at about this time even without these factors. As Lowry Nelson observes, a growth and decline trend is typical of new settlements.[50] The agricultural and grazing base in Castle Valley was inadequate to support further growth in population. Indeed, with mechanization and falling prices for farm products, farms were merged into larger units, providing a livelihood for fewer families. To an extent this limitation was offset by the availability of employment in the Carbon County coal mines. The town of Mohrland, just inside the Emery County line, was a sort of Huntington satellite for the twenty years between wars, but at a distance of eight miles even that closest coal camp was too far away for commuting. Some men still tried to divide the year, living in the mining camps during the winter and returning to the farm in the summer, but increasingly they tended to relocate more or less permanently, reluctantly (in most cases) accepting a different way of life as the price for economic survival. At the same time, the growing commercial predominance of Price led to a decline in business activity in Huntington.

The combined effects of national and local conditions can be traced in single representative example. J. W. Nixon opened his store in 1900 and for two decades conducted a prosperous business, making as much as $90,000 per year, much of which came from wholesale dealings in locally produced alfalfa seed and honey.[51] In 1919 Nixon sold his operation to my grandfather, Edward G. Geary, and moved to Provo (just one of several prominent citizens to move away from Huntington at about that time). Grandpa did not continue the wholesale part of the business, but the retail store remained in about the same competitive position as it held under Nixon. The retail sales gradually declined from $28,636 in 1921 to $23,978 in 1928, then more sharply in the 1930s, reaching a mere $6,415 in 1938, the last year of operation. Grandpa's net worth, reflecting his farm and other activities as well as the store, rose from $14,506 in 1921 to $30,486 in 1930, then fell to $21,206 in 1936.[52]

This decline was not apparent at first in an actual drop in population but rather in the cessation of growth, indicating that most young people, as they came of age, were leaving the community. And those people who could make the strongest contribution to church and civic institutions were most likely to leave. In the late teens, for example, the talented Johnson brothers, James and Evart, who were leaders in dramatics and music, moved away, as did such other community leaders as J. Fleming Wakefield, Jr., and Don C. Woodward.[53] At the same time there came a decline in building activity in the community. Although several new homes were built in the years following, they were nearly all more modest in size and more commonplace in design than the solid brick houses of the flowering period. The high school building was erected in 1923, after fire destroyed the schoolhouse built in 1908. But that was virtually the end of major construction for twenty-five years until a new Mormon chapel was built in 1950. The building of schools was symbolic in a way, for increasingly the high school became the focus of community activity in drama, music, and sports, which became the province of young people rather than of the community as a whole.

This general pattern is probably typical of rural Utah in this period. In Huntington, however, some special factors led to an even more obvious decline. Much of the land on which the town was built began to turn swampy after several decades of irrigation, killing the orchards and causing whole sections of town to be abandoned. This shale soil also proved to be a poor foundation for heavy brick buildings, and most of the houses and public buildings were gone by the 1960s. An additional problem was a quirk in local construction methods which made the brick houses especially liable to chimney fires. My grandfather, in 1950, could remember seeing more than sixty homes burn down in town.[54]

The decline was gradual at first, as I have suggested, but obvious by the period of second-stage depopulation. This is the period of my own childhood, and I must counter the easy assumptions of decadence by saying that it was an excellent time for a boy to grow up. To be sure, the town was badly run down by then, but that only added to the sense of eternity which Charles Peterson has mentioned in his recollections of Snowflake. There is a dignity, a richness, a sense of accumulated life in an old house or a weathered barn, or most especially in a spacious old meetinghouse that embodies the sacrifices and loving craftsmanship of the whole community—a dignity which simply cannot be expressed to those who have not experienced it for themselves. I feel that I grew up in a town that was as rich in its sense of the past as a thousand-year-old European village. Indeed, when I have since visited such thousand-year-old villages, I have felt immediately at home there; I have felt the same spirit that I had grown up with.

But there was the additional advantage in Huntington of seeing daily those who had been there at the very beginning. It was like the opportunity to discuss the founding of Rome with Romulus or the early days of Plymouth with William Bradford. At the same time there was still a large contingent of young people and a strong community pride in the schools and the achievements of the youth even though it was taken for granted that those achievements would take them away from Castle Valley. In short, it was a genuine community of a kind increasingly remote from the experience of most people, a three- and sometimes four-generation community with a common involvement in communal life.

But this stage, too, eternal though it may have seemed to me as a child, was passing. After 1950, the trend of depopulation accelerated, the population falling from 1,442 in 1950 to 787 in 1960. I was part of the out-migration during that decade. It is difficult to say where the trend might have gone from there. Indeed, we will never know. For in the 1970s development in Huntington took a radically new direction which has almost completely changed the character of the community. With the development of power plants and the opening up of coal mines to serve them, the depopulation of Castle Valley was abruptly reversed. Emery County led the state in the rate of population growth during the 1970s, and for part of that time, during the peak construction period of the power plants, it also led the state in average personal income—a far cry indeed from the early days of hardship on Prickly Pear Flat. Consequently I can also say, with Charles Peterson, that "the changes in the town since my youth dwarf the changes that had taken place before."[55] Huntington is no longer the community I once knew, but it would be wrong to say that the new development has brought more bad than good. It is disappointing that the physical development of the community and improvement in the quality of life have not kept pace with its growing prosperity and that prosperity itself is at the mercy of the ups and downs of the coal industry. On the other hand, there is at last an answer to the decades-old dream that the town's young people might have an opportunity to remain at home and contribute to the building up of their own community.

In any case, the developments of the 1970s have brought to an end the period in which Huntington and the other Castle Valley towns could be considered as representative of the development of the Mormon town. If they are representative now, it is of the problems of boomtown development which face wide areas of the West in the next several years. This change is so radical that it perhaps makes the past irrelevant to an understanding of the future. It is interesting to note, however, that the rapid growth of the last ten years is similar in some respects to that of the first ten years of the town. In the first instance, that period was followed by a period of flowering, when community institutions were strengthened and the quality of life improved. Perhaps we may look forward to a second flowering.

NOTES

1. Charles S. Peterson, *Utah: A Bicentennial History* (New York: Norton, 1977), 41.

2. Virginia Sorenson, *Where Nothing Is Long Ago: Memories of a Mormon Childhood* (New York: Harcourt, Brace, and World, 1963).

3. Charles S. Peterson, "A Mormon Town: One Man's West," *Journal of Mormon History*, 3 (1976):3.

4. Lowry Nelson, *Boyhood in a Mormon Village: A Turn-of-the-Century Memoir* (Privately published, 1972), foreword.

5. *Journal History*, May 24, 1875, quoted in John H. S. Smith, "Census Perspectives: The Sanpete Origins of Emery County Settlement," in *Emery County: Reflections on Its Past and Future*, ed. Allan Kent Powell (Salt Lake City: Utah State Historical Society, 1979), 46.

6. Smith, "Census Perspectives," 46.

7. Stella McElprang, ed., *Castle Valley: A History of Emery County* (Emery County: Daughters of Utah Pioneers, 1949), 27.

8. Ibid., 22-23.

9. Ibid., 17.

10. The anecdote is recounted by Peterson, *Utah,* 137.

11. Leonard J. Arrington and Melvin A. Larkin, "The Logan Tabernacle and Temple," *Utah Historical Quarterly*, 41 (1973):302.

12. J. Albert Jones, *A Story of the Settling of Huntington, Utah* (Privately published, n.d.), 12.

13. Ibid., 12-14.

14. Ibid., 15-22.

15. Ibid., 27.

16. Ibid., 28.

17. Ibid., 18-22.

18. Mary Ann Rowbury Brown Gordon, "A Life Sketch of Mary Ann Rowley Brown Gordon," Huntington Daughters of Utah Pioneers Collection, Manuscript Division, Harold B. Lee Library, Brigham Young University, Provo, Utah (hereafter referred to as Huntington DUP Collection).

19. This anecdote was related by Sunny Seely Redd, November 19, 1980.

20. "Minutes of Huntington Manufacturing and Agricultural Company," January 9, 1880, April 21, 1884, February 7, 1885, Manuscript Division, Harold B. Lee Library, Brigham Young University, Provo, Utah.

21. Jones, *Settling of Huntington,* 38-40.

22. McElprang, *Castle Valley*, 228.

23. Lowry Nelson, *The Mormon Village: A Pattern and Technique of Land Settlement* (Salt Lake City: University of Utah Press, 1952), 141.

24. Andrew Jenson, *Encyclopedic History of the Church of Jesus Christ of Latter-day Saints* (Salt Lake City: Deseret News Publ. Co., 1941), passim.

25. Edward G. Geary, "Personal History" (unpublished manuscript in possession of the author), 8.

26. Gordon, "Life Sketch of Mary Ann Rowbury Brown Gordon."

27. Nelson, *Boyhood in a Mormon Village*, 4.

28. McElprang, *Castle Valley*, 223-24.

29. Gordon, "Life Sketch of Mary Ann Rowbury Brown Gordon."

30. Smith, "Census Perspectives," 47.

31. W. H. Lever, *History of Sanpete and Emery Counties, Utah* (Ogden, 1898), 508-9.

32. Talitha C. Avery, "A Sketch of Talitha C. Avery's Life," Huntington DUP Collection.

33. This list is drawn from personal knowledge and the brief biographies that appear in Jones, *Settling of Huntington.*

34. Nelson, *Boyhood in a Mormon Village*, 7.

35. Allan Kent Powell, "Castle Valley at the Beginning of the Twentieth Century," in Powell, *Emery County*, 1-34. Powell's paper gives a comprehensive picture of some key changes between 1880 and 1900.

36. Nelson, *Boyhood in a Mormon Village*, 10.

37. *Autobiography of James William Nixon* (Washington, D.C.: Privately published, 1937), 30.

38. For a detailed account of the emergence of this second generation in Huntington life, see Elmo G. Geary, "A Study of Dramatics in Castle Valley from 1875-1925" (Master's thesis, University of Utah, 1953), 87-104.

39. McElprang, *Castle Valley*, 29-31.

40. Elmo G. Geary, "Dramatics in Castle Valley," 72.

41. Ibid., 73.

42. Ibid., 74.

43. Ibid., 88.

44. Ibid., 54.

45. Nelson, *Boyhood in a Mormon Village*, 39-40.

46. Ibid., 15.

47. Ibid., 46.

48. Powell, "Castle Valley," 22-25.

49. Quoted in Jay M. Haymond, "Natural Resources in Emery County," in Powell, *Emery County*, 58.

50. Nelson, *Boyhood in a Mormon Village*, 9.

51. Nixon Autobiography, 46.

52. Personal papers of Edward G. Geary.

53. Geary, "Dramatics in Castle Valley," 120-26.

54. Personal papers of Edward G. Geary.

55. Peterson, "A Mormon Town," 4.

4

Generations of Elites
and Social Change
in Phoenix

G. Wesley Johnson

While Edward Geary examines the growth, decline and rebirth of a small community in central Utah, G. Wesley Johnson, Professor of History at University of California-Santa Barbara, looks at the growth of Phoenix, the large and sprawling metropolis in Arizona. Dr. Johnson points out that it was not merely the sunny climate that brought about the growth of Phoenix but "sustained activity of many boosters, entrepreneurs, and civic leaders over several generations that lifted the desert hamlet up from obscurity to become a great regional capital." After explaining the methods of gathering material for the Phoenix History Project, Dr. Johnson divides into four groups those who helped develop the area, namely the Town Elite, the Old City Elite, the New City Elite and the Metropolitan Elite. The Town Elite (1885 to 1901) encouraged railroad construction to Phoenix, promoted Phoenix as the state capital and persuaded the federal government to build a dam for irrigation. The Old City Elite (1910 to 1935) encouraged boosterism and created publicity for the city as a desert oasis. The New City Elite (1935 to 1960) consolidated power and laid plans for the postwar expansion. Finally, the Metropolitan Elite (1960 to 1980) represents the creation of many power groups within the large urban sprawl.

In the fall of 1870, federal census takers visited a new village near the banks of the Salt River in Central Arizona. Here they found about three hundred new settlers who had excavated some of the old Indian canals and had begun irrigating the harsh desert floor. One of these pioneers was Darrell Duppa, an Englishman of some education, who marveled at the great expanse of canals left behind by the Hohokam, the ancients who had first inhabited this Sonoran valley. Duppa succumbed to American frontier boosterism and predicted the settlement would one day become a great city, rising Phoenix-like from the ashes of this old civilization. In fact, the Egyptian bird of mythology caught the fancy of the townsfolk, and Phoenix was the name given the new town. It proved to be an apt foretelling of the future, because in 110 short years, that desert hamlet grew to become a metropolis of 1.5 million persons, the ninth largest city in the nation.

Why did Phoenix attain such spectacular growth? Its beginnings were hardly auspicious: founded near a non-navigable desert stream, isolated from the mainline railroads for decades, and situated in the midst of the great Sonoran Desert which rivaled Death Valley in summer temperatures, its future seemed similar to hundreds of other frontier towns—marginal at best. In this essay, I attempt to answer the question of "why did Phoenix grow" in human terms, by looking at the people who presided over its rise to prominence. I look briefly at economic and political factors, but my focus is upon social factors, especially the formation and continuity of elites in presiding over the development of Phoenix. In his study of Houston elites, William D. Angel found that "natural conditions did not dictate the future success of cities like Houston. The entrepreneurial behavior of a few prosperous capitalists did."[1] In the case of Phoenix, it was the sustained activity of many boosters, entrepreneurs, and civic leaders over several generations that lifted the desert hamlet up from obscurity to become a great regional capital. It is my basic argument that a major factor for rapid social change and development in Phoenix was the activity of these community leaders I will refer to as the "elite." With so many handicaps, like Houston, the ascension of Phoenix was closely linked to the quality and ability of its local leadership class and its capacity for action over several generations.

The Methodological Approach

Few American cities offer a more striking example of social change in several generations than Phoenix, where most of the period of intense community development is within the memory of people living today, This is fortunate since the citizens of the new city were far too busy to keep systematic written records on society, politics, and economy. When the Phoenix History Project was planned during the national bicentennial period to collect materials for a history of Phoenix, it was determined that oral history interviews should be given a high priority to make up for the lack of written documentation that characterized Phoenix in the 1970s. Lack of a local historical society until 1973 and no city archive meant that the community's written legacy of its past was sparse or nonexistent.[2] The Phoenix History Project planned and carried out five hundred oral history interviews with a variety of Phoenicians, chosen as knowledgeable informants, over a five-year period. These interviews are prime evidence for examining the reasons for the rapid growth of Phoenix and the development of local leadership, since many informants had participated in or had firsthand knowledge of community "turning points."

These informants represented a wide variety of occupations, social classes, family backgrounds, ethnic groups, religions, geographical locations within the city, and educational backgrounds. A number of informants served as members of an informal panel to advise on who should be interviewed (if still alive) or be studied (if dead or moved from Phoenix). Publicity in local news media about the project resulted in hundreds of phone calls and letters from the general public, from which suggestions for further interviews were compiled. In addition, local political, economic, and social leaders were contacted for suggestions, and their participation became the equivalent of another panel to advise the project.

The persons interviewed were asked to comment on the development of community leadership and to identify persons who had contributed; the results from the interviews were added to the results of the informal panels mentioned above, and these results were compared with research in so-called "mug" books (biographical dictionaries) and an extensive chronological investigation of Phoenix newspapers (from 1878 to 1970) carried out by Aimee Lykes. On the basis of the synthesis of these data, names of "elite" members were suggested. More detailed results will be published later, but for this essay the focus is upon the leaders identified and their actions during several generations. From a methodological perspective, the Phoenix History Project used elements of both the reputational and decisional approaches for analyzing elite behavior and power relationships. Decisions on major questions of public policy were analyzed as a source of determining who participated in decision making and this was contrasted with the members of the community "nominated" by the panels. The result presented here is a synthesis.[3]

The elites under study were divided into different cohorts—not birth cohorts, but period cohorts; that is, periods during which members demonstrated measurable activity within community affairs. As is set out below, the five cohort groups correspond with five periods of growth and social change within the community. One can argue that these five periods of change derive partially from the activity of these cohorts (in addition to economic and political factors) during that time. In fact, the activity of these cohorts during the first four periods was a prime causal factor for change. As Glen Elder has observed, "An understanding of change thus entails comparative investigation of the setting, composition, and process of cohort flows and their relation to social institutions."[4] These cohort groups of elites built up Phoenix during three successive stages—first as a town, second as a well-defined city, and third as an expanding metropolis. During the first two stages—Phoenix as town and city—it is necessary for this analysis to divide each stage in two. Hence, five period cohorts as a part of the urban biography of Phoenix are:

the Founding Elite, the Town Elite, the Old City Elite, the New City Elite, and the Metropolitan Elites.[5]

The Founding Elite—1870 to 1885

The first period cohort, the Founding Elite, provided an initial burst of leadership in Phoenix. By the late 1860s, Salt River Valley was attracting veterans of the Civil War because of lucrative U.S. Army contracts to provision the needs of Ft. McDowell. The army camp, located on the Verde River north of its junction with the Salt, was established to protect new settlers and travelers from Apache Indian attacks. John Y. T. Smith was the first to grow hay for army horses on the banks of the Salt, but it was Jack Swilling, a Confederate veteran, who sized up the ancient Hohokam Indian canals, abandoned for centuries, and realized they could be utilized to grow crops on a more systematic basis than the capricious river would allow. The Swilling Ditch Company attracted mustered-out soldiers from McDowell and miners from nearby Wickenburg, where mines had peaked. William Hancock, who served at McDowell, decided to stay in the Salt River Valley once he was mustered out; in 1870 he was commissioned by leaders of the emerging settlement to survey a town site. John Alsap, a medical doctor who farmed and who later practiced law in Phoenix, was a guiding force in gaining recognition for the young community, and by fall of 1870 a rudimentary local government was organized.[6]

Smith, Swilling, Hancock, and Alsap were joined by Darrell Duppa, who suggested the name "Phoenix" for the new town, as five of the major founders. Of modest means, all had been attracted to life on the frontier for the "main chance": some for mining, such as Swilling and Duppa, some for farming, such as Smith and Hancock (and later Swilling). And in that quest for the main chance, all shared an optimism that saw well beyond the bleak desert that at the outset met their gaze.

Swilling and Duppa had the broadest vision of the future, yet they were reduced to marginal importance within a few years. Swilling stood accused of robbery and murder, was sent to Yuma prison, and died shortly afterward; Duppa became a saloon keeper who dabbled in mining. Smith became a prosperous farmer and big landowner, and married Phoenix's first schoolmarm. Hancock and Alsap both practiced law at times, traded in real estate, and in 1881, when the settlement was finally incorporated as a city, Alsap was elected first mayor.

Other settlers of greater means and much energy arrived during the 1870s, and apart from Smith, after the mid-1880s all the founding fathers were either dead or no longer influential in the community. One such early newcomer was Charles Trumbull Hayden, prosperous merchant of Tucson, who staked a claim to a strategic valley location and built Hayden's Ferry, at a point where the Salt River during flooding was easiest to cross. He built a flour mill there and within a few years the second community in Salt River Valley was born: it was called Tempe, named (again by Duppa) for the valley of the gods in Greek mythology. When R. G. Dun, the forerunner of Dun and Bradstreet, did the first survey of economic life in the valley, he found Hayden to be the most creditworthy merchant in Phoenix or Tempe. Others, such as the Goldwater family, were still emerging frontier merchants and were not yet impressive to Dun.[7]

The Founding Elite can be characterized in the following terms: most were marginal actors, people of insubstantial means who came to the frontier in search of opportunity. Only latecomer Hayden was a man of some affluence and, interestingly, only he achieved lasting influence—through his son, Carl, who sat in Congress for Arizona for more than five decades. Most were from the Midwest or had Yankee origins—although a few, such as Swilling, were southerners. While these southerners continued to play an important role in town affairs during the first decades, they never succeeded in making Phoenix, like Tucson, a southern city. Phoenix bore the stamp of the Midwest from its foundings down to modern times.[8]

The Town Elite—1895 to 1910

It is rather in examining the Town Elite that patterns of continuity characterizing later growth are found; it was this group of aggressive entrepreneurs who brought two spur rail-roads to Phoenix, captured the state capital from Prescott and Tucson, and persuaded the federal government to build Roosevelt Dam to provide crucial water storage for extended irrigation. Whereas some frontier towns were limited by the actions of their founders, who settled down to mediocrity, Phoenix was able to attract in the 1880s and 1890s a remark-able group of actors both men of means and men of vision. This group inherited a small frontier village, built it into a pros-perous town that became Arizona's territorial capital in 1889, and set the stage for overtaking Tucson as the area's largest city by 1910.[9]

Key members of the new Town Elite were men with excellent financial connections such as Colonel William Christy, William J. Murphy, Emil Ganz, and Moses H. Sher-man. Christy had served as state treasurer of Iowa before coming to Arizona for his health; he was a man of means who bought large acreage on the west side in Phoenix and experi-mented with new crops. But his main contribution was in helping found and direct the Valley Bank which quickly became the leading local financial institution. Christy, with excellent connections to the Midwest, brought Phoenix a touch of "class."[10]

Also arriving in the early 1880s was William J. Murphy, a railroad contractor who had helped build the Atlantic and Pacific through northern Arizona. He took over the herculean task of financing and building the Arizona Canal, the valley's largest irrigation canal more than forty miles long. Murphy gained access to great acreages of land the behemoth canal would water, then he helped finance the canal by selling bonds in Chicago, New York, and Great Britain. In the process, Murphy more than anyone publicized the mild winter climate, the twelve-month growing season, and other unique attrac-tions of Phoenix to the rest of the country and Europe. Murphy also helped form the Arizona Improvement Com-pany, the largest local corporation which dealt in land and water rights. He was also allied with Christy as a backer of his Valley Bank.[11]

Emil Ganz, a German immigrant who had first tried his fortunes in Georgia, later came to Arizona and quickly achieved prominence with his Bank Exchange Hotel. After Phoenix was incorporated in 1881, it had a succession of weak mayors until 1885, when Ganz was elected. Here was the first cosmopolite, a man with a breadth of experience and vision, who put the city on a sound financial basis and inaugurated new services. Ganz later became chief of the rival banking group to Christy; the spirited competition between his Phoenix Bank and the Valley Bank benefited Phoenix, as each vied to finance new commercial and real estate projects.[12]

In real estate, none surpassed the shrewd Yankee, Moses Hazeltine Sherman. A classic example of the Horatio Alger myth, he came to Prescott, Arizona from his native New York State as a penniless schoolteacher. But Sherman confidently borrowed heavily and invested in cattle when prices were down and sold at a handsome profit when prices skyrocketed He moved to Phoenix and invested in land before the land boom of the later 1880s, financed the street railway system in Phoenix, became a prime participant in the Valley Bank, and by 1890 was the largest taxpayer in Phoenix. Sherman had a flair for organizing syndicates and using other people's money to create his own fortune; this was facilitated by the fact that he had married the daughter of an important Southern Pacific official.[13]

In a seminal essay published in 1957, Robert K. Merton separated and compared two archetypes of influential individuals, namely those whose primary interests were local and those who were more cosmopolitan in outlook.[14] One sees this clearly in examining the Founding Elites, who were local in orientation, as opposed to the Town Elites, who were wide ranging in their connections, such as Sherman who had financial allies in San Francisco and Los Angeles, Christy who had friends in Iowa and adjacent midwestern states, and Murphy who had bankers in Chicago and the East. It was this type of activity which distinguishes the two generations of elites, and suggests why Phoenix may have taken off economically, compared to neighboring towns such as Wickenburg or Florence,

where purely local interests and perspectives predominated—
and where little growth occurred after the 1880s.

The mild climate as a haven for health seekers was probably the single most important factor in attracting high quality
newcomers with experience and expertise to Phoenix.[15] Consider for example the young Dwight B. Heard, heir apparent to
the largest hardware company in the nation, who forsook
Chicago for Phoenix in the hope of being cured of pulmonary
illness. His move was influenced by another Chicagoan, John
C. Adams, a former attorney for Marshall Field, who had
recently moved to Phoenix—also for family health reasons—
and had founded the city's premier hostelry, the Adams Hotel.
Moreover, both Adams and Heard were influenced by the
presence of winter visitor Whitelaw Reid, publisher of then the
most important newspaper in the nation, the *New York Tribune.* Following his unsuccessful bid for the vice-presidency (on
the ticket with Benjamin Harrison) in the 1892 election, Reid
traveled to regain his health and spent two winters in Phoenix.
Reid boasted to his eastern friends of the pure air, mild winter
climate, and abundant sunshine. The image of Phoenix as a
hospitable place for winter visitors was enhanced, and soon W.
J. Murphy and his son Ralph founded Ingleside Inn, the first
resort hotel in Phoenix. There was a snowball effect. Heard
wrote to his family in Chicago, justifying his decision to stay on
the frontier because people of the "quality" of Whitelaw Reid
recognized the uniqueness and desirability of Phoenix and
were investing in it. Heard then emulated Murphy and Sherman by persuading midwestern and New England visitors to
invest in Phoenix land, but because his connections were even
more extensive than Murphy or Sherman he became an even
greater economic success with more impact on civic affairs.[16]

Other recruits to the Town Elite were Jewish merchants
such as the Goldwater and Goldberg families, each who found
leading mercantile houses that survive to this day (Goldwater's
and Hanny's); George Luhrs, a German immigrant who built
the Luhrs Hotel and whose sons later built up a real estate
dynasty in Phoenix; John C. Adams, mentioned above, who
was soon elected mayor and became Republican party chief
for many years.

Still another cosmopolitan New Elite was Benjamin F. Fowler, who moved to Phoenix just before 1900. Soon after his arrival he led the fight to have a storage dam built on Salt River so that the capricious water flow could be controlled for irrigation. A major water storage dam had been discussed since the 1880s. Private dams were financed and partially built but the projects failed in the 1890s, and by 1900 talk centered on the idea of getting the federal government to help. But how could a town of 5,000 population, in Arizona Territory (statehood was not attained until 1912), persuade Washington, which had not yet financed reclamation projects, to pick Phoenix as its first major venture?[17]

Fowler was one major reason. He had connections in the East, and he used influence in lobbying in Washington to convince Department of the Interior engineers to pick Phoenix for a massive demonstration project of what could be accomplished in the arid lands of the West. To be sure, other elite members such as Dwight Heard, who was a personal friend and political confidant of President Theodore Roosevelt, helped out. In 1902, after Roosevelt signed the Newlands Reclamation Act, development of the Salt River was announced as the first major national endeavor. In one bold stroke, Fowler and other elite members harnessed the financial power and technical know-how of the federal government to do a job where private enterprise had failed. When the dam was formally dedicated (by former president Theodore Roosevelt) in 1911, a new era of agricultural abundance opened for Phoenix and its adjacent Salt River towns of Mesa, Tempe, and Glendale.[18]

Two other major accomplishments of the Town Elite were obtaining spur lines to Phoenix from the Southern Pacific to the south and Santa Fe to the north by 1887 and 1895, respectively. This meant that the agricultural produce of the valley, then still its main economic resource, could now be sent to California and eastern markets. At the same time, as their town grew and its economic potential soared, the Town Elite literally absconded with the state capital. Phoenix community leaders reasoned that if their town were going to have any pretensions for greatness, it must become the seat of the state capital. In 1889 they "induced" the legislature, sitting in Prescott, then the capital (it had also been in Tucson for a time), to remove to Phoenix—by parlor car, via California, with all expenses paid. Phoenix delegates mustered votes and the victory was celebrated all the way to Phoenix. In one coup, the entrepreneurs of Phoenix put the ornament in the crown they planned for their fair city. Centrally located, sited in the midst of a huge agricultural plain, the future of Phoenix seemed certain when the dam was dedicated and regular water assured. By 1912 President Taft signed Arizona into statehood and Phoenix became the state capital. The big desert town had now become a small city.[19]

The Old City Elite—1910-1935

Statehood brought a new vista for leading business and civic leaders. For several years until the First World War, boosterism flourished and publicity for Phoenix as a garden city and a desert oasis flooded the country. Some members of the Town Elite survived into this period—Heard especially —but Fowler, the primary mover in obtaining the dam, had been replaced by John Orme as head of the Salt River Valley Water Users Association, which controlled the dam, power, and irrigation districts. Sherman moved to Los Angeles. Others of the elite founding families continued to be active: Lloyd Christy continued for his family, heading the Valley Bank and serving as mayor of Phoenix; Sylvan Ganz followed in his father's footsteps as a leading banker. The Goldwater family produced two sons who became active by the end of this period—Robert and Barry—and who would furnish continuity for this pioneer family for another generation. Ralph Murphy managed Ingleside Inn and other properties of his father, W. J.[20]

New faces appeared in Phoenix after the dam and statehood. This group is called the Old City Elite. Largely from the Midwest, they sought opportunity in what now appeared to be the largest city in Arizona, for in 1910, Phoenix at 11,134 was edging up on Tucson at 13,193.[21] George Mickle arrived in the valley soon after statehood, recognized the need for neighborhood markets, and soon founded the largest chain in Arizona—the Pay 'n' Takit markets. In 1927 Mickle sold out to Safeway Stores and plowed his millions into creating the Phoenix Title and Trust Company and building a new skyscraper in Phoenix. Mickle changed business interests and became the very model of the successful entrepreneur who made his fortune in Phoenix, unlike Heard who arrived with a silver spoon. Mickle was active until the 1950s.[22]

Another newcomer was Charles A. Stauffer, publisher of the *Arizona Republic* and *Phoenix Gazette*. Stauffer lived in the shadow of Dwight Heard for many years as his chief assistant, but upon Heard's death he took over Heard's *Republic* and merged it with the *Gazette*. Stauffer became Phoenix's first true press lord by the early 1930s. A mild-mannered, sensitive man, he was well liked in the community. Stauffer also had a golden touch for investments, and he learned how to be an anonymous philanthropist from his mentor Heard. Unlike most members of either the Town or Old City Elite, Stauffer had been reared in the valley. His period of maximum influence was in the 1920s and 1930s. Toward the end of the depression, his brother-in-law, Wesley Knorpp, increasingly ran the newspaper, radio station KTAR, and other enterprises. For an entire generation Stauffer was the chief opinion molder in the community.[23]

It was the Town Elite that had founded and nourished the institutions which became so important in helping to define community leadership during this period, but it was the Old City Elite that initiated the service clubs, such as Rotary, Kiwanis, and Lions; the social clubs, such as the Arizona Club, El Zaribah Shrine, and the Phoenix Country Club; and the Chamber of Commerce, which grew out of the old Board of Trade. This group became conscious of having a "correct address," and members sought exclusive neighborhoods like Los Olivos (pioneered by Heard) between Central Avenue and Third Street; Palmcroft between Seventh and Fifteenth Avenues, north of McDowell Road; and Country Club Estates, surrounding the new clubhouse of the Phoenix Country Club. These prime locations became new seats of power for business, professional, and industrial leaders, with the Country Club area housing affluent winter visitors who now made Phoenix their private residence. These new areas replaced the Bennett and Churchill additions south of McDowell, which had been prime residential locations for the Town Elite.[24]

It is not surprising that during this period an attempt to create a "polite" society in Phoenix occurred. Since Phoenix had never been a western town with stereotypic manners and mores, there was no "uncivilized" past to erase or conveniently forget. Since there was no industry in Phoenix, there was no division between blue-collar workers and managerial or bureaucratic workers. Rather Phoenix was a city dominated by a commercial elite, who benefited from the wealth of the farmers who managed the region's agricultural enterprises. (It was during this period that many farmers, laden with profits from cotton, citrus, and melons, moved to the city.) Perceptions of who was to be in "polite" society centered on including a number of families who dated from Town Elite days, a few from Founding Elite days, and many who were in the process of settling in Phoenix. The first edition of the Phoenix Social Register appeared in 1914, and appeared infrequently for the next two decades.[25]

A far more important means of demarcating who was really part of "Old Phoenix" was the founding shortly after the turn of the century of Iron Springs, a summer resort in the pine forest near Prescott. Early Phoenix families joined together to organize an exclusive summer vacation retreat for women and children, since most husbands stayed in Phoenix to work during the sweltering summers and took the train to visit on weekends. Acceptance into this self-defining community was far more conclusive about a person's status as compared to inclusion in the Social Register.[26]

The Woman's Club was founded in 1900 and would continue to be a focal point for feminine activities for the next fifty years. Social life in pre-World War II days was rooted in personal entertainments, informal parties, and several seasonal

balls, the most famous of which was the St. Luke's Ball,
founded in the 1920s, still given today as a benefit for St.
Luke's Hospital. Ironically, a woman who remained an out-
sider at heart was the dominant person in Phoenix social life.
This was Maie Heard, wife of Dwight, who survived his death
in the late 1920s for another twenty years. Mrs. Heard directed
numerous charities, founded an American Indian art museum,
privately financed the major community welfare operation
before the New Deal, and helped innumerable community
service organizations, such as the Boy Scouts. Yet Mrs. Heard
never bought a house at Iron Springs, and the guest book of
her home, Casa Blanca, kept from about 1902 to her husband's
death, reveals precious few local Phoenicians who dined at her
table—most of her guests were visiting notables. In a sense, she
typified a few families who considered themselves above local
polite society. In her case, her father was one of Chicago's most
respected and influential citizens. Maie Heard took her social
status from Chicago, not Phoenix, even though Phoenix was
her home for fifty years.[27]

Domination of the Chamber of Commerce after World
War I was in keeping with a Harding-Coolidge era preoccupa-
tion with business-as-gospel; in the Phoenix instance, the
1920s and 1930s became an era of weakness in city government. This was a cruel disappointment to some progressives,
who had sponsored a new city charter in 1913 and put Phoenix
in the vanguard nationally in moving to a city manager-
commission form of government. Unfortunately, no attempt
was made to find professional city managers and the position
became a part of the local spoils system. Never rising above
local squabbles, city politics were dominated by second and
third echelon community leaders. Petty vice-lords arose in the
1930s and 1940s, payoffs were common on municipal contracts, and a seamy side appeared to city life. But Phoenix
never became a corrupt fiefdom for a city boss or clique; it
suffered rather from neglect of the true community leaders,
who were busy in commerce, agriculture, and the professions.
In this latter category, a host of lawyers and doctors who
would become important in local affairs now surfaced; the Old

City Elite included such affluent medical doctors as R. W. Craig, E. Payne Palmer, Sr., and W. J. McLoone, and prominent attorneys such as J. L. B. Alexander, Louis Chalmers, Alexis Baker, and Richard Sloan.[28]

A consolidation of power among families also took place: this was the era of greatest growth for the Jewish merchant families like the Goldwaters, Diamonds, and Korricks. The O'Malley family, arriving from St. Louis in the early 1900s, emerged during this time as a major factor in lumberyards, building materials, land, and development. The McArthur brothers, Warren and Charles, perhaps best typified the success of family enterprises. Moving from Chicago soon after statehood, they became distributors for Dodge motor cars and by the 1920s had become two of Phoenix's leading entrepreneurs. They conceived of an international resort hotel on the desert in Phoenix—decades ahead of their time—and found backing to build the world famous Arizona Biltmore, finished in 1929. The McArthurs typified the cosmopolitan aspect of the Old City Elite, with their connections in Chicago. However, the depression cut short their plans and the Wrigley family took over the Biltmore. Indeed, the Wrigleys had built the ultimate mansion in Phoenix atop an adjacent knoll to the Biltmore, from whence they could watch Phoenix at work to the south and the Biltmore crowd at play to the east. (The Wrigleys heralded another group to be considered below, the Expatriate Elites.)[29]

What was the accomplishment of the Old City Elite? They presided over the transition from town to city, by pushing Phoenix into a building boom without precedent in the 1920s. The Phoenix skyline for the next four decades was created as in quick succession the Heard, Luhrs, Security, Luhrs Tower, and Title and Trust buildings were constructed. George Luhrs, second-generation member of the local elite, was put in charge of his family's two major edifices and struggled during the depression to keep them open. It was this modernized American skyline of high-rise buildings that was the main legacy of this group for the city, a reflection of their determination to convert Phoenix from a garden town into a well-defined city, with a downtown area of shopping and professional services.[30]

The New City Elite—1935-1960

Growing out of both the Town and Old City Elites, the New City Elite became the group that tightened control over the city by maintaining power at the Chamber of Commerce and in 1949, by means of Charter Government reform, taking control of city politics. In practice little different from the Old City Elite, there were old names but a new generation: second generation O'Malleys, third generation Goldwaters. This was the group that, after consolidating power, laid plans for post-war expansion of Phoenix and managed to direct and control the city until about 1960, when Phoenix became a metropolitan area far transcending even the most grandiose Chamber of Commerce projections of 1945.[31]

A further example was Walter Bimson, who personified the new element in Phoenix. Bimson, a native of Colorado, became a talented young executive at Harris Trust in Chicago. Like Heard forty years before, Bimson, who visited Phoenix on bank accounts, saw his future in Arizona and accepted an offer to take over the ailing Valley Bank. Bimson's success in saving the bank provided the foundation for other Phoenix businesses in coping with the depression and rebuilding. Bimson founded a banking dynasty and provided cosmopolitan leadership for Phoenicians for three decades. Furthermore, Bimson brought a new level of sophistication and maturity to the city by stressing cultural activities. He assembled his own first-rate art collection, persuaded his bank to invest in art, then became the catalyst for the community to build the Phoenix Art Museum in the 1950s.[32]

In fact, one can argue that aside from political reform, this elite cohort group's greatest accomplishments were cultural. Dr. Howell Randolph, a medical doctor of taste and sophistication, became the prime mover in creating the Phoenix Symphony Orchestra in the mid-1940s. Pre-World War II Phoenix was a city of limited cultural life; but the postwar surge of population brought with it newcomers interested in providing Phoenix with cultural institutions hitherto neglected.[33]

By 1940, as this new group became consolidated, other newcomers beyond Bimson appeared. Preeminent among attorneys were Orme Lewis and Frank Snell; within a few years both founded law firms which became the most prestigious firms in town and still bear their names. Snell especially emerged during the war as a community "power broker" when he was able to convince a weak City Hall to clamp down on rampant vice conditions, this in part as an inducement to lift restrictions on weekend liberty of thousands of servicemen stationed at nearby Luke and Williams Air Force bases. After the war Snell joined forces with ally Edward O'Malley on a variety of projects, and a list of his accomplishments in bringing community projects to life (working with Bimson on the Art Museum and founding the Thunderbird School of Foreign Trade, for example) is long indeed. Snell and O'Malley were successful in helping Phoenix gain control of its second largest utility, Arizona Public Service, and Snell later served as board chairman. Snell never held office, preferring to work through a close group of allies to make certain that community affairs went in the "right direction." It was a measure of agreement at the top that no one ever suggested that either Bimson or Snell were city bosses; rather, they personified the aspirations of the directing group they led.[34]

The attitude of shared agreement characterized the direction of city life in Phoenix from the beginning; for such a meager population base, perhaps this is not surprising. It proved to be essential as the middle New City Elite period approached—just after World War II. Phoenix had benefited immensely from war industries (e.g., Goodyear, AiResearch, and Aluminum Company of America) plus five army air training facilities, a navy depot, and an army training ground. When peace came, the local economy was immediately in trouble as these war industries closed down. The business community of Phoenix feared a return to a prewar agricultural economy. Lewis Haas, an experienced executive, was brought in to revivify the Chamber of Commerce, and under his direction, Chamber staff and citizen committees launched an ambitious drive to bring industry back to Phoenix. International events intervened to aid the cause, since the Korean war build-up meant electronics manufacturers, such as Motorola, took a fresh look at Phoenix and built new plants. By the end of the

1950s General Electric and Sperry Rand had been lured to the valley—and with them a host of related smaller manufacturers, jobbers, and suppliers.[35]

Before the local "economic miracle" could succeed, however, it became clear to the directing elite that control over City Hall was essential before industry could be convinced to bank on Phoenix. Although under Snell's influence vice had been cleaned up during the war, politics in the immediate postwar period lapsed back into the apathetic situation of the 1930s. In this instance, a crusading *Republic* and *Gazette*, now taken over by "Hoosier" publisher Eugene Pulliam, who had bought out Stauffer and Knorpp, led the way by exposing the unfortunate return of vice, graft, and pay offs at City Hall. A citizen's committee, appointed by Mayor Ray Busey, who was struggling to reform the system he had inherited, came in with recommendations to revamp the City's charter. The result was that the commission form of government, with each commissioner presiding over certain prerequisites, such as police or streets, was thrown out and a council system with members elected from the city at large was instituted. Moreover, the requirement that the city manager be a legal resident of the city when appointed was abolished, since for years this had precluded hiring a professionally trained manager from another city. New elections were called in 1949, and a slate of candidates (henceforth known as the Charter Government ticket), who were drawn from the New City Elite, took over City Hall. Nicholas Udall, Mormon lawyer and scion of the famous Udall family, was elected mayor; Harry Rosenzweig, member of the prominent jeweler family, and others were elected to the council. Rosenzweig made political history by convincing another son of an old elite family to run for Council—a person who had made a name for himself as an outstanding photographer and adventurer, organizing boat trips down the Colorado River through Grand Canyon when few mortals attempted such a feat. This newcomer to local politics proved to be so adept and popular that he stayed only one term on the reformed council. In 1952 he audaciously ran against Ernest W. McFarland for Arizona's U. S. Senate seat. McFarland,

Harry Truman's majority leader, mentor of Lyndon Johnson, was retired by this brash upstart who had cut his teeth in city politics—Barry Goldwater.[36]

For the next twenty-five years, local politics were controlled by Charter Government's political committee, which met in secret every two years to handpick a slate of candidates to run for city office. It was clearly dominated by members of the New City Elite, and opponents derided the fact that most of Charter's candidates over the years lived in the more affluent suburbs, belonged to many of the same clubs, and had a "WASPish" orientation. Charter's managers were not foolish and attempted to provide ethnic and religious representation. Hence, at various times Charter handpicked Mexican-American, Asian-American, and black candidates, and regular spots were assigned to Jews, Mormons, and Catholics. One of Charter's wisest decisions was to pick Ray Wilson as city manager in 1950. Wilson, prior associate manager at Kansas City, brought the first hand of professional management to Phoenix and left an indelible mark of expertise that helped transform the city. Phoenix now became a showcase of municipal government. An example of the city's excellence in this regard was the inauguration of a prestigious internship program that ranks today as one of the nation's finest. The reform thereby provided the reputation for honest municipal administration that helped attract the new industry the Chamber of Commerce was seeking.[37]

Whereas elected city government participants between the wars included relatively few able community leaders, the lists of Charter Government-picked candidates during the 1950s and into the 1970s reads like a Who's Who of local business and professional leadership. During the 1950s the high point of elite influence was reached because there was still only one major group running Phoenix—Charter ran politics and Charter's informal backers, such as Snell, Bimson, O'Malley, and Pulliam (none of whom ever held office) provided the link to the Chamber of Commerce and Lewis Haas. Politics and economic development worked hand in hand, and when Jack Williams, well known local broadcaster, was elected mayor in the mid 1950s, the media was recruited as part of this directing group. Williams, whose voice had been known to Phoenicians for twenty years, was an authentic New City Elite member. He had grown up during the Old City Elite period, but he now helped articulate the goals of the newer cohort group. Many Charter members and allies became part of the Goldwater wing of the Republican party, but Williams's successor as mayor after four years, Democrat Sam Mardian, demonstrated that Charter remained essentially bipartisan. Williams went on to become governor of Arizona for several terms—an exception, since most Charter candidates never ran for state office, viewing their turn at City Council a "civic responsibility."[38]

Phoenix during the 1950s was firmly in the hands of the generation which emerged in the mid and late 1930s—Bimson, Snell, O'Malley, Orme Lewis, the Rosenzweig brothers, Harry and Newton, and others. They were joined by newcomer publisher Pulliam and Chamber of Commerce head Haas in the 1940s; indeed, as Phoenix's population quadrupled, other newcomers arrived, but their major influence and activity was deferred to the decade of the 1960s and beyond. The 1950s, the period of Eisenhower normalcy, was also the classical period of one-elite-group rule in Phoenix, with all the economic, political, and media bases covered. This was a time when Frank Snell could still, as members of the elite had done for several decades, sit down for lunch at the Arizona Club with a few friends and develop either public or private policy for Phoenix, as the occasion demanded. It was a time when the directing elite welcomed the onrush of growth in Phoenix, since everyone was becoming affluent; it appeared as though this group had promoted a demographic revolution that would assure an economic bonanza for the old families.[39]

The Metropolitan Elites—1960-1980s

The very success Charter and the Chamber of Commerce provided proved to be the eventual undoing of the New City Elite. With Phoenix expanding from 100,000 in 1950 to more than 400,000 in 1960, the unprecedented influx of newcomers meant this ruling elite faced problems of recruitment (who would be allowed to enter their ranks?) and maintenance of power (how to replace aging or dead members?). A more serious problem was the spatial development of the city, because the demographic revolution was spreading the city over hundreds of square miles newly annexed to the city. The greatest expansion took place during the regimes of Mayor Jack Williams in the late 1950s and Mayor Sam Mardian in the early 1960's. By the late 1960's this Los Angeles-like urban sprawl resulted in the creation of multiple power centers throughout Salt River Valley.

First, within Phoenix, the midtown area developed after Ralph Burgbacher's new Park Central Mall stimulated a decentralization from the original downtown nucleus. Soon a host of high-rise buildings mushroomed in the corridor along Central Avenue, containing new corporations, new ventures, and newcomers with different agendas from the old elites. This was particularly true in banking, where old-line banks like Valley Bank, First National Bank, and Arizona Bank built new headquarters in thirty-and forty-story skyscrapers, but placed them downtown, while most of the newer financial entities built in midtown. Walter Bimson of Valley and Sherman Hazeltine of First National committed their institutions to remain in the old town center which had been the home of four generations of elites. With no such nostalgia, the newcomers, the Metropolitan Elites, chose midtown.[40]

Or they chose other valley locations that proved attractive. Scottsdale, just northeast of Phoenix proper, is an example. Once a tourist mecca with cheap, westernlike store facades, Scottsdale emerged from curiosity status in the 1940s to become a full-fledged modern city by the late 1950s and 1960s. After battling Phoenix and successfully annexing a huge slice of the northeast residential area, Scottsdale increasingly became the home of affluent newcomers; some were retired, winter visitors prolonging their stay, and others were ambitious younger professional business people. In fact, Scottsdale became a symbol for an ambitious, often nouveau riche group of people who set up their own standards of exclusivity. Another power center was the Mesa-Tempe complex, adjacent to the southeast; these two cities both reached more than 100,000 people by 1970, and no longer could be considered mere bedroom communities of Phoenix. Talley Industries located in Mesa and Tempe, home of Arizona State University, became a center for research and high-tech industries, and, together with Chandler further to the southeast, have been the biggest growth area in the Valley in the late 1970s and early 1980s.[41]

An embryonic power center emerging during the end of this period was Northwest Phoenix-Glendale, an area long dominated by agricultural interests. But with completion of the gigantic Metrocenter Mall, the area gained a more specific focus. By the early 1980s, a fourth power center within Phoenix seemed to be in formation: the Camelback-Biltmore corridor on east Camelback Road, northeast of downtown Phoenix, near the resorts that had grown immensely after the war and firmly established the desirability of Phoenix climate and life-style. Each one of these new centers had its own group of economic and civic leaders. Even veterans such as Frank Snell admitted it was no longer possible to sit down for lunch at the Arizona Club to decide the fortunes of the city. There were now too many clubs, too many players, too many interests.

Phoenix had reached the size and status of a metropolis by 1980, and this gave rise to what political scientists call pluralistic power centers and pluralistic elites. The decade of the 1960s was the period of transition, as the old single-focus elite waned and the multiple new power centers came to the fore. In politics, Charter Government held on but almost lost out under Charter mayor Milt Graham, whose own popularity caused him eventually to abandon Charter and win successful reelection as an independent. But the die was cast, and after Charter mayors John Driggs and Tim Barrow had finished their terms of office, Margaret Hance emerged as an independent by the mid-1970s. An aging Charter Government Committee finally abandoned politics by the end of the decade and Phoenix by 1980 was in the midst of a political realignment, with ethnic groups and disadvantaged economic groups coming forward to claim more representation in the city's councils.[42]

From an economic perspective, diffused power throughout the city was the order of the day. One exception was the media, however, which was still firmly in the hands of the old elite (McFarland and Chauncey's television stations, Pulliam's newspapers). But even the media changed when Chauncey sold out and Pulliam died. While one could find examples of younger generations of older elites active in Phoenix (e.g., Richard Snell of Ramada Inns, Gary Driggs of Western Savings, and Ed Korrick on the City Council), the most obvious fact about the metropolitan Phoenix area was that its directing elites were metropolitan and dispersed.

Another way of looking at leadership in contemporary Phoenix is suggested by the five hundred interviews completed by the Phoenix History Project, where a pattern of influentials has been suggested. This can briefly be summarized as follows, as a further articulation of the Metropolitan Elites.

1. The Technicians. These are the highly trained bureaucrats who run City Hall and its services, who work in the multiple layers of staff and bureaucracy which characterize an expanded state government. These are also the high tech engineers of Motorola, General Electric, and Sperry.

2. The Managers. With the rise of big industrial corporations in Phoenix, dozens of top executives have invaded the valley. Some, such as the head of Greyhound who preferred Phoenix to Chicago, have moved the entire corporation to the valley.

3. The Entrepreneurs. These are the David Murdocks and Karl Ellers, who built syndicates, conglomerates, and skyscrapers. One of them, William Schulz, who became the apartment king of Phoenix, dared to challenge Barry Goldwater for the Senate in 1980—and almost won.

4. The Cultural Brokers. Postwar Phoenix needed cultural institutions, and although old elite Walter Bimson helped move the city in new cultural directions, it was members of the

new Metro Elite such as newcomer Lewis Ruskin who put a stamp of quality and cosmopolitanism on Phoenix's new cultural institutions. This also includes the famous Phoenix Zoo, which the Maytag family of Iowa helped found.

5. The Intellectuals. Singularly absent from Phoenix life until the 1960s, this group has grown parallel with Arizona State University (40,000 students in 1984), which has become one of the largest urban centers of research and higher learning in the country.

One can query whether these approximate interest groups belong within a larger elite structure, and it is possible that the notion of multiple power centers and pluralist elites may be tempered by interest groups and coalitions. Groups increasingly interested in gaining access to power include ethnic minorities and retired persons, both of which are important factions willing to take action.

There is yet another group which has made an impact on Phoenix—the so-called "Expatriate Elites." Since the beginning of the twentieth century, Phoenix has attracted winter visitors, but some of them, from Whitelaw Reid on, such as the Wrigleys, McCormicks, and John Lincolns, have been a special force in the community, endowing institutions and making major investments. The fact that both Harris Trust and Northern Trust of Chicago, two of Illinois' largest banks, have recently opened branch offices in Scottsdale suggests the scale and importance of expatriate activity in Phoenix.[43]

These preliminary impressions of the new Metropolitan Elites suggest the fluidity of the present situation in Phoenix. It is a period of transition and realignment in all spheres. In a city which has been characterized by rapid social change, the pace of change has accelerated even more since 1960. Frank Snell said he thought Phoenix had always been relatively open for newcomers, and that those who aspired to participate in the direction the community could be accommodated. The bulk of research supports this view—that is, provided you were not a member of a minority or ethnic group. Phoenix had few original-entry ethnic enclaves; almost all ethnic groups (save some Mexican Americans) had lived elsewhere before migrating to Phoenix—they were what is often called "redirects." Thus it was possible for some Italian American and Jewish families to penetrate the ranks of the Old City Elite in the early 1900s. Save for the early country clubs, Phoenix rarely showed much anti-Semitism. But access to power for Mexican Americans and blacks had to wait until the 1950s and 1960s, when representatives were admitted to City Hall on Charter tickets. By standards of the 1980s, appointing these leaders was probably tokenism, but at the time Phoenix was proud to admit such ethnic minorities to the levers of power. Only Native Americans have been totally excluded from beginning to present. And this is a special case, since local Indians have failed to take advantage of the Federal Indian School at Phoenix, which has trained generations of Indian leaders for nations such as the Navajo, far removed from Phoenix. Local Indians such as the Maricopas, Papagos, and Pimas have been unsuccessful in putting enough young people into the educational system to bring forth a new generation of aspirants to leadership until the present; perhaps their day at City Hall will come.[44]

The data do not allow further speculation on the crucial theoretical question of "circulation of elites," but it seems apparent that the post-1960 period will be viewed by future historians as the time when the old elite structure crumbled, when great population increases resulted in new power centers and pluralist elites as well as dramatic spatial expansion, and when minority and other ethnic and special interest groups became a part of the metropolitan structure. No longer does one group direct the political and economic affairs of Phoenix.

Though they have not created a modern Utopia—as some have proclaimed—the several generations of successive controlling elites have had a predominant influence on the development of one of the nation's largest (ninth in 1980), fastest growing, and most cosmopolitan cities. Will this growth continue, as city fathers and most of the Metropolitan Elites wish? Or will Phoenix slow down for the balance of the twentieth century, to assimilate its hundreds of thousands of newcomers?

The period 1985 to 2000 may prove to be still another turning point for the community, as the city strives to consolidate and create a new formula for leadership.

One other major factor affecting the post-1960 period in Phoenix is the fact that local influentials have lost control not only because of the demographic explosion that changed the face of Phoenix, but also because Phoenix has become a part of the national Sun Belt phenomenon. Growth of federal government programs has meant that even City Hall, ironically the very bastion of Goldwaterism, has become dependent upon Washington for many programs and services. New factories and new service industries, such as American Express, that have located in Phoenix are national in scope and have had few (if any) local ties. Phoenix has become a national institution, and as one wit has observed, "Every winter that plunges below normal temperatures brings ten thousand new recruits to Phoenix." Even Frank Snell, who helped orchestrate the postwar growth, admitted in 1980 that he never imagined it would become so large.[45]

The larger significance of this study may lie in the fact that Phoenix as a frontier community was able to control its own fortunes until quite late, when other, older cities had succumbed to economic, political, and social forces of a national character. We have seen how during the formative years the quality of leaders Phoenix attracted made it possible to surpass other frontier communities, to become the state capital, and to obtain federal backing for building the storage dam. Later, other dynamic civic leaders helped garner air force, navy, and army facilities for Phoenix during World War II, and even later, this group of elites, now several generations in time depth, presided over convincing the entire nation of Phoenix's virtues. The result was spectacularly successful, as the rich agricultural base was built upon by light manufacturing and service industries, buttressed by a tourism industry now one of major proportions. To a casual visitor in the 1970s, it might have appeared that after a century of growth, it was inevitable that Phoenix should have become one of the nation's Sun Belt capitals. But getting from 1870 to 1970, as this study has attempted to show, was made possible by the willpower and energy of its elites, who so dramatically transformed the desert hamlet on the banks of the Salt.[46]

NOTES

1. William D. Angel, Jr., "To Make a City: Entrepreneurship on the Sunbelt Frontier," in *The Rise of the Sunbelt Cities* eds., David C. Perry and Alfred J. Watkins, (Beverly Hills: Sage Publications, 1977), 125-26.

2. Some materials on Phoenix history had been collected as part of a general collection on Arizona at the Arizona State University Library's Arizona Room, and some materials were on deposit at Phoenix Public Library. Otherwise the first century of history in Phoenix awaited documentation. Newspapers had been preserved at the Arizona State University Library and the State Archives and Library, Phoenix. The situation, however, was not comparable to such Western cities as Denver or Salt Lake City.

3. Materials and methodology are discussed in the forthcoming monograph study on Phoenix, "Phoenix Rising," by the author. As for a rationale for studying elites in the community, one of the best syntheses is in Robert Presthus, *Men at the Top: A Study in Community Power* (New York: Oxford Press, 1964); see especially Chapters 1, 2, and 12. See also Geraint Parry, *Political Elites* (New York: Praeger, 1969), for a general introduction on elites; Carl V. Harris, *Political Power in Birmingham, 1871-1921* (Knoxville: University of Tennessee Press, 1977), for an informed discussion by a historian using the decisional approach, especially pp. 39-95; Jocelyn M. Ghent and Frederic C. Jaher, "The Chicago Business Elite: 1830-1930: A Collective Biography" *Business History*, 50, 3 (1976): 288-328; John Walton, "Community Power and the Retreat from Politics: Full Circle After Twenty Years?" *Social Problems* 23 (1976): 292-303; and the imaginative treatment in Edward O. Laumann, Lois M. Verbrugge, and Franz U. Pappi, "A Causal Modelling Approach to the Study of a Community Elite's Influence Structure" *American to Sociological Review* 39 (1974): 162-4.

4. Glen Elder, "History and the Life Course," in *Biography and Society: The Life History Approach the Social Sciences,* ed. Danel Bertaux, (Beverly Hills: Sage Publications, 1981), 88-89.

5. The main approach to urban history of the Phoenix History Project has been to construct an urban biography of the city. This entails developing a basic chronology, a narrative history, and a number of problems for analysis, such as elite formation, analysis of the census, economic growth, and public policy.

6. See biographical folders on Smith, Swilling, Hancock, and Alsap in "Biographical Research Files," Phoenix History Project, Phoenix (hereafter cited as Project Biographical Files.).

7. Duppa and Hayden, Ibid.

8. See U.S. Census for Phoenix and Salt River Valley for 1870 and 1880.

9. For a detailed discussion of some of these early Town Elite members, see Geoffrey Mawn, "Phoenix, Arizona: Central City of the Southwest, 1870-1920" (Ph.D. diss., Arizona State University, 1979).

10. On Christy, see extensive materials furnished by the Christy and Fulwiler families in the Project Biographical Files.

11. Murphy's grandson has published a full portrait of this remarkable entrepreneur: Merwin L. Murphy, *W. J. and the Valley* (Alhambra, Calif.: Merwin L. Murphy, 1975). See also Project Biographical Files and excerpts from National Archives, Washington, D.C., materials on the building of Roosevelt Dam.

12. On Ganz, see Project Biographical Files.

13. Aside from materials at the Phoenix History Project, there are several important bound books of correspondence by Sherman at the Sherman Foundation Library in Corona Del Mar, California.

14. Robert Merton, *Social Theory and Social Structure* (Glencoe, Ill.: The Free Press, 1957); see especially Chapter 10, "Patterns of Influence: Local and Cosmopolitan Influentials," 387-420.

15. Recruitment of elites is related to Pareto's concept of the "circulation of elites," and, for this essay, is viewed simply as the process by which certain elite cohorts were formed in Phoenix. As Nadel remarked concerning recruitment, it was "the movement of people in and out of positions of pre-eminence." See S. F. Nadel, "The Concept of Social Elites," *International Social Science Bulletin* 8 (1956): 413-24; see also Parry, 97-105 for a more specific focus on recruitment and elite background.

16. On Whitelaw Reid, see Bingham Duncan, *Whitelaw Reid: Journalist, Politician, Diplomat* (Athens: University of Georgia

Press, 1975), Chapter 12; in addition, the letters of Whitelaw Reid in the Library of Congress tell much about his sojourn and impressions of Phoenix life.

17. On the Jewish merchants, see Blaine Lamb, "Jews in Early Phoenix, 1870-1920," *Journal of Arizona History* 18 (1977): 299-318.

18. For a full treatment of Fowler's activities and influence in Phoenix, and the best account yet on the winning of the Roosevelt Dam, see Karen L. Smith, "An Uneasy Alliance: The United States Reclamation Service and the Salt River Valley Water Users' Association, 1890-1917" (Ph.D. diss., University of California,-Santa Barbara, 1982).

19. See discussion of transference of the capital in Jay J. Wagoner, *Arizona Territory, 1863-1912, A Political History* (Tucson: University of Arizona Press, 1970), 245-47.

20. See materials on boosterism in Arizona Collection, Arizona State University Library, and in the Phoenix History Project file.

21. U.S. Census for 1910.

22. George Mickle, Project Biographical Files.

23. Stauffer left some of his papers to the Arizona Historical Society in Tucson; there are some documents in the Arizona Room at the Arizona State University Library; and a special collection of materials was given on Stauffer to the Phoenix History Project by his daughter, Sylvia S. Laughlin.

24. See social and civic club files at Phoenix History Project; on the early additions to the town site, see Karen L. Smith, "From Town to City: A History of Phoenix, 1870-1912" (Santa Barbara: University of California, 1978); on the role of Dwight B. Heard in the development of new residential areas mentioned above, see interview with Bartlett Heard, son of Dwight, in tape recorded interviews at the Phoenix History Project.

25. On the changing role of agriculture, see series of interviews on agricultural history in Phoenix by Karin Ullmann for the Phoenix History Project.

26. See the excellent article by Sylvia Laughlin, "Iron Springs, Arizona: Timeless Summer Resort," *Journal of Arizona History* 22 (1981): 235-54.

27. See G. Wesley Johnson, Jr., "Dwight B. Heard in Phoenix: The Early Years," *Journal of Arizona History* 18 (1977): 259-78, and the taped interviews with Bartlett Heard at Phoenix History Project.

28. On early Charter reform, see Stephen Rockstroh, "An Analysis of Phoenix Municipal Administration, 1881-1952" (Master's thesis, Arizona State University, 1952); also, Joseph C. Smith, "The Phoenix Drive for Municipal Reform and Charter Government," Arizona Collection, Arizona State University Library. On members of the elite mentioned, see Project Biographical Files.

29. On the McArthur brothers, see Project Biographical Files.

30. For information see taped interviews with George Luhrs, Phoenix History Project, about the building of the Luhrs family properties.

31. See Michael Konig, "Transformation of Postwar Municipal Government in Phoenix," typescript (1982) Phoenix History Project; see also Bradford Luckingham, "Urban Development in Arizona: The Rise of Phoenix," *Journal of Arizona History* 22 (1981): 197-234.

32. On Bimson, see Ernest J. Hopkins, *Financing the Frontier* (Phoenix: The Arizona Printers, 1950), and files and interviews with Bimson at Phoenix History Project.

33. On the founding of the symphony and art museum in Phoenix, and the role of community leaders, see Cultural Files, Phoenix History Project, and interviews with Frank Snell and Walter Bimson; see also interview with Oscar Thoeny, M.D., in Arizona Medical History collection, Flinn Library, Maricopa County Medical Society, Phoenix.

34. See Snell interview, Phoenix History Project.

35. See files of the Phoenix Chamber of Commerce at Phoenix History Project; see also "Research Memo Overview on Phoenix Business," a report by Nancy Edwards at Phoenix History Project, on interviews with postwar business leaders in Phoenix carried out by Edwards. On Motorola's move to Phoenix, see interview by Richard Lynch with Dr. Dan Noble, vice-president of Motorola, Phoenix History Project.

36. The best overview on postwar politics and charter government is Brent Brown, "An Analysis of the Phoenix Charter Government Committee as a Political Entity" (Master's Thesis, Arizona

State University, 1968); also see Konig "Transformation," and Konig's forthcoming Ph.D. diss. on postwar Phoenix politics (Arizona State University, Department of History).

37. Brown, and interview with Dix Price, former Charter Committee chair, Phoenix History Project.

38. See interviews with Williams and Mardian, Phoenix History Project.

39. See interviews with Orme Lewis, Harry Rosenzweig, Newton Rosenzweig, and Frank Snell, Phoenix History Project.

40. See U.S. Census for Phoenix, 1950 and 1960. See taped interviews with Ralph Burgbacher and Sherman Hazeltine, Phoenix History Project. The two high-rise clusters, distinctly separated by several blocks of much lower buildings, present a dramatic and rather unique city skyline to those flying into Phoenix for the first time.

41. See demographic and economic figures for changing growth patterns in Salt River Valley in *Foresight Eighty: Insights and Foresights for the Phoenix Metropolitan Area* (Phoenix: Western Savings, 1980), a compendium commissioned by the largest savings and loan in Phoenix.

42. See the interpretation on the demise of Charter in G. Wesley Johnson, Jr., *Phoenix: Valley of the Sun* (Tulsa: Continental Heritage Publishing, 1982), 159-65. See also interviews with John Driggs, Newton Rosenzweig, Dix Price, and Sam Mardian, Phoenix History Project.

43. No major study has yet been written on the impact of the expatriates, winter visitors, or health seekers in Phoenix. On the activity of a leading community entrepreneur, see interview with Karl Eller, Phoenix History Project.

44. Phylis Martinelli, "Beneath the Surface: Ethnic Communities in Phoenix, Arizona," typescript, Phoenix History Project. Mrs. Martinelli was in charge of carrying out research on ethnic and minority groups at the Phoenix History Project. Also see series of articles published by Robert Trennert on the Phoenix Indian School.

45. Johnson, *Phoenix: Valley of the Sun,* 144-76; and forthcoming monograph, "Phoenix Rising."

46. I should like to acknowledge funding support for research on this paper from National Endowment for the Humanities, Research Division, and Arizona Humanities Council.

5

Apostolic and Patriarchal Financing: The Economic Life of Heber C. Kimball

Stanley B. Kimball

The large polygamous families of nineteenth-century Mormon leaders quite often formed communities by themselves. The leaders usually had several homes, extensive gardens, orchards and farmlands, and they developed a pattern of dealing with their various households of wives and children. In this article, Stanley B. Kimball, Professor of History at Southern Illinois University at Edwardsville, points out that we do not know very much about the economic setup of these families, and that by studying the arrangements of Heber C. Kimball, apostle and member of the First Presidency of the Church, we can better understand how other Mormon leaders planned their finances.

What follows is a study of a family community. Dr. Kimball briefly explains Heber C. Kimball's financial dealings before coming to Utah, then describes how Kimball organized his households physically and economically. He paints a picture of equal division of chores and responsibilities that were controlled by the patriarch. This equality continued with the settlement of Kimball's estate which provided for Kimballs' wives and children.

"Nobody pays my bills for me. I pay my way or go without."
—H. C. Kimball—

The economic affairs of the early church apostles and leading patriarchs, especially polygamists, are not well known. From what is known, however, of the economic life of Heber C. Kimball we may be better able to generalize about others.

Kimball's economic life divides conveniently into three periods: (1) from 1815, when at the age of fourteen he went to work for his father as an apprentice blacksmith to his acceptance of Mormonism and his move to Kirtland, Ohio in 1833, (2) from 1833 to his second entry into the Great Basin in 1848, and (3) his life in the Great Basin from 1848 to his death in 1868. The first and last periods are fairly well documented, but little is known about the second.

As was customary at the time, Heber's childhood ended at age fourteen and he went to work for this father as an apprentice blacksmith in West Bloomfield, New York, a new and promising village on the Ontario and Genessee Turnpike. (His older brother, Charles, had already set up a pottery shop on his father's property, a fact which would subsequently influence Heber.)

Five years later, as a result of his father's financial reverses occasioned by the Panic of 1819, he found himself a slightly schooled and unemployed blacksmith. His past had been uneventful, his present was bleak, and the future promised nothing. As he later wrote:

> My father, having lost his property and not taking the care for my welfare which he formerly did, I was left to seek a place of refuge or home of my own at this time. I saw some days of sorrow; my heart was troubled, and I suffered much in consequence of fear, bashfulness and timidity. I found myself cast abroad upon the world, without a friend to console my grief. In these heartaching hours, I suffered much for want of food and the comforts of life, and many times went two or three days without food to eat, being bashful and not daring to ask for it.[1]

In the meantime, Heber's brother Charles had established himself as a potter in the nearby township of Mendon, close to the village of the same name. Organized in 1812, Mendon was another promising location along the Ontario and Genessee Turnpike and a good place for a pottery. All of the necessary natural resources—clay beds of high silica content, water, and timber—were close at hand. At the invitation of Charles, Heber moved to Mendon in 1820 and became an apprentice potter.

After Heber married in 1822, he bought out his brother's pottery, went into business for himself, and built a home. Land records suggest that this first home was located about one-quarter mile east of "Tomlinson's Corners" on the north side of Boughton Hill Road, where he eventually owned property on both sides of the road.[2]

Ambitious and hard working, he chopped wood, planted an orchard, raised pigs, and built a barn and other outbuildings. His industry enabled him to make several additional land purchases. The Kimballs lived comfortably. As a potter, Heber took pains to get good clay, even if it meant hauling it a great distance, and on a good day he could turn out as many as twenty dozen milk pans. Apparently he specialized in common brownware, fine textured clay burned to a very high degree and finished with a hard brown glaze. It was used mainly for simple kitchen and table items—jars, crocks, pitchers, bottles, mugs, pots, milk pans, cups, churns, and plates. Despite his great output, no completely authenticated piece of Heber's work has been found.

After Heber joined the Church in 1832, both his spiritual and economic life changed. When he moved from Mendon to Kirtland, Ohio in 1833, the time of generally steady, documented employment was over.

It is not entirely clear how he supported his family in Kirtland. Initially he probably lived off the money he brought with him from Mendon which he obtained from selling his property there. It appears he did some work as a potter and may have planted some crops, but his many activities in the Church, especially the Zion's Camp march, his call as a member of the Quorum of Twelve, and a mission to England, would have interrupted seriously such economic activities. The same is true of the Missouri and Illinois periods. Almost nothing is known 'about his economic life in Missouri.

After his arrival in Kirtland in 1833, Heber worked almost full time for the Church. In Nauvoo, however, there is some evidence he worked as a potter, perhaps at The Pottery Association located east of the temple on Knight Street or at the Earthen Ware Manufactory managed by a J. Crocott. He also bought and sold building sites from which he may have derived additional income. In 1842, for example, he sold one lot for $120 and another in 1844 for $164.[3] Also at this time the Church helped him. His brick home in Nauvoo, for example, was built for him by the Church, or at least by church members, and he occasionally received money and provisions both from the Church and from generous Saints.[4]

Whenever possible his family members earned money as best they could. In Winter Quarters, by way of illustration, Vilate, his first wife, rented out her dining room to two non-Mormon merchants from Nauvoo who had freighted out a line of goods, groceries, and fine wines and liquors, and Presendia Huntington, another wife, kept house for two brothers. Some of his family may have handcrafted things to sell, as many others did, like willow baskets and washboards.

His growing polygamous family imposed continually increasing economic burdens on him. When he took the bulk of his family from Winter Quarters to Zion in 1848, he was responsible for seventy-one individuals and needed 23,000 pounds of flour alone.[5]

Much more of his economic life is known after his final arrival in the Valley in 1848 (he was in the pioneer company of 1847). To properly care for his large family's physical wants, Heber worked hard, protected what he had, was enterprising, and engaged in many different kinds of economic activities. Although a member of the First Presidency, he was expected to support himself. "Nobody pays my bills nor my expenses for me," he wrote some absent sons. "I pay or go without."[6] Although he eventually had forty-three wives, sixty-five children, and an unknown number of adopted and foster children, he never was responsible in Utah for more than sixty at any one time and perhaps never for more than forty-one. Still, that is a good-sized family, even in Mormon terms. In 1854 he wrote to a son in England, "I furnish the wood and fuel, bread, beef, and vegetables, for twelve families, and the most of them their clothing."[7]

Because of his industry he was able, in 1852, to assure his brother Solomon back in New York that he had plenty of groceries, wheat, cheese, beef, pork, potatoes, "and almost every luxury you can obtain in the states."[8] He added in 1857, "I have everything here almost for my comfort and the comfort of my family that you have in that land"—flour, cornmeal, every kind of vegetable, peaches, apples, pork, beef cakes, fritters, sugar, tea, coffee, and rice. "I can say, I am about ten times better off and more comfortable than I was in Mendon."[9]

In 1855 he assured his son, William, who was in England on a mission, that all was well at home.

> Now I'll speak of things in the family. . . . Heber [Parley, a son] is at Utah . . . assisting to take charge of the Church cattle, also Brigham. . . . David . . . is now commenced drawing wood . . . as I have now three teams running. My mill has grain so that it runs every day. . . . I have got a stone wall nearly round my possessions. I have bought out John Nebeker, the house that he built above Bro. Heywoods. I gave him 1,800.00 which is less than what it cost him. As for our horses, cattle, and sheep, they are all doing extremely well, where there has only been 300 lbs. of wool, this year I have had 425 lbs., almost as many lambs as there are sheep this year. My stock all look well now. . . .
>
> Wm. left us a few days before . . . to assist in driving cattle to California.
>
> I put in 20 acres of wheat at my mill . . . my garden seems well, everything looks well and fresh.[10]

His immediate economic concern was his "plantation" (as he liked to call it)—his ten-acre lot cater-cornered to the north

east of Temple Square, which he developed both agriculturally
and industrially. He was proud of his plantation and improved
it in many ways, planting shade and fruit trees and gardens,
surrounding it with a cobblestone wall, and building several
barns and storehouses on it.[11] Between 1849 and 1860 he also
built three schools on this property, largely for his own children and grandchildren. Later he set aside a family cemetery.
(Today this 82-by-75 foot cemetery is all that remains on this
site from Heber's day.)

Heber enjoyed showing off his industry. Several non-
Mormon visitors were impressed with his garden. During the
summer of 1859 while en route to California, Horace Greeley
paid Heber a visit. Heber proudly showed Greeley around and
pressed fruit, berries—and some Mormon doctrine—on his
guest. Greeley later wrote that it was the "most magnificent
garden I have been invited to visit."[12] A New York writer, Fitz
Hugh Ludlow, also treated to fruit, was unsparing in his
praise. "I must confess," he wrote:

> that if there ever could be any hope of our conversion, it
> was just about the time we stood in Brother Heber's fine
> orchard, eating apples and apricots between exhortations,
> and having sound doctrine poked down our throats, with
> gooseberries as big as plums, to take the taste out of our
> mouths, like jam after castor-oil.[13]

Ludlow also left behind a detailed description of this
plantation which is worth recording in full.

> Mr. Kimball's city establishment (he is a large prop-
> erty holder elsewhere) is situated on a rise of ground but a
> few rods from the Temple corner and the Presidents
> inclosure. . . . [His house is] neat and commodious but,
> unostentatious, like the residence of some principal select-
> man in a New England village. Utah has not yet had time
> to grow the noble elms which shade such a residence; but
> everything which money, keen business tact and indom-
> itable energy can do has been done by Heber Kimball at

least, to make his place a paradise of luxuriant vegetation. In picturesquely selected places he has contrived to create pretty little groves of maple, poplar, acacia, and box elder, transplanting the young trees from the Wahsatch [*sic*] cañons, and by plentiful irrigation making them grow so rapidly that they had already attained the respectable height of twenty-five or thirty feet.

In this matter of irrigation I noticed that both Brothers Brigham and Heber seemed to be "not under the law, but under grace." The chief water supplies of the Mormon city may without metaphor be said to run through each apostle's back yard, and no hand but their own shuts the gate on their trenches. The lower level of Heber Kimball's place, toward the city, is a garden laid out under its owner's supervision by an old Mormon gardener . . . . The plan of the garden is as simple and natural as a path through the woods, the walks wandering hither and thither among intersecting rivulets, and under green arches of apricot, apple, peach, plum, and nectarine, whose pleasant-scented fruit, ripe already or mellowing to ripeness, bowed their overweighted branches together above our heads.

Heber's melons and cucumbers were very thrifty: Indeed, the soil and climate of Utah are finely suited to the cultivation of all gourd fruit. It was a week too late for strawberries, or, Heber told me, I should have seen a sight,—Brother Brigham's crop had amounted to over eighty bushels, and he had gathered an almighty lot himself. Heber was cultivating a kind of currant which he had introduced from the cañons, and which by high science had been so far domesticated and improved that its fruit was very pleasant having an abundant juice, less acid, and a flavor no less pronounced, than our own large white currants at the East; furthermore, attaining the weight of a good-sized gooseberry.[14]

Utilizing the power of City Creek, Heber was able to develop on his lot one of the earliest "industrial centers" in

Utah. He first built an oil mill or press to make linseed oil out of flax seeds.[15] Heber got off a little joke in reference to this mill. "A gentleman," he related, "desired to inform me, the other day, how to adulterate my oil with lye; but as I did not believe in *lying*, I did not procure the recipe."[16] While he would not lie, he was all business. "I can get over a gallon of oil," he told the Saints in 1861, "if you have money, I want it, and you shall have the oil. . . . If the Gentiles bring oil here and sell it at three dollars per gallon, I will under sell them."[17]

To the *Deseret News* Heber's mill was "another step towards that social independence so much desired by all who know the blighting consequences of importing, instead of manufacturing those things that are necessary to the comfort, existence and happiness of the people."[18] This comment suggests clearly what Mormondom's greatest economic problem was—no exports. An imbalance of imports over exports leads to a weak economy and was the economic reason for the Isaiahan denunciations from the pulpit of female finery, as well as tea, coffee, tobacco, and all other nonessentials. Such imports drained Utah of specie.

To his oil press he later added a run of stones to grind wheat, a cane mill, and a circular saw. Ludlow also described Heber's industrial complex. "We visited upon the same ground," he remarked,

> on the bank of one of those streams heretofore mentioned as traversing apostolic back yards, a cider-mill, a grist-mill, a feed-grinder, a workshop with lathes, belts, and shafting, and almost every conceivable mechanism for economizing human power in the management of a large estate demanding constant supplies and repairs.
>
> Among other apparatus operated by Heber's water-wheel I observed a carding-machine, and was told by the proprietor that he had the entire gear of a woolen factory on a small scale, and when it was set, could manufacture from the fleece excellent yarn and durable cloth, sufficient at least for all household uses.[19]

Prior to the development of his mills in Salt Lake City, Heber had built a gristmill in 1852 a few miles north in Bountiful, Davis County, where much grain was then grown. In seeming contradiction to the policy that water and timber should not be privately owned, the general assembly granted him exclusive rights to North Mill Creek Canyon—the first good canyon for water and timber north of Salt Lake City. Such grants, however, gave the grantee development and regulatory rights only. This mill at the mouth of his canyon was a burr type, two stories and an attic high, powered by an overshot wheel. It was the largest in the territory and stood until 1892.[20] The ruins are located at approximately the intersection of 4th East Street and 9th South Street in Bountiful and are marked by a plaque placed there by the Daughters of Utah Pioneers. Also, in order to develop the timber resources of this broad and gentle canyon, in 1849 Heber built a two-and-a-half-mile road and extracted a toll of 25 percent of all wood and poles taken out of it. (The upper canyon is known as Mueller Park today.)

In addition to the ten-acre lot and eleven building lots in Salt Lake City mentioned above, Heber acquired other land for homes, farming, and ranching. Near present-day 23rd South and 3rd East in Salt Lake City, he owned twenty-seven acres, and north of his home he took a section of bench land, on Capitol Hill, which no one wanted. Later, when poor emigrants came into the valley, he permitted them to build homes on this bench property for free or for very little. (After his estate was partially settled in 1875, deeds were issued to fifty-four individuals who had built on this and other Kimball property.)[21] This part of Salt Lake City today is known picturesquely as the Marmalade District because at one time a lot of short streets there were named after such fruits as apricot, plum, cherry, and peach. He also engaged in real estate. In 1858, for example, he bought three homes for $1,300 and completed the purchase of the Townsend Hotel.[22] Furthermore, he owned a meadow, building lot, and home in Provo, and part of the "Big Field" in Brigham City.

Heber was likewise involved extensively in ranching. He ran cattle, horses, and sheep in Cache Valley, in Tooele Valley near Grantsville, on Kimball (Stansbury) and Antelope Islands in the Great Salt Lake, and near Black Rock on the shore of the lake. He was grazing cattle near Black Rock as early as 1849. Today copper smelters give the area the look of the sixth and seventh circles of the *Divina Commedia*, but then meadows flourished near the springs at the base of the Oquirrh Mountains. By 1860 Heber had built a substantial ranch house, bunkhouse, barns, and other buildings out of rock, all surrounded by a rock fence. (The ruins of this ranch house were destroyed when Interstate 80 was constructed.)

Heber had at least two stock brands. The first, a simple "H", branded on the left hip, was recorded December 29, 1849. Since other cattlemen soon used the same brand and applied it on the left shoulder, right shoulder, right hip, and left thigh, Heber may have changed brands to avoid confusion. In May 1852 the *Deseret News* pictured his brand as probably a fancy H on its side—in cowboy lingo a lazy H—or maybe an attempt to make a monogram out of his initial.[23]

In the mid-1850s Kimball grazed about sixty head of cattle and eight horses with the church herds in Cache Valley. Kimball Island does not seem to have been grazed extensively. More important was Antelope Island, which was reserved mainly for the benefit of the Perpetual Emigration Fund, but Heber and Brigham Young also kept cattle and sheep there. The island was a particularly good winter range, for the winds blew the snow off the low mountain tops, exposing the grass. He also did some ranching in Parley's Park, east of Salt Lake City. In 1855 the legislature granted him, Jedediah M. Grant, and Samuel Snyder the area as a herd ground. Heber's son William later operated a stone hotel there (which is still standing just north of I-80 at the Kimball Junction). It became a regular stop on the Overland Stage, and Horace Greeley, Walt Whitman, Mark Twain, and many others stayed there.

Heber's most extensive ranching was done seven miles south of Grantsville. In 1857 the territorial legislature granted him and William McBride a 25-mile square herd ground.[24]

Heber built a ranch house there, and two of his sons, David Patton and Abraham, lived there at different times.

In addition to farming, ranching, and milling, Heber was involved in freighting. In 1855 he became one of several vice-presidents in the Brigham Young Express and Carrying Company (popularly known as the Y.X. Company). Later, after the U.S. Army located in Utah, he and some of his sons kept several wagons busy carrying freight for the army. Such trafficking with the Philistines was frowned on by some and Heber wanted it understood that he was not selling the army any locally needed supplies, especially wheat. "I have hauled wheat to the camp," he explained, "that the merchants have bought of this people, and I have got my pay for it."[25] If some of the Saints insisted in going against church policy and selling wheat to the army, then others in the Church, including himself, might as well profit from the freighting as did the Gentiles.

In addition to all these activities, in 1853, Heber, along with a few others, privately incorporated the Great Salt Lake Water Works Association to pipe water to homes and businesses in the city. Its shares were offered at $100 each.[26] Because of the political offices he held, first in the state of Deseret and then Utah Territory, he was sometimes paid for "services rendered the Territory." On February 25, 1853, for example, he received a draft for $195.00.[27]

Not only did he strive to support his own family well, but he helped and encouraged others to do likewise. A consistent advocate of self-sufficiency and "home manufacture," he believed the Saints in Utah could become self-sufficient and preached this theme often, from the pulpit and in the legislature. On January 6, 1852, for example, he made a powerful and enlightened speech in the Legislative council (Senate) advocating home manufacture.

> It is my opinion that measures can be entered into for the encouragement of home manufacture, by nourishing men that have a disposition to go into business, with public funds of either the church or state. . . . I know of a great many men that seem to be anxious to do something

in this way, but have nothing to help themselves with. . . . I have this disposition as well as any other man. I am trying with all my might to dispose of all the capital I can raise to lay the foundation for my existence, and for the existence of my family, that they may be independent.

Until we take a course to assist such men, and nourish and cherish them we shall [not] accomplish anything . . . . If there is anything we can manufacture ourselves let us go at it right straight and not sit here on our harses [*sic*] doing nothing. . . . Let those who have surplus property, let us lend it to the state, and by and by the state will pay it back with usury, or lend it to the Church and the Church will turn around and pay you again.

In this same speech he criticized the sisters for insisting on expensive imports in favor of homemade items and accused them of "teasing us all the time to buy such a little nasty shitten things."[28] Most of the assembled brethren probably enthusiastically agreed.

He was also greatly concerned with the storing up of foodstuffs, especially grain, against poor crops and famine. For years he preached preparedness. On August 13, 1853, for example, he warned the Saints to take care of their grain "for you will see hard times."[29] When a near famine did come in 1856 he had to put his own family on half rations in order to feed the heedless.

Heber supported the organization of the Deseret Agricultural and Manufacturing Society, which was organized by the general legislature in January 1856 "to promote the arts of domestic industry, and to encourage the production of articules [*sic*] from the native elements," and which eventually became the Utah State Fair Association. In recognition of his own economic enterprise, Heber was made an honorary member from the beginning.

The sources provide a few more glimpses of Heber's economic activities and philosophy.

During the winter of 1848-49 and for several years thereafter his families lived in the one-room homes within the fort, with other families, in tents, wagon-boxes, and other temporary shelters. (We know, for example, that Vilate used her wagon-box as a private bedroom for four years until Heber finished his large family home. She obviously preferred that privacy to the crowded cabins with only blankets for partitions.) They also lived in "adobe row," some small dwellings he built on the south side of his ten-acre lot along present-day North Temple.

During the following spring the fort was generally abandoned and the Saints began to build more substantial homes. Heber commenced a large home on the lot which took nearly three years, until February 1852, to finish. This home, facing west, years later was officially designated 142 North Main Street. It stood until the 1920s, when it was razed and the Kimball Apartments built in its place. It consisted of a white two-story frame rectangle thirty feet wide by fifty-six feet long containing sixteen plastered and painted rooms. To this core were added wash, wood, and storehouses. Several years later Heber added a splendid two-story porch on the west end, which commanded a full view of Temple Square, most of the city, and the Valley.[30]

On the main floor, Vilate's quarters were in the front and Sarah Peak's, his first plural wife, in the rear. A "girls' parlor" opened off Vilate's rooms and there was a large dining room. In the parlor was a huge piano which, although several pianos were hauled west from Winter Quarters, Heber most likely imported from St. Louis to keep a promise he had made to his daughter, Helen, before they left Nauvoo. In the Old West a piano was as much a symbol of permanence, stability, respectability, and dignity as it was a musical instrument. On the second floor was Heber's private bedroom. The spinning room was in the front. Elsewhere were the storage room and several large and small bedrooms for some of his wives and children.

The Kimball household was so extensive that Heber kept his own storehouse on the premises. Later in her life one of his daughters recorded a charming little story about an incident with her father in this storehouse, one which demonstrates how adroitly Heber could handle little family economic problems.

> My sister Sarah was two years younger than me and one day when we were very small, father took us to his store-house where he kept supplies of shoes, drygoods and whatnot for his family. He was going to give us each a pair of shoes. Like all little girls we went in delighted with the prospect of having some pretty new shoes. Father placed us on a table or counter, and took off our old shoes. He took down from a shelf two pairs of old ladies' shoes. I can see them now, low topped, wide soles, low heels. He put them on our feet, laced them up and tied them, then told us to walk. We were horrified. I kept a stiff upper lip but I saw that Sarah was weakening. Father gave one of his characteristic laughs, sat us up on the table again and took them off. Then he put on our feet some shoes that were anything but pretty, but they came somewhere near fitting us, and we went home rejoicing.
>
> This puzzled me for a long time. Why should my father who seemed to know everything take the time to put such shoes on the feet of two little girls when anyone could see that they would not do at all? It finally dawned upon me that had he, in the first place, given us the shoes that finally pleased us we would have been greatly disappointed. But after our first shock we went away happy and contented.[31]

Heber was particularly critical of women's love of finery. It was hard to build the kingdom of God "while you take a course to make slaves of your husbands through love of finery." He mocked them—"Oh, dear, I want to know if we ain't going to have any more ribbons." He had to "pay every dime I can get for morocco shoes, for my women to wear to meeting; and they will wear out a pair while going to meeting." He excoriated men for being under "pettycoat government," and considered bonnets "a cursed disgrace to the Saints." The sisters should have been content with homespun cloth as he was.[32]

In a less irritated manner, he once wrote a friend, "The sisters of our city are commencing to bring about a reformation in regard to dress, to carry their dresses on their shoulders instead of their hips, and they reduce the quantity from 10 to 15 yards to 6 and 7, and dispense with girting; it makes a wonderful stir with the ladies, and is a great relief in expense to the brethren.[33] This was the "Deseret Costume" introduced in 1855, but of very brief popularity.

Everyone had to work in his large family. One wife, Adelia Hatton, noted she went to live with several of Heber's wives, Sarah Ann Whitney, Lucy Walker, Ellen Sanders, and Martha McBride, "all eating at the same table, but each one having their own separate rooms." The worst they had to contend with "was having so many children together for when they were all in the house they made a good deal of confusion. This we got along with as well as we could be expected for each woman tried to cultivate her share of patience. . . . all trying to do their part in the good cause they were engaged in." They were plenty busy mending, spinning, making clothes, and such chores. Occasionally, she said, "when our Lord [Heber] could find time he would come in and visit us and instruct and teach us our duty and if he saw anything he thought was wrong in any one of us he was not slow to tell us."

Sometime later Adelia went to live in the "big house" on North Main Street with Vilate, Mary Ellen Harris, Christeen Golden, Ruth Reese, Sarah Peak, Mary Smithies, Laura Pitkin, and nine children. "I found them all good women," she said, "each one took their share of work and everything went in order." Laura spun, knitted, and laid out dress patterns; Ruth was a good tailor and made Heber's clothes, and Christeen did his washing and saw that his clothes were kept in order. They all shared in the general housework, doing Vilate's for her as "her health was very delicate."[34]

Heber, of course, could not tolerate waste. One day several of his wives got a lecture on prudence and economy when he found some good bread thrown in the swill pail and scum on the homemade beer.[35]

Heber's estate papers have been preserved and reveal much about his economic life in Utah.[36] For all of Heber Kimball's prudence, and despite his threat to leave all his property to the Church, he died intestate. He was survived by thirteen inheriting wives, forty-one inheriting children, at least eight other wives who had not formally separated from him, and an undetermined number of adopted and foster children. Ten of his inheriting wives had children; the other three were entirely dependent on him. The eight other wives appear to have been living with relatives and friends elsewhere, mainly in Utah.

Kimball's economic life seems to be an archetypal example of one "doing the best he can." He worked hard, tried everything feasible, did his best to provide a good standard of living for himself and his huge family, sometimes made mistakes, was very patriarchal, helped others, and, on occasion, appears to have taken some advantage of his ecclesiastical position.

Above all, however, his economic life, as we can reconstruct it from scattered and scanty sources, gives us a model through which to generalize about the economic problems of life in large polygamous families in nineteenth-century Utah.

APPENDIX[37]
H. C. Kimball's estate

The gross value of his estate was figured at $100,580 (or the equivalent of more than a $2,000,000 estate today), less debts of $15,255, leaving a net of $85,324, or approximately $1,600 per heir.

The estate procedures were very complicated and were not finally completed until 1875. In fact some undistributed property was discovered in 1887 and a question about one city lot came up as late as 1938.

A general inventory of his estate at his death follows:

Personal property (main home, homes of other wives, Grantsville ranch)	$20,150
Real estate (Salt Lake City lots, houses, gristmill, carding mill, San Pete Valley farm and ranch, Provo house, lot and meadow, Davis County farm and flour mill, Richfield farm Cache Valley farm, Grantsville herd ground and house)	72,750
Livestock (Grantsville, Salt Lake City)	5,955
Accounts receivable	1,725
	$100,580

The first act of the court was to order an inventory of his property. This extremely detailed document reveals much about the life and economics of his family. The listing of personal property in his main home, for example, includes several copies of the Book of Mormon, thirty-one other assorted books, furniture, carpeting, pens, needles, stamps, lamps, belts, bolts, hinges, tools, brooms, lobelia, tea, coffee, and a spitoon, for a total value of $5,052.

The personal property used by his thirteen inheriting wives was retained by them in 1868 and accounted as part of

their inheritance. The distribution of Kimball's property to
wives and children was as follows:

	1869	1875	1876	Total
1. *Lucy Walker*	456	5,850 *(plus home)*		
2. John H.				
3. Lidia H.				
4. Ann S.			1,355*	7,661
5. Eliza				
6. Washington				
7. *Ann Gheen*	333	5,900		
8. Samuel H.				
9. Andrew				
10. Daniel H.			1,172*	7,405
11. Alice A.				
12. Sarah				
13. *Sarah Ann Whitney*	394	5,300		
14. David H.				
15. Newell W.				
16. Horace H.			1,440*	7,134
17. Sarah M.				
18. Joshua W.				
19. *Amanda Gheen*	355	5,775		
20. William C.				
21. Albert H.			315*	6,445
22. Jeremiah H.				
23. Moroni H.				
24. *Mary Smithies*	297	4,400 *(plus home)*		
25. Malvina				
26. Wilford			1,697*	6,394
27. Lorenzo				
28. Abbie				
29. *Christeen Golden*	806	2,825		
30. Jonathan G.				
31. Elias S.			661*	4,292
32. Mary M.				
33. *Harriet Sanders*	310	2,925		
34. Hiram H.			484*	3,719
35. Eugene				

	1869	1875	1876	Total
36. ***Ruth Reese***	364	3,000		
37. Jacob R.			264*	3,628
38. Enoch H.				
39. ***Prescendia Huntington***	448	825 *(plus home)*		
40. Joseph			32	1,305
41. ***Ellen Sanders***	264	925 *(plus home)*		1,189
42. Jedediah Heber				
43. ***Mary Houston***	121	200 *(plus home)*		321
44. ***Sarah Peak***	309	200		509
45. ***Mary Ellen Harris***	147	200		347
†46. Heber P. Kimball (Vilate)		2,090		2,090
†47. Helen M. Whitney (Vilate)		1,500	470	1,970
†48. David P. Kimball (Vilate)		1,500	225	1,725
†49. William H. Kimball (Vilate)		1,500	178	1,678
†50. Rosalia William (Ellen Sanders)		900	127	1,027
†51. Abraham A. Kimball (Clarissa Cutler)		550	395	945
†52. Solomon F. Kimball (Vilate)		700	232	932
†53. Isaac A. Kimball (Emily Cutler)		600	190	790
†54. Charles S. Kimball (Vilate)		300	237	537
55. Daniel Davis (adopted)		500		500
Totals	4,604	48,465	9,474	62,543

At the final distribution in 1876 the gross breakdown was:

Total value of the estate	$100,580
Less estate debts	15,255
Distributed to wives	53,069
Distributed to children	9,474
Living expenses 1869-75	22,782
Balance	00

---

†Children who were of age. The name of each individual's mother is given in parentheses. Daniel Davis was the sole adopted child to inherit. It is clear from his diary that he was very close to Heber and treated as a member of the family.

*The total distributed to all the children combined.

From these figures it appears that his ten inheriting wives and their thirty-two minor children were treated equally, similarly the three childless wives. Apparently family responsibility and the amount of property previously received from Kimball determined the distribution to his ten married children.

NOTES

1. "Synopsis of the History of Heber C. Kimball," *Deseret News,* March 31, 1858.

2. Monroe County Deeds, 27:144, Liber 24:435, and Liber 26:325.

3. Winslow Whitney Smith Papers, September 1842, March 12, 1844, LDS Church Archives, Historical Department, Church of Jesus Christ of Latter-day Saints, Salt Lake City (hereafter referred to as LDS Church Archives).

4. See H. C. Kimball Journal, January 25, 28, 1845 for example, LDS Church Archives. In St. Louis, on February 5, 1858, "Daniel D[avis] Kimball, agent for H. C. Kimball," received "seventy-five dollars from Frederick Froerer as a donation to help Brother Heber C. Kimball remove to the Valley of the Great Salt Lake." I would like to thank Darrell Stoddard for bringing this receipt to my attention.

5. H. C. Kimball Journal, October 10, 1846, LDS Church Archives.

6. H. C. Kimball to David, Charles, and Brigham Kimball, November 20, 1864, H. C. Kimball Papers, LDS Church Archives.

7. H. C. Kimball to William Kimball, December 21, 1854, *Millennial Star,* Vol. 17 (April 21, 1855), 252.

8. H. C. Kimball to Solomon Kimball, February 29, 1852, H. C. Kimball Papers, LDS Church Archives.

9. H. C. Kimball to Solomon Kimball, January 2, 1857, H. C. Kimball Papers, LDS Church Archives.

10. H. C. Kimball to William Kimball, May 29, 1855, H. C. Kimball Papers, LDS Church Archives.

11. *Deseret News,* September 24, 1856. He sometimes over-extended himself. Once he bought 5,000 peach trees and then, according to the *Deseret News* of March 11, 1857, offered to dispose of them at the rate of half of what he paid for them two or three years before.

12. Horace Greeley, *An Overland Journey from New York to San Francisco in the Summer of 1859* (1860, reprint, New York: Alfred A. Knopf, 1964), 204-5.

13. Fitz Hugh Ludlow, *In the Heart of the Continent . . . with an Examination of the Mormon Principle* (1870 reprint, New York: AMP Press, 1971), 347.

14. Ibid., 348-49. On at least one occasion in 1855 Heber did use too much water, but Water Master Phineas W. Cook was afraid to fine him. When Heber heard of this, he told Cook he "would cuff his ears if he did not fine him, told him not to be afraid of the big men, he was Water Master and expected to act like it." Heber paid the fine. *The Life and History of Phineas Wolcott Cook* (n.p., n.d.), 81-83, Utah State University Library, Logan.

15. Kimball said he was using the hydraulic presses "brother Taylor brought to this country, and they are performing wonders. They will each press equal to a hundred and twelve tons weight." *Journal of Discourses*, 26 vols. (London: Latter-day Saints' Book Depot, 1854-1886), 9 (April 7, 1861): 28. These are probably the same presses imported from France in an unsuccessful attempt to make beet sugar.

16. H. C. Kimball to "Brothers," May 15, 1861, *Millennial Star* 23 (July 27, 1861): 478.

17. *Journal of Discourses* 9 (April 7, 1861): 28.

18. *Deseret News*, June 20, 1860.

19. Ludlow, *Heart of the Continent*, 349-52. Heber later built a second carding machine on Fifth North between Second and Third West.

20. The Account Book of Daniel Davis, 1852-67, LDS Church Archives, suggests how busy and complex were some of Heber's business affairs.

21. H. C. Kimball Estate Papers, Order Confirming Acts of Administration, August 24, 1875, Utah State Archives, Salt Lake City.

22. Historian's Office Journal, May 20, 1858, LDS Church Archives; Journal History, July 12, 1858, LDS Church Archives.

23. The records of brands in early Utah are fascinating. See William Clayton, "Book of One Thousand Marks and Brands Alphabetically Arranged," Salt Lake City, 1855, LDS Church Archives; "Historic Utah Brands," Subject File, Utah State Historical Society, Salt Lake City; and "Record of Marks and Brands," Utah Territorial Archives, Salt Lake City.

24. *Journal of the Legislative Assembly of the Territory of Utah, 1856-57*, 14, 24.

25. *Journal of Discourses* 8 (July 1, 1860): 109.

26. *Deseret News*, March 5, 1853. Nine men bought thirty-four shares, of which Heber acquired three. See Ledger A, Great Salt Lake City Waterworks Association, LDS Church Archives.

27. Document 718, February 25, 1863, Utah Territorial Archives.

28. "Speech by Counselor Kimball. . . . ," January 6, 1852, H. C. Kimball Papers, LDS Church Archives.

29. *Journal of Discourses* 2 (August 13, 1853), 105.

30. In the Salt Lake Temple Stone Cutters Record Book, 1852-57, 1870-75, LDS Church Archives, dated March 1855, the following is recorded: "A bill of timbers for a porch on H. C. Kimball's house, T. O. Angell, Archt." I am uncertain whether Kimball received the timbers free or paid for them.

31. Alice K. Smith, "Musing and Reminiscences on the Life of Heber C. Kimball," *Improvement Era* 33 (June 1930): 559.

32. Ibid., 8 (July 1860): 111.

33. "H. C. Kimball Discourse, March 23, 1853," H. C. Kimball Papers, LDS Church Archives.

34. Adelia Almira Hatton Memoirs, 18-19, in possession of author.

35. Mary Ellen Kimball Journal, October 24, 1858, LDS Church Archives.

36. See appendix.

37. This analysis of the Kimball estate is based on three documents. The first is the "Inventory and Appraisement of the Personal Effects and Estate of Heber C. Kimball, deceased, made January 1, 1869" which is in the Utah Historical Society Archives, Salt Lake City. The other two, the "Order Confirming Acts of Admin-stration, Aug. 24, 1875" plus "Exhibit B," and the "Decree of Court Authorizing Distribution of Property, September 7, 1876," are in the Utah State Archives, Salt Lake City.

The Inventory, an extremely detailed document of 132 folio pages, is the source of the 1869 figures which represent the value of the household items of each of Kimball's thirteen inheriting wives.

The Order is the source of the 1875 figures which represent the value of goods and property distributed to Kimball's wives at that time.

The Decree is the source of the 1876 figures which represent the value of goods and property distributed to his surviving children at that time.

The detailed and lengthy Inventory is also the source of the information listed as "Living expenses 1869-75." (All figures have been rounded to the nearest dollar and because the documents are not always accurate there may be some small differences in the totals.)

There are three wives listed in this appendix who did not inherit: Vilate pre-deceased Kimball and Clarissa and Emily Cutler did not follow Kimball west. The estate records do not explain why only five wives are shown to have received the homes they lived in as part of their inheritance. According to various Salt Lake City directories, however, most of Kimball's wives remained in Salt Lake City. They lived in the big Kimball home (which went to Kimball's oldest son, Heber Jr.) and in other homes throughout the city.

6

Family Life and Rural Society in Spring City, Utah: The Basis of Order in a Changing Agrarian Landscape

Michael S. Raber

Most scholars of Mormon history have argued that the Church played a dominant role in Utah community life in the nineteenth century and that the control declined during the twentieth century. In this article, Michael S. Raber, a consulting anthropologist with Raber Associates in Cobalt, Connecticut, argues that individual households and families had a greater effect on the development of the Mormon town than the Church. Using the information he gathered in Spring City for his dissertation, he points out that while ward leaders directed early cooperative efforts in Spring City, heads of households actually controlled these efforts. Rather than the Church retreating on economic issues in the late nineteenth and twentieth century, Dr. Raber sees the decreasing church control as the result of the successful development of independent farming households.

When present-day Mormons from the Intermountain West look back at their history, they often make nostalgic contrasts. In Brigham Young's day the Church supposedly played a commanding role in the economy and society of local communities and in the Mormon region as a whole. Under the

direction of church leaders, households and families cooperated in creating farmlands, irrigation systems, or stores.[1]
Modern Mormons sometimes see the present as a falling away
from a cooperative past, as church-directed community efforts
now often emerge only in the context of emergencies or special
projects.

I spent nearly two years in Sanpete County during the
mid-1970's studying the history of small-scale farming and of
farming households in Spring City. At the time I wondered
how this town of very independent farmers and other folk
originated from what was supposed to have been a well-organized, centrally directed program run by the Church. My scrutiny of that town, and of regional patterns of church authority,
land tenure, and marketing of farm products, led me to conclude that strong central or church direction was limited.
Spring City people as I knew them in the 1970s were not
products or descendants of a program or a society run by the
Church because central planning, direction, or organization
did not extend very far into many of the most important
aspects of pioneer Mormon life. For people from places like
Spring City, the most important element in social life has never
been the Church; it has been the households and families living
in these towns.

Many social conditions of rural Mormondom in the modern Intermountain West seem to be directly descended from
Euro-American domestic and agricultural patterns which predate the Church by at least several centuries. While there is still
no comprehensive history of such patterns, my immediate
interest here is in the limited effects of church programs or
church leadership on the development of rural society in Mormon Utah, and in the apparently greater importance of pre-
Mormon patterns on this development. In the first section of
this paper, I outline the relationships between family organization and the Church, and the effects of family relationships on
the role of the Church as a central force in social action. I then
discuss the persistence and direction of local Mormon family
organization during three or four generations using Spring
City as a case study, along with some tentative remarks on the

pre-Mormon patterns from which so much of this family organization seems to derive. Finally, I present conclusions on the implications of church-family relationships for understanding the economic and social aspirations of early church leaders.

Households, Families, and
Pioneer Church Organization

The earliest Mormon attempt to settle the Spring City area was in 1852, when closely related members of the Allred family began to establish large contiguous farmsteads without a nucleated village center. The Allred settlement was soon abandoned, however, in the face of the Ute threat during the 1853 Walker War. A more classic form of Mormon settlement began at Spring City in 1859, when English, Danish, and American settlers laid out a gridiron pattern of town lots surrounded by irrigated fields. Spring City was called Springtown until 1870, when it was incorporated under its present name. Within the framework of Mormon-written territorial laws, and of a county court system which worked closely with church leaders, Springtown acquired rights to the waters of three creeks and to several thousand acres of land for herd grounds south and east of the town lots. These resources were nominally in the charge of the Springtown bishop who, with his counselors and several elected committees, supervised the construction of the earliest irrigation system, the allocation of water turns, the management of small town herds, and the distribution of farmland. Farmland was not actually allotted to towns through the territorial government, but since farmland was useless without water at this time, and since water rights originated with the county court and passed to the towns as represented by their bishops, towns essentially created their own farmland. The legal system changed in 1869 when a federal land office was finally set up in Salt Lake City, and towns could no longer create and distribute rights to farmland.

During this most collective period of Spring City history, the bishopric administered town affairs in public meetings with those townspeople who actually received the rights to land and water. These people were usually married priesthood holders in the Church. The few who did not fall into this category were unmarried adult men who were probably eligible for the priesthood, younger unmarried men representing their widowed mothers, and perhaps widows having no adult sons.[2] The distinctive feature of these people, whose identities are clear from 1860s tithing lists and genealogical reconstructions, is that they were all heads of households or people likely to become heads of households within a few years.[3]

There are important differences between *households* and *families*.[4] I see family as a series of kinship relations into which most people enter at different times of their lives. These relations include roles or responsibilities which can vary among different cultures, but the genealogical positions associated with such roles are usually fairly limited. Most of us live first with parents as children, later with spouses and children, and sometimes with other combinations of kin and non-kin. Family relationships also pertain among kin who may never live together. Residence is only one aspect of family relations, and as such should not define families. Households are more nearly defined by residence, although the familiar case of a Mormon polygynist with distinct residential groups of wives and children suggests that a single household may include more than one home. Households are perhaps best seen as groups of people who share the use and immediate control of particular sets of assets or resources such as land, livestock, equipment, or money. Usually these groups consist of close kin, but boarders and servants appear in many historical situations. Households sometimes include more distant kin, or kin not usually expected in various cultural definitions of households (e.g., orphaned or destitute relatives who otherwise would live elsewhere). For pioneer rural Mormons, who lived sometimes with unfortunate kin but rarely with servants or boarders, these definitions mean that households were the groups which effectively owned—through the husbands or widows who usually led them—the farmland, houses, gardens, town and hay lots, and water rights which were the principal real property assets needed at the time.

During the 1860s the transfer of these assets of land and water rights to households by the local ward was permanent, and apparently unrelated to one's church standing. In several cases where men were disfellowshipped, their rights to such assets were not revoked or impaired.[5] The only kinds of agricultural rights not divided among individual households very early in the settlement process were rights to appropriate or claim irrigation water and to use pastureland. Water was administered by the town—and by the ward—when the household heads met together. The various unirrigated pasture areas could not be legally claimed by individuals without fencing,[6] which in practice meant virtually no private pasture. Limited regulations on access to timber in nearby canyons rarely called for cooperative efforts other than road construction. From the size of irrigated farm holdings distributed—five to ten acres at a time—and the universal distribution of farmland to households living in the ward, it seems clear that the aim of settlement from a local perspective was to make each household as self-sufficient as possible with grants of permanent, privately held rights to land and water. This objective is a familiar feature of Mormon colonization, but there are less familiar implications in these arrangements for the relationship of the Church to member households.

It was the responsibility of each household to take care of itself except in dire circumstances. There were few instances of ward-organized economic activities which were not based on the pooling of individually held assets such as livestock or labor for proportionate returns to each individual household, even during the most collective era of town history. Town herds were simply groupings of various households' livestock. All herding operations sponsored or administered through the ward were oriented either towards caring for stock such as milch cows used primarily for household subsistence, or towards increasing the size of sheep and dry stock (i.e., non-milk producing) herds for home use and private sale. The preparation of allotted land for cultivation was not usually managed by the ward. Each household had to clear off the brush, prepare the ditches, and do the plowing on its own ground, with whatever help it could get.

Only in emergency situations, notably after the influx of refugees from the Piute County area during the Black Hawk War of the mid-1860s, did the entire Springtown ward mobilize for the preparation of all fields in a new division of farmland. In several other cases it appears that groups of men within the ward organized themselves to make new divisions, with the permission and participation of the bishopric, and these self-selected groups jointly did the land clearance and ditch digging necessary during the first season.[7] These latter cases are similar to participation in dry stock or sheep herding arrangements. Investments were made on a relatively short-term basis with all returns going to the individual participants in direct proportion to their inputs. The ward-wide distributions required few responsibilities to the ward or the town on the part of the grantees other than prorated ditch maintenance tasks—involving some work each spring—and one-time construction duties for fencing and ditching irrigated fields.[8]

The most striking negative evidence for the lack of ward management or involvement in household economics is the rapid failure of the "united order" begun in Spring City in May 1874. United orders were set up in nearly every Mormon town in a final attempt to achieve regional self-sufficiency, and most failed soon after they were initiated. As with most of these organizations, the Spring City effort was modeled on the first united order set up in St. George, in February 1874. In theory, each united order was a collective in which members contributed their labor and farmlands to be managed by local order directors, with each member receiving wages and dividends in proportion to capital and labor inputs, and drawing against united order products for sustenance between wage or dividend distributions. There was no attempt in this type of united order to change domestic housing or eating arrangements. The actual operating procedures of these united orders were rarely if ever worked out at the time of establishment, however, and given the short histories of most orders little useful evidence survives that clarifies how they functioned.[9]

Apparently, only nineteen men in Spring City originally subscribed to the united order, all but one contributing livestock in return for shares.[10] At this time, there were over 130 household heads or adult males in the community. Several other men are known to have joined after May 1874, and it is possible that the articles of incorporation included only the names of directors and other men in formal leadership positions. At least some of the irrigated farmland owned by Spring City households was managed collectively under the united order, but the order broke up "before the harvest."[11] Taken together with the fact that the Spring City United Order was set up in the late spring of 1874—after planting of the spring wheat on which the local economy depended—and that directors of the order there were appointed as late as March 1875, the single agricultural season of collective effort implied by this statement could have been in 1875.

I can draw several implications for my arguments about limits to church-managed community agriculture from this limited united order evidence. Subscription of shares in the Spring City United Order may have been understood by participants as more of a joint-stock endeavor, similar to those I described for herding operations, or to the cooperative store established in 1869, than as the kind of total commitment of labor and capital envisaged by General Authorities. The similarity in recorded form between subscriptions to the store and the order suggests this understanding, as does the lack of any detailed operating instructions to the contrary which plagued nearly all the united orders.[12] The apparent continuation of household-managed farming through the 1874 agricultural season—after the order was set up—also suggests a preference for joint efforts only in well-defined, short-term efforts. There was a strong preference for limiting agrarian labor organization to household members in Spring City, as I mention below, in part because of uncertainties about the results of cooperative farming activities.

If these conjectures about the Spring City United Order are true, a previously unexplored factor in the failure of so many united orders between 1874 and 1876 may have been the timing of initial organization (late spring 1874) relative to the agricultural season, since many people may have been wary of collective efforts after seasonal work on their farms was already underway. Resulting delays in full implementation of united order agriculture could have seriously diminished any momentum for participation being developed by Church leaders.

The material presented in this section strongly suggests that church-led or community-level economic activity in Spring City never extended into agricultural production. The only long-term example of such activity not limited to herding or irrigation management was the Spring City Co-operative Mercantile Institution, a local arm of the ZCMI movement.[13] This cooperative venture was designed to *distribute* products, not to create them. Households managed production. In the next two sections, I explore why they did so, as the positive side of the negative evidence outlined so far.

Household Autonomy in Mormondom

The features of Spring City life just outlined were not accidental or just cases of people failing to live up to Mormon standards in some way. Rather, these features were part of a contradictory pattern established early in church history: plans for regional self-sufficiency and independence were based on autonomous producer households.

The dividing line between church authority and household autonomy appears most clearly in nineteenth-century records of church meetings and church courts, and these are a good place to begin looking at why Mormon households were *expected* to be essentially autonomous. Surviving ward minutes from the 1860s are filled largely with the land, water, and herding affairs I have reviewed. These affairs were treated in gatherings labeled as business meetings in the records, and in content and form the business meetings were very different from more strictly ritual gatherings such as sacrament meetings despite the presiding presence of the bishopric at both kinds of meetings. Business meetings were evidently attended only by the household heads, sometimes referred to as the "male citizens"—not as the "elders." There was often much discussion, and some dissent with bishopric opinion, on pragmatic problems of individual responsibilities and assessments for public projects. Votes were taken which were not always unanimous, and dissenters were not singled out for sanctions. The bishopric did not stand on its authority in influencing decisions, unless someone insulted or verbally abused the bishop or other men present. Such action was held to be unchristian-like, and subject to possible disfellowshipping, if public apology was not forthcoming. There was a line between a citizen's right to protect his own interests as those interests were commonly held by the ward community, and his right to act in an unchristian-like manner toward others in the pursuit of those interests. The ward as an administrator of public resources was not identical to the ward as a ritual community. Consensus rather than ritual authority was generally the source of decision making in the former sphere.[14]

A similar and perhaps even more informative line appears in church court records of the nineteenth century. Men could be called to account by the bishopric or stake presidency for failing to support wives or children, for cheating or abusing others, for apostasy, or for adultery, but a man's management of his own resources and his own household was never questioned—provided that standards of Christian-like conduct and priesthood responsibilities toward kin were maintained.[15]

Even attempts to eliminate competition of private stores with ZCMI outlets during the 1870s halted short of using ritual authority. In 1875 Spring City's resident Apostle, Orson Hyde, apparently threatened to excommunicate two men from nearby Moroni for running a store in competition with the Moroni branch of ZCMI. The two men were in good standing in the Church, and either directly or indirectly they brought the matter to the attention of Hyde's superiors in the First Presidency of the Church. Apostle Hyde was overruled. He was told that it was best "not to hold over men under such circumstances the terrors of excommunication. Cooperation should be able to hold its own . . . upon its own merits." Hyde was advised to combine the two stores on some basis that would not involve loss to either so as to end the rivalry.[16] Even economic programs of the greatest importance to church leaders could not be enforced through ritual authority. The fact that the men from Moroni tested Apostle Hyde's authority in this case suggests some general understanding of this principle.

I do not think the Church retreated on issues of economy, in its use of ritual authority during the later nineteenth century, as is sometimes maintained. Decreasing ward and stake involvement in matters of property, water, and other generally economic concerns is certainly evident in church court records, but I think this is because once the Church had successfully implanted all these farming households, and once the legal system making all these community-run, land grant programs possible was changed in 1869, there was no reason for the ritual authority of church leaders to be applied to such problems. Some leaders in other Mormon towns did try to run things more closely, but except in unusual cases they generally failed. Spring City was probably not an atypical community in this regard.

The division between church authority and household autonomy in economic matters was a critical limiting factor in regional plans for Mormon independence. Church leaders hoped to organize the economy of Mormondom to become self-sufficient, and to do this they needed to produce things which could be sold to non-Mormons in exchange for equipment, tools, and other things most Mormons did not have or could not manufacture at this time. Shortages of all kinds of metal products and machinery were particularly vexing since they limited productive capabilities even on small farms. At the same time, the Church essentially located the source of potential exports—which initially had to be agricultural products—in church-member households. Households were the basic productive unit in agrarian Mormondom. Since households were responsible for themselves, they could not and did not always contribute to church programs to the extent that its leaders wished. Springtown tithing records for the 1860s are clear on this point. Most households, between 82 and 94 percent, paid *some* tithing between 1860 and 1868, but the extent to which payment was made in the valuable regional commodities—especially wheat—varied greatly with market conditions and harvest sizes.[17]

Households had to take care of themselves before they could support the Church, and so the Church apparently had problems collecting enough surplus commodities to further plans for regional autonomy. Despite the fact that Mormon farmers produced crops such as wheat which were always in some demand in the intermountain regional economy, Brigham Young's merchandising or manufacturing projects were evidently plagued by shortages of the cash needed to deal with eastern U.S. or European suppliers. The detailed financial histories of these projects are still in part matters of conjecture, as are the precise dimensions of cash and produce flows between farmers and nonfarmers in the region. It is clear, however, even in a qualitative sense, that there was a large traffic in produce by Mormon farmers as well as merchants supplying non-Mormon miners and the urban population of Salt Lake City. The Church was never able to control or effectively regulate this important source of cash, and it is hard not to see a connection between this "lost" cash and some of the problems with Young's projects.[18]

In my theory of Mormon farmer households, cash crops were sold, directly or indirectly, by farmers to secure the finished or unfinished goods they wanted or needed from the eastern United States, or the cash needed for capital investments in their own operations. These individualized exchanges tended to preclude the consolidation of Mormon marketing power, and—I suspect—limited the diversification of ZCMI efforts in nonfarm production by concentrating on similar short-term exchanges geared to household economies. There is still a tremendous amount of research needed on all the topics touched on in these last two paragraphs, but the cumulative effects of household autonomy on regional plans seem clear even if many of the quantitative details are presently unavailable.

The primacy of household units in Mormon economic plans is not all that surprising, given the great emphasis placed on the priesthood of each adult male and the ultimate glorification of people as husbands, wives, and children—not as church members as such—in Mormon doctrine. The importance placed on household units and family relations is fundamental to this doctrine. God rules the Mormon universe as a divine father, with many children and probably a wife or wives. While all males will remain sons of God forever, they may also become gods themselves, ruling their own immortal households and perfecting the organization of physical matter. A properly performed earthly marriage, enabling a couple to prepare for eternal life together, is necessary for the achievement of celestial glory. The priesthood held by men is preparatory to their potential being as gods, and they are given the responsibility and authority to manage their households as an important part of the process of preparation. Despite presumed relations of filial obedience among related divine households, there is an autonomy of authority *within* households under the father/husband/god-to-be. Since single households, and related households ordered in genealogical hierarchy, are the models for eternal, celestial government, no earthly form of church or civil government has priority over a priest's authority as husband and father, provided he does not abandon or pollute his position by nonsupport or adultery.

The Church is a temporary organization in this scheme, designed to provide an earthly framework in which households can better prepare for eternity, and ordered in a hierarchy of priests and their dependents. A priest as household head is responsible to this hierarchy of other priests for the proper management of his household; his wife, wives, or children are for the most part more responsible to the priest/husband/father than to the Church hierarchy as such. Priesthood holders, then, are more responsible for the individual achievement of divinity than the Church. The Church provides instruction and guidance; the priest-led household provides the personal relationships in which personal and familial perfection can occur.[19]

It was for these reasons that priesthood authority within households was largely unregulated, within the broad limits I outlined in reviewing Church court data. There is a direct relationship between priesthood authority and the economic and social independence of households in Spring City, and, I suspect, in many other Mormon towns. The Church encouraged this independence in its colonization practices, outlined in the preceding section, and both Church leaders and members hoped for a fairly egalitarian distribution of agricultural resources among the member households. The Church did not actively regulate economic relations among households to achieve any particular distribution for the same reasons that it did not regulate relationships within households, but it did establish standards of behavior among households to allow for the orderly achievement of household objectives. These standards injected an important element of temperance into the autonomy of households, as I outline in the next section.

Households and the Moral Order in Spring City

The social identities of members in Spring City households were similar to those in most non-Mormon American and European households of the nineteenth century; indeed, the similarity would seem to pertain to the non-Mormon norm over a much longer period—from at least the eighteenth century to the present—if recent social historiography and demography is correct. The "extended family," in which kin other than parents and unmarried children lived together, was not a very common occurrence in the Euro-American world. Most households had few such other kin.[20] In much of Euro-America one could also find boarders or servants in some households. However, this appears to have been more of an urban phenomenon during periods of migration and mobility than a rural one, in post-colonial America.[21] There were rarely boarders or servants in Spring City, although these people appear in the larger Mormon towns and cities with more wage laborers. People in Spring City households who were not parents or unmarried children were almost always grandchildren with one or both parents dead, and widowed or divorced children who were often the parents of the grandchildren in question. These were exceptions, though. Between 1860 and 1900, a period in which both census and genealogical data are available, 85 to 95 percent of all Spring City households were

composed of parents and unmarried children, whether poly-
gyny was involved or not. Other kin appeared in Spring City
households only when misfortune or other unusual circumstances prevented parents and unmarried children from living
together. It was expected that children would form their own
households once they married.[22] All of this is as familiar to us
today as it was to our ancestors.

Historically, much of Mormondom can be seen as *added
onto* these basic features of Euro-American household organization. Priesthood authority was given to the men who were
also household heads, and the basic social units of agricultural
production were carried over from at least some of the societies
from which early Mormons came. Church authority and general settlement ideals also elaborated on these earlier models in
several ways. In theory, all households were defined as equal
by the nearly universal granting of priesthood status. The
strengthening of family relationships among households was
allowed for, ideally, by setting up a legal system featuring more
or less self-created land grants, making it possible—again,
ideally—for related households to live near each other. Finally,
a moral framework of conduct expected between households
was established, a framework which countered some of the
more antisocial or even anarchic tendencies which might have
been expected in a context of completely unfettered household
autonomy.

Although Church ritual authority could not be imposed
on households for most types of behavior, membership in
communities where Christ-like conduct was an ideal, if not
always a reality, made for a good deal of face-to-face civility.
There have been very few acts of intentional violence in Spring
City history. Settlement of differences by force, theft, or destruction of property among community members has never
had any institutional or moral basis, a state of affairs which
continues to the present. Since many Spring City people during my sojourns there had lukewarm, neutral, nonpracticing,
nonexistent, or even hostile associations with church matters,
the strength of this tradition of orderly coexistence seems
clear. Nearly everyone in town in the mid-1970s was at least

descended from a church member, usually one who moved there before 1900. However, I do not think that abstract principles of behavior alone account for the palpable order of Spring City and other Mormon towns where I have spent time. The equality fostered by priesthood and pioneer settlement programs gave some sanctity to all households and their property, even if at the same time it did nothing to discourage competition or inequality among households in most instances.

The sources of disaffection with the Church in this and other rural towns have never been systematically explored, but my research experiences suggest two avenues of inquiry: (1) misunderstandings by local church leaders of the importance of treading lightly in areas of legitimate priesthood or household autonomy; and (2) a general inability of the Church at all levels to deal with the inequalities of agricultural development which emerged shortly after the settlement era.[23] In coping with historical conditions of development, Spring City families and households have made adjustments which indicated the strength and durability of the cultural patterns imported into Utah and the Mormon West.

Family Organization
in a Contracting Agricultural Economy

Despite the opportunities for the development of family life offered by church settlement programs, few groups of related households in Spring City were able to remain very intact in any spatial sense after about 1875. By family life I mean kin from different households being able to live near one another and associate on a continuing basis. Work on the emotional or psychological content of such associations has only recently become an object of serious study, and the scattered nature of research materials available in this emotional field has so far daunted any systematic efforts to integrate personal relationships, domestic settlement patterns, and historical development in any defined locality in Mormondom. The evidence I present below, relating inheritance and mobility patterns, does suggest the importance of proximity in the content of family relationships, however.

Face-to-face, continuing relationships among related households in Spring City were often as fragmented and as infrequent for several generations after 1875 as they are sometimes believed to be today for rural and urban Mormons alike. However, I suspect that family relationships beyond the range of parent/child households are probably stronger today in Spring City than they were one hundred years ago. There has not been a decline or breakdown of support and contact between related households in recent times. I would argue instead that in many ways there has been an increase in support and contact, with greater opportunities to achieve a model of family organization which was initially attempted under inherently unfavorable agricultural conditions in the nineteenth century. This latter-day growth of family relations may have occurred precisely *because* early Mormon Utah agrarian conditions became less stable, as a review of events and patterns in Spring City would seem to indicate.

Definitions of household have remained unchanged throughout Mormon history, and much of Euro-American history generally. There is some evidence, most of it indirect, for an ideal family pattern in Mormonism involving the households of married sons being in close contact with the households of fathers. This was not new to Mormonism. At least in the eastern United States and Canada, it seems that cycles of movement into unsettled areas, and movements away from areas perceived as crowded, were often grounded in attempts to maintain this pattern.[24] We will need more case studies and syntheses of Euro-American landholding, inheritance, and migration for clearer outlines of this ideal and of historical variations in it.

There is a conspicuous example of this ideal pattern among the Allreds who settled Spring City in large numbers in the 1850s and 1860s. The Allreds were from the American South, and for at least a generation before they joined the Church they apparently settled in clusters of dispersed farm households centered around fathers and married sons, with slightly more distant spatial relationships among each of these clusters and similar groups headed by the brothers of the fathers in any group in question. In other words, each male household head was living closest to his father, brothers, or sons, and living somewhat further away from uncles, cousins, or nephews on his father's side, depending on who he was.[25] The Allreds tried exactly this pattern in early Spring City, in a very dispersed manner of settlement, and had to give it up because of Indian attacks.[26]

It is interesting to note that the Allreds tried to settle on large farms, which was the only way groups of households like these could hope to remain intact for any period of time. There were good reasons for kin to settle in this way, not the least of which was the heavy demand for labor needed to clear off new land in the first season of settlement. Regardless of how common or desirable this pattern was among the societies from which Mormons came, it was encouraged at least tacitly by Mormon land policies in the self-created ward land grants and the lack of community labor available for most tasks. The family groups to which I refer are essentially collections of the basic household units. Clusters of households centered on fathers and sons were the most common single immigrant groups I found in early Spring City history, encompassing 20 percent of household heads arriving before 1870 with any genealogical links to other households. However, when the opportunities for obtaining land rights were greatest, other groups centered on in-laws or brothers were also present.[27]

In Spring City the conditions of agricultural production have usually not been favorable to sustaining long-lasting kin relations of proximity and assistance beyond household limits. Until the development of the turkey industry in Sanpete beginning in the 1930s, virtually all agriculture in Spring City was based in some way on the production of irrigated crops. The only exceptions were a very small number of men who were able to build up large sheep herds at the end of the last century without having an irrigated farm. Otherwise, wheat remained the most important cash crop until the end of the First World War. Afterwards, restrictions on grazing activities by the U.S. Forest Service made the production of livestock feed, expecially alfalfa, critical for maintaining the small live- stock operations on which most Spring City households relied during the long depression after that war. Even most large sheep operations required sizable farms for feed production. Almost no livestock men tried to rely completely on pasture, and this was still the case in the 1970s. So there has been, and for some Spring City people there continues to be, a long tradition of heavy reliance on irrigated farming.

Irrigated farms were initially very small in Springtown— five to fifteen acres. Pioneer irrigated agriculture and the ways in which it was established were directly related to the size and arrangement of farms; farm size and arrangement had direct impacts on household and family development. Beyond the general understanding that land shortages began within a few decades of Mormon settlement, there is still no comprehensive assessment of the origins and history of village-based irrigated farming in this region. In the next few pages, I present some of the more apparent effects on the history of Spring City farms which were too few and too small.

Small Mormon farms were always expected to produce commodities as well as subsistence products. Households needed saleable surpluses to buy tools, consumable items such as sugar or coffee, and sometimes land. The production of irrigated crops has usually been associated in Spring City with the labor of people within the household owning the land, particularly the labor of fathers and adolescent or adult unmarried sons. This pattern was particularly obvious before the advent of mechanized harvesting equipment in Sanpete at the beginning of the present century. Most irrigated farming tasks could be completed by one man, but grain harvesting operations before mechanization required several people to cradle, bind, and shock.

Women and children helped in harvests if men and boys were lacking, but it is clear from census data and interviews I have had with older farmers that the labor of women and child- ren was not preferred in fieldwork. Women and children were more important in equally necessary work done on houselots, such as the management of chickens and cows, or the processing of food crops for home use.

At the same time, it appears that the exchange of labor between households in the nineteenth century was very limited. Most available evidence suggests that the labor of more than one household was needed to clear off new fields and prepare them for irrigated cultivation, but extra household labor was not used much once more normal, annually recurring farm activities were underway. To a large extent, then, it seems that each household was rather isolated within the limits of its own labor power for the most important elements of Spring City agriculture.[28]

The reasons for this isolation are not entirely understood at this time, but I can suggest several possible reasons before discussing the effects of these conditions on family relationships. There was, and for the most part continues to be, little wage labor available in Spring City to work with household members at farm tasks, probably because of both limited demand from households which usually had little surplus to spend or exchange as wages, and a limited supply of unattached men in the area with no commitments to their own households. There was also the fact that many grain harvests occurred at the same time and had to be completed quickly, so households may have been reluctant to jeopardize their own harvests by assisting others. In addition to grain harvests, there was a great deal of other farm work and canyon work to be completed in the fall. Considerations such as these made united order ventures short-lived.

The perceived need to confine most labor within households created many problems for these people, since continuing work relationships between fathers and sons, or between brothers, were jeopardized by the creation of new households as men married. The responsibilities of each household were first to itself, and second to closely related households. In order to continue critical work relationships, two conditions probably had to be met. Enough additional land had to be acquired for each son to support his own household, and enough labor power had to be acquired to allow for effective production on these hypothetical, larger farms or combinations of farms.

After the era of free land divisions under ward supervision in Springtown ended in 1869, a period of about forty years followed in which the effects of these conditions were played out in several ways. In a few cases, closely related households—often headed by brothers—left the town to homestead new and larger farms as the children in these households were growing up and approaching marriageable age, a time which was potentially the most critical point of fission in family relationships for these farmers. A small number of men succeeded in acquiring larger farms in and around Spring City, through combinations of homesteading, purchase, or inheritance. Some among these latter men had been able to establish larger-than-average sheep or cattle herds between 1880 and 1900, and profits from these operations served to enlarge their holdings in irrigated land. For the most part, it was these men and their descendants who survived as the full-time farmers of today. They were the first to use steam-powered mechanized harvesting equipment around the turn of the century, and some of their children were the first to use gasoline-powered tractors and harvestors around 1940. Much of the incentive to invest in machinery came from a combination of traditionally limited household labor forces and the enlarged holdings needed to keep these farms and farm families together. Expansion of labor power on the larger farms was also most responsible for an expansion of wage labor from a pool of less-successful people at about the same time the machinery was first introduced.[29]

For most households, however, including many whose heads were sons of the farmers just described, an inability to increase farm size resulted in outmigration from Spring City. Migration away from farms by second- or third-generation sons is an old story in Utah, but what is less familiar is the extent to which these migrations damaged family relationships. Support among relatives until well into the present century was usually in the form of aid given in person. In periods with little cash money and horse-powered travel over long distances on bad roads, relatives who moved away were often much less directly involved with their Spring City kin than those who stayed. The most dramatic documentary evidence of the importance of proximity is in records of inheritance. Few sons of pre-1870 Spring City settlers received any property rights from their fathers if they were not living in Spring City when the land was distributed. Distribution was rarely by probate or will, and usually land was deeded to children in a sale or as a gift as illustrated in this table.[30]

Receipt of Property
Rights from Fathers
By Adult Males

	Resident at Time of Devolution	Non resident at Time of Devolution	Totals
Received Rights	59	3	62
Received No Rights	38	36	74
Totals	97	39	146

The inheritance data also give great weight to the idea that a man's first responsibility was to his own household before those of his children, because in many cases even resident sons were passed over in favor of their mothers, especially if there were minor children to be cared for by a widow. Nearly half of the sons in this sample who received no land directly from their fathers were residents of Spring City with minor siblings. It seems clear from these materials that when household resources were limited and nonmobile, only children who actively participated in the maintenance of their parents' households were given shares in the parental resources—and only then when all parental responsibilities to unmarried children had been fulfilled to the degree possible.[31]

A small number of the inheritances in this sample, and an apparently larger number in later generations which I have not yet completely calculated, were different in that they involved more or less equal land distributions among all children regardless of residence. Early cases of equal land distribution occurred only when men had much larger than average holdings, in line with the observation that the continued residence of sons required the expanded holdings of fathers. These cases, increasing with frequency through time, suggest again my hypothesized ideal pattern of continued associations of households headed by fathers and sons. In the later cases, though, it was not always land which was being distributed, but rather the monetary value of land and other assets. This pattern was not the result of any legal changes since Utah inheritance laws have been virtually unchanged since 1897. While some of the change may be related to a greater tendency to leave wills, I think it is more a result of the breakdown of Utah's older agricultural economy and the involvement of people in either nonfarm wage labor, or in the kinds of expanded farm operations mentioned above. With specialization in sheep, dairy, or turkeys, or with people working in industrial or service jobs outside of Spring City, or with combinations of wage labor and part-time farming, family relationships of material and moral support have intensified. Familial assistance is no longer as limited by considerations of distance and can take forms other than actual on-the-scene effort. Increased participation in cash economies allow Spring City people to help their relatives with money, to take advantage of faster and easier (albeit more expensive) forms of transportation, and recently to revive the ideal pattern of related households living nearby, using money earned elsewhere to resettle in Spring City.

The changes in inheritance and residential conditions in this century suggest a return to patterns of multigeniture or partible inheritance and familial proximity which seem to underlie the earlier ideals of family organization.[32] We should perhaps see the settlement, growth, decline, and readjustment of the economy in the Mormon West as a long *interruption* in family ideals, a difficult period in which hard choices were made about the distribution of family resources.

The resettlement of kin in Spring City during the last five to ten years suggests that rather than encouraging a further fissioning of family relationships, the end of the old rural order has finally begun to strengthen family relationships—in at least a geographic sense—in ways which have not been possible in Utah for about a century. This has not happened simply because there was more money and easier travel, since in many parts of the world such benefits can lead to increasingly distant relationships. Something else is involved here, and I believe that two apparently contradictory conclusions can be drawn from this discussion about Mormondom and its members, both of which concern the fundamental social bases of the Church.

The combination of restrained behavior between neighbors and presumed autonomy of households has proven to be an attractive one for many Spring City people. Despite some divisions in the town along lines of church authority or membership and income, the pattern established in the 1850s and 1860s in Spring City has allowed for a relatively class-free society in which most people move about with great freedom. This is in contrast not only to urban or suburban environments in Mormondom, but to many small non-Mormon towns with more complex divisions of labor and established elites. Spring City may be part of a disappearing kind of Mormon town, though, since the spread of urban values and tastes along with increased populations is introducing more civil authority and less autonomous relations among people in other Mormon towns only slightly larger. Once civil government starts to regulate conditions of waste disposal or even the aesthetic appearance of peoples' houselots, much of the quality which continues to attract people to a small town like Spring City starts to fade. Yet it seems that for a long time a church famous for its lines of authority and central planning has been the basis for a very unhierarchical, decentralized rural society. The basis of continuity has been the organization of the Church on a foundation of independent priest-led households. This organization has not been sufficient to give much definition to communities beyond their constituent households, but that definition alone has proven to be a distinctive one.

Finally, I think that for this household base to develop into the network of continuing family relationships which church leaders have always encouraged, the original social and economic programs of Joseph Smith and Brigham Young *had* to fail. Except under ideal conditions of a constantly expanding land base which were probably impossible under any circumstances—especially with individual households as the landowning, basic units of production—the isolated agrarian ideals of early Mormonism were actually destructive of most kin relationships beyond the household. Mormons were never as separate from the rest of the world as church leaders wished, but to succeed in many of the most basic ambitions of patriarchal and family relationships, Mormons had to enter even more completely into the ways of the world. Mormon social policies and aspirations may have been better suited to the world the pioneers were fleeing than to the agrarian haven they hoped to build.

NOTES

1.   The model of a centrally directed Kingdom of the Saints has been developed explicitly over the last three decades. For the most general treatments of this model, see Leonard J. Arrington, *Great Basin Kingdom: An Economic History of the Latter-day Saints* (Cambridge: Harvard University Press, 1958), and Leonard J. Arrington, Feramorz Y. Fox, and Dean L. May, *Building the City of God: Community and Cooperation Among the Mormons* (Salt Lake City: Deseret Book Co., 1976).

Interpretations of post-statehood Utah history have also been heavily influenced by this model, since there is a presumed contrast between the relatively uncommercialized, isolated, church-managed territorial economy propounded by Arrington and others, and the commercialized, national or international, and corporation-controlled economy of the present century in Utah. On this contrast, see Leonard J. Arrington and Thomas G. Alexander, "A Dependent Commonwealth: Utah's Economy from Statehood to the Great Depression," *Charles Redd Monographs in Western History*, No. 4 (Provo: Brigham Young University, 1974). As I argue in this paper, and at greater length in my dissertation on which parts of this paper are based, there are problems with assuming that the Brigham Young era Mormon economy was isolated or centrally directed in any effective sense; see Michael S. Raber, "Religious Polity and Local Production: The Origins of a Mormon Town" (Ph.D. diss., Yale University, 1978). Less direct suggestions of decentralization in Utah appear in L. Dwight Israelsen, "An Economic Analysis of the United Order," *BYU Studies* 18 (Summer 1978): 536-62, and in J. R. Kearl, Clayne L. Pope, and Larry T. Wimmer, "Household Wealth in a Settlement Economy: Utah, 1850-1870," *Journal of Economic History* 40 (September 1980): 477-97.

2.   The priesthood in the Church of Jesus Christ of Latter-day Saints has always been restricted to male members. While there was apparently some evolution in the two orders of priesthood regarding the ages of eligibility for different positions, for practical purposes and at all times, only males regarded as adults have been ordained as elders (the lowest grade of the priesthood in the higher, Melchizedek, order). Springtown public meetings and participants are discussed in Raber, "Religious Polity," 193-94 and 216-18.

3.   Springtown tithing schedules 1860-1868, LDS Church Archives, Historical Department, Church of Jesus Christ of Latter-day Saints, Salt Lake City (hereafter cited as LDS Church Archives). The genealogical reconstruction is discussed in Raber, "Religious Polity," Appendix I.

4.   Aspects of this distinction are discussed in Tamara Hareven, ed., *Family and Kin in Urban Communities, 1700-1930* (New York: New Viewpoints, 1977), 1-15.

5.   Compare Springtown Ward Record of Business 1869-1904, LDS Church Archives, with the tithing schedules of 1867 and 1868. I have no examples of the extreme case of excommunicants.

6.   See an act passed by the territorial legislature in February 1851, in Dale L. Morgan, "The State of Deseret," *Utah Historical Quarterly* 8 (1940): 65-251.

7.   Livy Olsen, "The Life Story of a Western Sheriff," Utah State Historical Society Library, Salt Lake City (hereafter cited as USHS).

8.   Springtown Ward Record of Business, LDS Church Archives; "The Diary of the City Council of Spring City, Commencing January 30, 1871," Special Collections, Harold B. Lee Library, Brigham Young University, Provo.

9.   Israelsen, "Economic Analysis," 542; Arrington, Fox, and

May, *City of God,* 146-47.

10.   Articles of Association, The United Order of Spring City, dated August 28, 1874, Book H-Incorporations, Sanpete County Courthouse, Manti, 25-28.

11.   "Hemming Hansen," in Hansen Family Book of Remembrances, copy in possession of Mrs. Edith Schofield, Spring City in 1976.

12.   Cooperative Meeting, February 1, 1869, in Springtown Ward Record, LDS Church Archives; Arrington, Fox, and May, *City of God,* 146-49.

13.   The Zion's Cooperative Mercantile Institution began as a wholesale and retail operation set up in Salt Lake City by Brigham Young in 1868 using the combined assets of the largest Mormon merchants in Utah. ZCMI was set up to distribute retail products, virtually all of them imports from outside Utah, through local stores set up in many Mormon towns in exchange for cash received by the local stores for local produce sold to regional mines. The entire effort was designed to counter the anticipated influence of non-Mormon merchants in the increased traffic in imports following the arrival of the transcontinental railroad in 1869. The cooperative store program featured heavy financial and ideological investments by Mormon leaders, and great emphasis was placed on eliminating Mormon competition with the ZCMI network. See Arrington, *Great Basin Kingdom,;* Arrington, Fox, and May, *City of God,* 88-104; and Raber, "Religious Polity," 280-83.

14.   Raber, "Religious Polity," 221-23.

15.   Springtown Ward Record of Business; also see Nels Anderson, *Deseret Saints: The Mormon Frontier in Utah* (Chicago: University of Chicago Press, 1966), Chap. 13.

16.   First Presidency to Orson Hyde, October 31, 1875, LDS Church Archives.

17.   Springtown tithing schedules, LDS Church Archives; Raber, "Religious Polity," 269-71.

18.   Arrington, *Great Basin Kingdom*; Raber, "Religious Polity," 90-105.

19.   Raber, "Religious Polity," 28-29 and 414-15.

20.   E.G. Peter Laslett and Richard Wall, eds., *Household and Family in Past Times* (Cambridge: Cambridge University Press,

1974); Peter Laslett, "Characteristics of the Western Family Considered over Time," *Journal of Family History,* 2 (1977): 89-115. Historians of Western Europe find suggestions of this pattern in place no later than the ninth century A.D. Georges Duby, *Rural Economy and Country Life in the Medieval West,* trans. Cynthia Poston (Columbia: University of South Carolina Press, 1968). Duby's discussion of agrarian households suggests striking parallels with Mormon farmers.

21.   John Modell and Tamara Hareven, "Urbanization and the Malleable Household: An Examination of Boarding and Lodging in American Families," in Hareven, *Family and Kin,* 164-86.

22.   Raber, "Religious Polity," 311-26.

23.   For an indication of this latter problem at a regional level, see Kearl, Pope, and Wimmer, "Household Wealth."

24.   Philip J. Greven, Jr., *Four Generations: Population, Land, and Family in Colonial Andover, Massachusetts* (Ithaca: Cornell University Press, 1970); Kenneth A. Lockridge, *The First Hundred Years: Dedham, Massachusetts, 1636-1736* (New York: W. W. Norton & Co., 1970); Richard Easterlin, "Population Change and Farm Settlement in the Northern United States," *Journal of Economic History* 36 (1976): 45-75; David P. Gagan, "The Indivisibility of Land: A Microanalysis of the System of Inheritance in Nineteenth Century Ontario," *Journal of Economic History* 36 (1976): 125-41; Darrett B. Rutman, "People in Process: The New Hampshire Towns of the Eighteenth Century," in Hareven, *Family and Kin,* 16-37.

25.   James T. S. Allred, "James Tilman Sanford Allred," Special Collections, Harold B. Lee Library, Brigham Young University; Redick N. Allred, "The Diary of Redick N. Allred," *Treasures of Pioneer History,* vol. 5, ed. Kate B. Carter (Salt Lake City: Daughters of Utah Pioneers, 1956), 297-372; Redick N. Allred, "Life Sketch," USHS; William M. Allred, "Biography and Journal," LDS Church Archives; Ruth Osborne, "History of James Allred," copy in possession of Canal Creek Encampment, Daughters of Utah Pioneers, Spring City, Utah.

26.   Andrew Jensen, "Spring City Ward, Sanpete County, Utah," LDS Church Archives; George D. Watt et al., *Journal of Discourses,* 26 vols. (London: Latter-day Saints' Book Depost, 1854-1866), 1:165.

27.   Raber, "Religious Polity," 386-90.

28.   U.S. manuscript census schedules for Spring City 1860, 1870, 1880, and 1900; personal communications, Henry S. Schofield, Osmer H. Beck, Joseph F. Hansen, and George Crisp, 1974-1976, in possession of the author; also see Leo Rogin, "The Introduction of Farm Machinery in Its Relation to the Productivity of Labor in the Agriculture of the United States During the Nineteenth Century," in *University of California Publications in Economics*, 9 (Berkeley: University of California Press, 1931).

29.   Most of the points made in this paragraph are based on unpublished comparisons of reconstructed genealogical and migration data from Spring City, described in Raber, "Religious Polity," Appendix I, with land tenure data on file in the Office of the Sanpete County Recorder, Manti, also noted in the same appendix. Additional sources include Diary of Redick N. Allred, 1956, and personal communications, Osmer H. Beck, George Crisp, John R. Baxter, and E. Kent Strate, 1974-1976, in possession of the author.

30.   This table is based on a sample of all 70 household heads who came to Springtown before 1870 and lived out their lives there, together with the 136 sons of these household heads living when their parents devolved property between 1870 and 1933. See Raber, "Religious Polity," 356 and Appendix I.

31.   Raber, "Religious Polity," 356-68.

32.   See Gagan, "Indivisibility of Land," and, for much earlier examples of European patterns, Jack Goody, Joan Thirsk, and E. P. Thompson, *Family and Inheritance in Western Europe, 1200-1800* (Cambridge: Cambridge University Press, 1976). Inheritance remains the most understudied element in the complex issue of family, household, landholding, and mobility.

7

"All Things Unto Me Are Spiritual": Contrasting Religious and Temporal Leadership Styles in Heber City, Utah

Jessie L. Embry

Like Michael Raber, Jessie L. Embry, Oral History Program Director of the Charles Redd Center for Western Studies at Brigham Young University, looks at some of the differences between the effects of the LDS Church on Mormon communities in the nineteenth and twentieth century. Unlike Raber, she finds support for the traditional view that the Church played a dominant role in the activities of Mormon towns in the nineteenth century that lessened in the twentieth century. However, individual church leaders were sometimes ahead or behind this trend, thus creating tensions. Using the example of two stake presidents in the Wasatch Stake, she shows how Abram Hatch's laissez-faire policy in the nineteenth century and William Smart's belief in the early twentieth century that the Church should control business and education led to conflicts with the LDS General Authorities and the residents of Heber City.

The function of the leader is to embody and to give expression to the needs and wishes of the group and to contribute positively to the satisfaction of those needs.

To the extent that he does this he may remain the leader; when he fails to perform this function he will be superseded and he fails as soon as the followers perceive his needs and his goals to be divergent from their own.[1]

Cecil A. Gibb's rather dogmatic definition in 1954 could apply to all types of leaders in business, government, and even religion. While it leaves unanswered the question of origins (do leaders originate goals which followers adapt as their own or do leaders simply reflect in a more perfect way the inarticulate goals of followers?), it is pragmatically true that only a narrow zone exists for discrepancies between leaders and followers where coercion cannot be used to enforce unpopular decisions. In a hierarchy, too, the levels of leaders and followers add interesting ambiguities with a mid-level leader playing both roles. For instance, stake presidents in the LDS Church achieve their goals only if stake members and bishops are willing to follow them and if the General Authorities are willing to support them.

Abram Hatch and William Smart faced these problems when they served as presidents of the Wasatch Stake. Both men had strong ideas about how Heber City should be developed and were just enough out of step with the philosophy of the Church at the time of their tenures that they were not completely accepted by either Heber City residents or by their ecclesiastical superiors.

When the Mormons arrived in the Great Basin in 1847, they welcomed the opportunity to shape a virgin land into the Kingdom of God and pursued an aggressive colonization pattern. Heber Valley, forty miles southeast from Salt Lake City and twenty-eight miles northeast from Provo in the Wasatch Mountains could not be settled until there was a wagon road through either Parley's or Provo canyons. By 1859 a road linked Provo and Heber Valley, and latecomers settled the little communities of Heber City, Midway, Charleston, Center Creek, Daniels, and Wallsburg.

Initially, Brigham Young called local settlers to be the presiding elders in the new communities. Later, when wards were established, these elders were designated as bishops. As the communities continued to develop, church authorities looked outside the Heber Valley area to find a leader with the administrative skills to assist in the area's growth. In 1867 Young called forty-two year old Abram Hatch to leave his prospering store in Lehi to serve as bishop in Heber City. Hatch had come to Utah from Illinois in 1850 and in 1852 married Penelia Jane Lott. He had worked as an apprentice in a store, established a small mercantile business, and served a mission in 1861. In 1877 when the Heber Ward was divided, Hatch was called to be the stake president in Wasatch County, and he served as the area's chief ecclesiastical leader until 1901.[2]

During the time Hatch was a bishop and stake president, and indeed during most of the nineteenth century, the Church attempted to follow the injunction given to Joseph Smith: "All things unto me are spiritual and not at any time have I given a law which was temporal."[3] People in early Utah saw little reason to separate church and state. Taking care of the community cattle herd, completing the irrigation project, and trading at the Church's cooperative store were considered religious duties. In addition to their ecclesiastical responsibilities, many bishops and stake presidents routinely served as mayors, businessmen, probate court judges, and presidents of school boards.

On the surface, Hatch acted like many of his peers, holding both civic as well as religious positions. He was a probate judge for six years in Heber and served in the territorial legislature for twenty-three years.[4] However, he distinguished between his church callings and his business and civic responsibilities in an unusual way. For example, Hatch reported in 1880 that Brigham Young had called him to establish a mercantile business in Heber so he started a co-op store. However, since he and Joseph W. Witt held 80 percent of the stock, some of the members complained that he was trying to monopolize the business. Hatch countered that the people could buy stock if they wished.[5] According to William Forman, bishop of the Heber City West Ward, Hatch did not support the Church's cooperative movement. Forman recorded in his journal that Hatch explained in a priesthood meeting that he would buy goods from the manufacturers. He would not give 10 percent to ZCMI, the Church-owned cooperative movement, to do his business. Yet Hatch was upset that ZCMI supported the store of a competitor, Mark Jeffs.[6]

During the 1870s when united orders were mushrooming throughout the Church and home industry was an important issue, Heber City also started an order and several cooperatives including a tannery and woollen mill.[7] These enterprises were not successful, and in 1878 William Forman and another bishop, Jonathan Cluff, appealed for more support for them at stake conferences and stake priesthood meetings.[8] Initially Hatch asked for greater support for home industry, but in 1888 he told the priesthood brethren that the united order had failed because adhering to it was impossible.[9]

Forman, who spoke out strongly in favor of home industry and the united order, had joined the Church in 1854 when he was twenty years old and had come to Salt Lake City in 1856. He married in 1859 and was advised to go to Heber City in 1860 where he became a prominent farmer and sawmill operator and was called to serve as a bishop in 1877.[10] He felt that Hatch failed to follow church policies at the time. For example, he recorded in his journal, "President Abram Hatch said he wished we had a few more honorable Gentiles among us. He is in favor of helping William Britt start a drug store."[11] If Hatch was supporting a gentile store, this was contrary to church policy at the time that members should buy only from members of the Church.

Forman also served as tithing agent in the stake and disagreed with Hatch on whether he should refer questions to Hatch or to the presiding bishopric. Forman wrote, "Brother Hatch does not want me to ask counsel from the presiding bishopric."[12] In November 1884 Forman resigned as bishop since Hatch had asked the presiding bishop, W. R. Preston, to have Forman serve as either tithing agent or bishop and Forman felt he could do the most good as an agent. Forman, however, felt that "it has been the desire of President A. Hatch for some time to get a bishop in my place for the West Ward and wished me to resign which I gladly did on Sunday so he and others can shoot at someone else."[13] When Hatch wrote to Forman and released him as tithing agent in September 1886 so that Hatch could take over the tithing office, Forman recorded in his journal that Hatch had told him "in the presence of ten leading men in the stake" that he had appealed to the presiding bishopric for Forman's release because he could not control him and Forman always went to the general church leaders for advice.[14]

Forman also disagreed with Hatch's store policies. Even though his store was not part of the ZCMI system, Forman felt Hatch tried to monopolize business and took "a course to crush every man in the stake that will not comply with his wishes and trade at his store." He rhetorically queried in his journal, "My thought is how long the Lord will let the wicked rule in Zion."[15]

Forman especially disagreed with Hatch's personal decision not to enter into plural marriage. Forman argued at a prayer circle in June 1881, "We were a humble and willing people [when we came to this valley] but now we're going after the farthing of the world and some of the sisters use up the means of their husbands to keep them from being able to obey the law of God celestial marriage."[16] In March 1884 Forman explained that Church President John Taylor had asked all presiding authorities to practice polygamy or resign. Hatch had announced he would not resign, adding that it had taken Wilford Woodruff seventy years to obey the Word of Wisdom and it might take him [Hatch] that long to live polygamy.[17]

Still, although Forman objected strongly to some of Hatch's policies, he felt he should remain loyal to his stake president. Several times the priesthood meeting minutes record his statements that it was important to follow church leadership. For example, in February 1878 he said that the quorum was not supporting the stake president and they should go to him if they had problems with him and not to their neighbors.[18] In December 1897 he explained it was the "duty of all to sustain Hatch. He was sent there by God."[19]

Hatch also differed from the contemporary position in regard to education. The Mormon system of education established ward or district schools, stake academies, and universities, all church-owned and operated. In 1867 the district elementary schools nominally became public tax-supported schools. Once out of the eighth grade, however, a student's only choices were to attend church academies, Protestant high schoois or the University of Deseret, which offered mainly high school courses during the nineteenth and early twentieth century. Although the University was initially controlled by the Church, it was considered a non-Mormon school by the 1870s and the two systems were in clear competition. In 1889 Karl G. Maeser, superintendent of the LDS academies, bluntly told the Wasatch Stake Academy board, "[I] would rather have [my] children exposed to the smallpox or the yellow fever or any other contagious disease than to have them exposed to the influence of an infidel school teacher."[20]

In July 1888 Wilford Woodruff wrote Hatch asking him to participate in the church educational system by organizing a board of education and establishing a stake school. Hatch appointed a board at the stake conference in August 1888 but it did not hold its first meeting until December. Members were assigned to canvass the wards for money to build an academy and also to determine where the school could meet before construction was completed. Arrangements were made to hold the academy in a church-owned building, and classes convened in September 1889. The curriculum included a wide range of high school classes from theology to bookkeeping.[21]

The academy struggled almost from the beginning. In May 1890 Hatch suggested at the stake board of education meeting that they should put off building an academy and the valley residents should support construction of the public school.[22] At another board meeting a month later, A. Henry Wootton, a teacher in Midway, reported that President Wilford Woodruff had said at a meeting of church academy workers that there was a stake president who opposed the church schools. Wootton added that Karl G. Maeser had told him President Woodruff was referring to Hatch. The principal of the Wasatch Academy, Enoch Jorgensen, then explained that he had told Maeser that he felt Hatch had given him "the cold shoulder."[23] Apparently at least momentarily chastened, Hatch commented at the stake conference in August about the academy opening for the new year and urged the Saints to "patronize it and the district schools."[24]

The academy continued to struggle. When the academy, still in temporary headquarters, closed for the year in May 1891, it was two hundred dollars in debt, and Hatch asked at the board meetings if it should not be closed. Apostle Francis M. Lyman commented that it was good that the school was no further in debt and the wards should split the cost.[25] In June 1892, however, Wootton reported that he was afraid the academy could not continue because of competition by the district schools. He pointed out that the academy still had no permanent place to meet and there were not enough students for even one teacher. Still, most of the members of the board felt the school should remain open. J. H. Moulton gave a stirring appeal for support for the school, "We send a number of our brethren to the nations to preach the gospel to them, but we are not willing to spend a little of the means that the Lord has blessed us with to teach the gospel to our own children. It is not the lack of money but the lack of faith that is the matter."[26]

Three months later Hatch agreed that the school was not successful because of a lack of faith, but he felt the school had too much competition from the free district and denominational schools. However, Maeser encouraged him to keep the school open and to have the board members ask church members to send their children to the school. He told the board members to be "not a drummer, soliciting patronage, but as awaking the saints to take their duties to their children." If they did, he promised the schools would be overflowing with students.[27]

The support for the academy did not come, and in 1894, after only five years of operation, it closed when the two teachers threatened to open a private school if they did not receive better salaries. LDS Church General Authorities recommended that Heber City and Wasatch County members send their students to the Brigham Young Academy in Provo for high school instead.[28]

In February 1901 Abram Hatch was released as president of the stake. The *Wasatch Wave* published an editorial quoting the *Deseret News* that the change was not due to "any misconduct in office or any desire on the part of the members under their direction." It was to give "a rest to the veterans who have for a long time borne the burden and heat of the day."[29] However, William Smart, who was called to replace Hatch saw the change differently. He recorded in his journal on January 25 that he had been asked to meet Apostle Matthias F. Cowley at the railroad station in Ogden and was there called to succeed Hatch "who was becoming infirm." According to Smart, Cowley also explained that "the people in Wasatch Stake are cold and unfaithful and the brethren felt that I [Smart] could do a good work among them."[30] In 1904, after Smart had been stake president for four years, he recalled that President Joseph F. Smith told him, "Brother Smart, you are doing a good work. I can see a change in unity coming over the people."[31]

The *Wasatch Wave* reported in a "History of Wasatch County" in December 1906 that when Smart took over as stake president "he at once adopted the policy of harmonizing the spiritual with the temporal . . . by affording a balanced and consistent growth among members of his church."[32] However, by 1906 Mormons had become Democrats and Republicans in preparation for statehood in 1896, businesses owned by non-Mormons competed freely with the LDS stores, and the Church gradually closed its academies and supported public high schools.[33]

This trend was well underway before Smart's call. A businessman from Rexburg, he had just been released as president of the Eastern States Mission before this new assignment. He believed that "the end of all spiritual work is the accomplishment of good and no stronger sermon can be preached than by our leaders taking a straightforward course in temporal matters."[34]

As part of his efforts to combine temporal and spiritual affairs, Smart formed a united order in November 1902 with his counselors and clerk. The last united order in the Church was in Cave Valley in Mexico. It had been phased out in 1895 and there had been no attempts to establish any since then, so Smart's order seems to have been an attempt to revert to a practice that had been abandoned by the Church.[35] His plan was to have all the stake presidency pool their resources and work together as a group. However, since Smart, his first counselor James C. Jensen, and his clerk Joseph W. Musser were not originally from Wasatch County, they did not own any property in the area. An attempt to invest their time and resources in the dairy and other property of second counselor Joseph R. Murdock was not successful and the order folded after only five months. Smart explained that they had tried to "manipulate" Murdock and their own businesses too much.[36]

Undeterred, Smart organized another cooperative effort in March 1904. In a letter to Church President Joseph F. Smith on January 30, 1902, he had explained, "There is a lack of unity of purpose which exists in regard to temporal condition and advancement of the people." Smart felt organizing a company where the people could work together would unite them. It would also direct community matters and would encourage additional development in the area. The company might also allow Smart to work with inactive Mormons in the area and recommit them to the Church.[37] Smart recorded in his journal that President Smith approved the aims of the company, but he was apprehensive of an exclusively church enterprise at a time when the Church was trying to broaden its economic base and establish a place in American society. He encouraged Smart to organize the company "under the auspices of the citizens rather than the priesthood."[38]

Smart persisted in his plans. He announced the future organization of the cooperative at a stake high council meeting on March 26, 1904, and appointed a committee to invite the bishops of each ward to send a representative. When the meeting was held two days later, most of those in attendance were members of the high council and bishoprics. The

Wasatch Real Estate and Development Company elected William Smart, president, Joseph R. Murdock, vice-president, and Joseph W. Musser, secretary. The board of directors was also made up of church leaders who attended the meeting.[39]

Under the auspices of the new company, several small retail businesses merged in 1905 and 1906 to form the Heber Mercantile Company. Smart explained that Mark Jeffs, who had owned a store in Heber since the 1860s, had asked him to help him incorporate his store. Several other small businesses including J. W. Buckley, Wootton Brothers, and the Midway Co-op also became part of the new company.[40] Abram Hatch was one merchant who did not become part of the new store, and Smart recorded in his journal that he was upset when "President Hatch and son Joseph, both strong financial men and large landowners" did "not show a more interested disposition in the store."[41] Even without Hatch's support, the new "merc" became the largest store in Heber City and was always closely associated with the Church. Years later many Heber Valley residents still believed they would be disloyal to the Church if they traded at another store.[42]

Just as Forman felt that Hatch had tried to force people to trade at his store, some people in Heber apparently felt that Smart was trying to create a "monopoly" and control all business in the community. In response to these comments, Smart explained in a stake conference in October 1905 that the new store was not "an accessory" to the Church and it was not trying to monopolize business in the valley. He went on to say that the store was a cooperative, and he encouraged others to invest in it.[43]

Despite this public disclaimer, Smoot continued to use his ecclesiastical influence to promote the Wasatch Real Estate and Development Company. One of the best examples involved the Timpanogos Canal. Joseph Hatch, a son of Abram Hatch who was not active in the Church, had organized a company in 1895 to build a canal with several other partners, all of whom were inactive Mormons or nonmembers. They planned to complete the canal in two years, but by 1905 no work had been done. Because the group was seen as non-

Mormon, local church members would not buy stock or encourage the construction.[44] Smart, however, saw the canal as a community project that in addition to improving valley farming would build rapport with the non-Mormons and reactivate men like Joseph Hatch. To get the project moving, he proposed reorganization of the canal company as another subsidiary of Wasatch Real Estate. Joseph Hatch had opposed the real estate company and did not hold stock in it, but he still accepted Smart's offer. In the reorganization that followed, Hatch remained president, but the rest of the directors were local prominent church leaders although Smart was not on the board. The canal project was completed and, in 1911, enlarged. The project did not achieve Smart's objectives, however; Joseph Hatch and the other inactive Mormons did not return to the flock. In fact, the original organizers became even more convinced that the Church had too much power in the community.[45]

Smart used his influence on a third project, one which would clearly perpetuate Mormon/non-Mormon differences. In 1902 the federal government began plans to open part of the Uintah Indian Reservation (about fifty miles from Heber City) to non-Indian settlement. Smart determined that the Uintah Basin should be settled exclusively by Mormons. In November 1903 he asked President Joseph F. Smith for permission to inform bishops and stake presidents that the reservation would be opening to settlement and that people interested in settling there should contact Smart.[46] Then Smart and other Wasatch Stake officials petitioned the state legislature to support a bill in Congress to put the land office in Heber City. When Congress placed the land office in Vernal, the *Wasatch Wave,* another subsidiary of Wasatch Real Estate, explained it was better to have the office in Vernal than in Price.[47] One of the reasons might have been because there were many non-Mormons in Price, and the Church could not control the settlement patterns. Smart's development company set up an office in Vernal, and according to the *Wasatch Wave,* helped settle many people on the newly released reservation lands.[48]

Wasatch Real Estate and Development Company's land policy led to disagreements with people outside of the Church. According to an article in the *Wasatch Wave* in July 1905, Smart had a letter published in the *Box Elder News* encouraging those interested in the reservation lands to contact him. The *Salt Lake Tribune* ran the same letter and published a reply claiming that Smart's offer was evidence of church control and "the great land steal." In response the *Wasatch Wave* said that church members had always worked together and Smart's letter was simply part of that plan.[49]

How did the average Mormon in Wasatch County view Smart's business activities? Smart dominated the community while he was stake president. Through Wasatch Real Estate, he was active in the mercantile business, a lumber company, the bank, the newspaper, a publishing company, and an abstract company. The minutes of the stake high council meetings and newspaper editorials reflect his viewpoint. However, there must have been some opposition because Smart's comment in stake conference that he was not trying to "monopolize business" was a clear defense against accusations that some people thought he was. Furthermore, when Smart was called as stake president in the Uintah Basin and moved to Vernal in 1906, his influence evaporated and the only legacy he left behind was the Wasatch Mercantile Company.

Smart's views on education were consistent with his business outlook. At a Wasatch Stake priesthood meeting in September 1902 Smart stated in much the same vein as Karl G. Maeser, "The Saints cannot afford to have their children receive sectarian education through which channels many evils frequently creep into their minds."[50] Again, however, Smart seems to have failed to see the changes the Church was making. Smart recorded in his journal that since there was no longer a church academy in Heber, President Joseph F. Smith suggested in June 1902 that there was no need for the stake board of education and it should be dissolved.[51] The stake leaders complied.[52] Smith also suggested that the lot owned by the Wasatch Stake Academy be returned to Elisha Averett, the former owner, at cost and the money raised for the academy be returned to the original donors or used some other way.[53]

Instead of a stake board of education, Smart organized a student association to help those students who were attending Brigham Young Academy in Provo. The association rented a home for the students and provided social activities. Smart also called young men to go to Provo to attend the BYA's missionary course.[54] In September 1903 he reorganized a stake board of education mainly to encourage religion classes and the church auxiliaries in Heber City.[55] He continued to encourage students to attend school in Provo and provide a support network for them.

In addition to sponsoring church schools, Smart felt that the Church should influence public education by assuring that spiritual men who were good examples were elected members of the school board and as the county school superintendent. In July 1902 he recorded in his journal that he was afraid that a group of "apostates, saloon keepers and patrons, girls of questionable report, secret society members and a few respectable Republicans" were trying to control the school elections.[56] That month, just before a convention to nominate school board members, Smart called a special prayer circle to encourage church leaders to support the people he had asked to run for office. He expressed displeasure in his journal about some church members who ran in opposition to his candidates, and he considered the election of his candidates a victory for the Church.[57] In November 1903 some members of the community, notably Joseph Hatch, campaigned on the platform that the schoolhouses should not be used for church meetings.[58] Smart took this as a direct challenge and "hustled our voters" so that John T. Giles, "our" man, was elected.[59]

Between 1902 and 1906, when Smart was stake president, he continued to select faithful church members to run for the school board. Inactive Mormons, non-Mormons and sometimes active members ran in opposition and the campaigns were often heated. Smart's candidates were elected, possibly because the people did not want to appear to be opposing the Church. Whatever their reasons for voting, when Smart left the area his successor did not take an active role in the school elections. Trustees sometimes ran unopposed, and the elections returned to, as the *Wasatch Wave* called them in 1908, "very quiet and exclusive affairs" with "only the trustees and a few of their intimate friends" voting.[60]

An interesting domestic example of Smart's staunch view of religion controlling all aspects of life took place when he and his wife discussed the need for someone to help Mrs. Smart at home. In 1903 Smart decided to call Josephine Jacobs, a widow whose husband had died a year before and whose baby had recently died, to help his wife. He told Jacobs she should see the call as a mission because Smart could be a better stake president if his house was in order. Jacobs explained she was in debt because of the funeral costs and she needed to make some money. Smart said that the calling was more important than making money but he would help her pay her debts.[61] While Hatch and others might have seen hiring a housemaid as a temporal assignment, to Smart it was an important part of his spiritual requirements as stake president.

In his attempts to unite church and education, Smart occasionally ran into what he felt was opposition from Abram Hatch and his family. When A. C. Hatch, one of Abram Hatch's older sons, graduated from the eighth grade, Smart recorded in his journal in August 1901, "He [A. C. Hatch] like the father and family at least takes no interest in religion knowing that preparations would be made for him to attend that state university in Salt Lake City. I have been anxious for him to attend the church academy in Provo."[62] In November 1902 Smart complained to his predecessor Hatch that his sons had not supported him and he would like to talk to them. At a meeting of Smart, Hatch, and his sons, Hatch said he would support Smart and asked his sons to also help him. Smart explained in his journal, "The boys seemed to be friendly but not cooperative and had not any disposition to do anything spiritual."[63] Smart may have also felt that Hatch's support was less than complete. At a school election in July 1902, Smart asked Hatch to support James C. Jensen, Smart's first counselor, for the school board. Hatch promised not to campaign against Jensen. Later Jensen told Smart that Hatch had told him he would not help him win the election.[64] These incidents, along with the disagreements over Hatch's store and over the use of school buildings for church meetings with Joseph Hatch, may have led Smart to apply to President Joseph F. Smith for help. In February 1904, Smart recorded Smith asked him to invite Hatch "to give him no cause to complain."[65]

Abram Hatch and William Smart were leaders whose views about the role of religion were out of harmony with those of the General Authorities and their followers. William Lindsay from Center Creek recognized the difference in leadership style when he explained, "President Smart was a very earnest man, much more spiritual minded than our former President Abram Hatch who, however, was also a good man but a very practical and a real business man."[65] Ironically, if their tenures as president of the Wasatch Stake had been reversed, Hatch and Smart might have received greater support from church leaders and members. As it was, even though neither were unsuccessful they did not receive total support from the LDS Church General Authorities or from the residents of Wasatch County.

NOTES

1. Cecil A. Gibb, "Leadership," in *Handbook on Social Psychology*, ed. Gardner Lindzey (Cambridge, Mass.: Addison-Wesley Publ. Co. Inc., 1954), 917.

2. William James Mortimer, ed. *How Beautiful Upon the Mountains: A Centennial History of Wasatch County* (Salt Lake City: Wasatch County Chapter Daughters of Utah Pioneers, 1963), 1-77.

3. Doctrine and Covenants 29:34.

4. Mortimer, *Wasatch County*, 374-75.

5. Wasatch Stake Council Meeting, March 27, 1880, Heber East Ward Minutes, April 3, 1880, LDS Church Archives, Historical Department of the Church of Jesus Christ of Latter-day Saints, Salt Lake City (hereafter referred to as LDS Church Archives).

6. William Forman Journal, January 1, 1884, Utah State Historical Society Library, Salt Lake City.

7. Heber Branch Historical Report, July 7, 1874, August 28, 1875, LDS Church Archives; Wasatch Stake Melchezidek Priesthood meeting, November 23, 1877, LDS Church Archives. Also see Leonard J. Arrington, Fermorz Y. Fox and Dean L. May, *Building the City of God: Community and Cooperation Among the Mormons* (Salt Lake City: Deseret Book Co., 1976) for a discussion of the united orders in the 1870s.

8. Wasatch Stake Conference, Heber East Ward Minutes, May 7, 1878; Wasatch Stake Melchizedek Priesthood meeting, February 23, 1878, LDS Church Archives.

9. Wasatch Stake Melchizedek Priesthood meeting, March 31, 1888, LDS Church Archives.

10. Mortimer, *Wasatch County*, 1065-66.

11. Forman Journal, February 7, 1879.

12. Ibid., March 11, 1884.

13. Ibid., November 3, 1884.

14. Ibid., September 20, 1886.

15. Ibid.

16. Ibid., June 1881.

17. Ibid., March 11, 1884.

18. Wasatch Stake Melchizedek Priesthood meeting, February 23, 1878, LDS Church Archives.

19. Ibid., December 4, 1897.

20. Wasatch Stake Academy Minutes, October 28, 1889, LDS Church Archives.

21. Ibid., December 22, 1888; *Wasatch Wave,* August 31, 1889, 3.

22. Wasatch Stake Academy Minutes, May 4, 1890, LDS Church Archives.

23. Ibid., June 7, 1890.

24. Wasatch Stake Conference Minutes, August 3, 1890, LDS Church Archives.

25. Wasatch Stake Academy Minutes, May 3, 1891, LDS Church Archives.

26. Ibid., June 12, 1892.

27. Ibid., September 4, September 6, 1892.

28. Ibid., September 2, 1893.

29. *Wasatch Wave,* February 15, 1901, 2.

30. William Smart Journal, January 25, 1901, LDS Church Archives.

31. Ibid., February 1, 1904.

32. "History of Wasatch County," *Wasatch Wave,* December 21, 1906, 10.

33. Thomas G. Alexander, "Twentieth Century Utah Introduction," in *Utah's History*, ed. Richard Poll et al. (Provo, Utah: Brigham Young University Press, 1978), 405.

34. Wasatch Stake High Council Minutes, April 2, 1904, LDS Church Archives.

35. Arrington, et al., *Building the City of God*, 310.

36. Smart Journal, November 26, 1902, LDS Church Archives.

37. William H. Smart, Joseph R. Murdock, and J. C. Jensen to Joseph F. Smith, January 30, 1902, Wasatch Stake Letterbook, LDS Church Archives.

38. Smart Journal, January 27, 1902, LDS Church Archives.

39. Ibid., March 26, 28, 1904.

40. Ibid., April 19, 1905; Wasatch County High Council Minutes, April 22, 1905, LDS Church Archives; *Wasatch Wave,* March 23, 1906, 3.

41. Smart Journal, March 26, 1904, LDS Church Archives.

42. Personal interviews with Heber City residents, Summer 1977.

43. Wasatch Stake Conference Minutes, October 28, 1905, LDS Church Archives.

44. *Wasatch Wave,* June 21, 1895, 2; Smart Journal, May 10, 20, 1904, LDS Church Archives.

45. *Wasatch Wave,* March 17, 1905, 2; Smart Journal, March 10, 1905, LDS Church Archives.

46. Smart Journal, November 13, 1903, LDS Church Archives.

47. *Wasatch Wave,* February 3, 1905, 2; May 19, 1905, 2.

48. Ibid., August 18, 1902; September 1, 1905, 3.

49. Ibid., July 14, 1905.

50. Wasatch Stake Melchizedek Priesthood Minutes, September 6, 1902, LDS Church Archives.

51. Smart Journal, June 1, 1902, LDS Church Archives.

52. Joseph White Musser Journal, June 5, 1902, LDS Church Archives.

53. Wasatch Stake High Council Minutes, September 27, 1902, LDS Church Archives.

54. Wasatch Stake Academy Minutes, July 5, 1902, LDS Church Archives.

55. Ibid., August 15, 1903.

56. Smart Journal, July 14, 1902, LDS Church Archives.

57. Ibid.

58. *Wasatch Wave,* July 11, 1904.

59. Musser Journal, July 11, 1904, LDS Church Archives.

60. *Wasatch Wave,* July 10, 1908, 5.

61. Smart Journal, December 9, 1903, LDS Church Archives.

62. Ibid., August 8, 1901.

63. Ibid., November 20, 26, 1902.

64. Ibid., July 14, 1902.

65. Ibid., February 1, 1904.

66. William Lindsay Autobiography, Special Collections, Harold B. Lee Library, Brigham Young University, Provo, Utah.

8

Grass Roots Entrepreneurship in the Frontier West: The Allens of Cache Valley and the Coreys and Wattises of Weber Valley

Leonard J. Arrington

Like Edward Geary, Leonard J. Arrington, Director of the Joseph Fielding Smith Institute for Church History and Senior Research Associate for the Charles Redd Center for Western Studies at Brigham Young University, looks at Mormon settlement after 1875. He describes how some Mormons left the settled areas along the Wasatch Front to establish new communities in Utah and surrounding states, Canada, and Mexico, and went on to become successful entrepreneurs. Some of these left their villages to work, in groups, and brought outside finances from their work in railroad and road construction to help stabilize the villages they had settled. The Allens, the Coreys, and the Wattises are three examples of families who, like the Argonauts, sought and found the Golden Fleece. In this case, they all got their start in railroad construction—first in Utah and then throughout the West.

In an article on Mormon migration after 1875, Richard Sherlock has described the atomistic process by which Mormon migrants left the settled valleys of Utah and founded communities in Star Valley, Wyoming; the Upper Snake River, Cassia County, and Oneida, Portneuf, and Gentile valleys in Idaho; valleys along the Little Colorado and San Juan rivers in Arizona and the Rio Grande Norte in New Mexico; the San Luis Valley and San Juan Basin in southwestern Colorado; the states of Sonora and Chihuahua in northern Mexico; and southern Alberta in western Canada.[1]

Rather than drawing from the entire Utah population at random, the newly settled areas were often closely identified with a given community or area. Chesterfield in Idaho had close connections with Bountiful, Utah. Other settlements were identified with Weber Valley. Particularly extensive was the outreach from Cache Valley in northern Utah, from which families moved north and west into Idaho and Oregon, east into Wyoming, and north into Alberta. "Little Cache Valleys" were established in all of these places; indeed, for a time most of the resulting settlements were considered a part of the Cache Valley Stake of Zion.

I should like to illustrate the movement from these valleys in the late 1870s and early 1880s by describing its impact on three families—one from Cache and two from Weber. As Sherlock points out, the migrations after 1875 did not consistently follow the Mormon village ideal and traditional pattern of settlement. Nevertheless, it is clear that the migrations presented challenges and opportunities which greatly improved the fortunes of these and other families. Hemmed in by a limited supply of irrigable land in Utah, seemingly doomed to progressively lower living standards as their numbers multiplied, some members of these families moved out to find opportunities that well repaid the wrenching effect of the dislocations. Moreover, in the process of finding remunerative work, Utah's young men and women showed remarkable resourcefulness and developed into notable entrepreneurs.

The first of these outward movements was the sending out of hundreds of men and teams to do the grading for the Utah & Northern Railroad, which, between 1874 and 1882, pushed north from Ogden to Dillon, Montana. Hundreds of families were benefited by the income from this labor. Having become acquainted with the "northern country" along the route, many young men—often recruiting brothers and brothers-in-law and their families—settled at favorable locations and established new settlements.

With their railroad-building experience behind them, these men and their friends and former neighbors often proceeded to take construction contracts in service of newly opened mining districts, such as those along the Wood River in Idaho and the Missouri River and its tributaries in western Montana. Or they assisted in the construction of the Oregon Short Line Railroad from Cheyenne to Portland; the Northern Pacific from Duluth to Portland, the Great Northern from Minneapolis to Seattle; and the Canadian Pacific from Montreal to Vancouver. During the early 1880s, the great era of railroad building in northwestern America and southwestern Canada, each of these mammoth projects provided employment for several "Mormon gangs."

* * *

The experiences of some individual families can be studied against this backdrop. The Ira Allens of Cache Valley are a good example.[2] A native of eastern Connecticut, born in 1814, Ira lived many years in Michigan, gathered with the Latter-day Saints in Illinois, and in 1850 came to Utah with his wife, Calista Bass, and their five children. At first they settled in Cedar City but after the unfortunate occurrences connected with the Mountain Meadows Massacre, they moved to Cache Valley in 1860. By that time Ira was forty-six, his wife was two years older, and their oldest children, Andrew and Simeon, were twenty-three and twenty-one. They and their friends, some twenty-one families in all, located available land in southern Cache Valley and founded the town of Hyrum, named for the brother of Joseph Smith. For the first year they lived in dugouts and wagon boxes and began to build their cabins in the usual Mormon fort style.

Ira, Andrew, and Simeon Allen were energetic colonizers. They joined with their neighbors to build a canal and road system; organized a steam sawmill enterprise to provide timber for homes; established a ranch (Hardware Ranch) for herding purposes; operated a dairy to furnish milk, butter, and cheese; and managed a general store called Allen Brothers. In 1875, under church direction, all of these were combined into the United Order of Hyrum, of which Simeon was treasurer. The Allens and their neighbors extracted lumber from Blacksmith's Fork Canyon and sold it in the rapidly growing community of Logan, and, in carload lots, to customers in Utah, Idaho, and Montana. Thousands of ties were sold to contractors and subcontractors as the railroad extended north from Ogden.

Meanwhile, Simeon had married Boletta Maria Johnson, five years his junior, whose family had converted to Mormonism in Norway and come to America in 1854 when Boletta was nine. Shortly after the Johnsons moved to Cache Valley in 1862, Boletta met Simeon, and they were married the next year. Their first child, Heber, was born in 1864 in their small dirt-roofed log house. Simeon had a farm of twenty-five acres, most of which he planted in wheat. Twenty-five acres was all he could handle, for he had to cut the wheat with an old-fashioned cradle, rake it into bundles with a homemade rake, and then, with Boletta working by his side, bind it by hand. The grain was hauled to a smooth threshing floor on the lot at home and there trampled out by horses and oxen. The straw was separated by a fork and the chaff and grain were separated by throwing the mixture up in the wind.

Like other women on the frontier, Boletta worked hard. She sheared the sheep, washed the wool, carded it into batts, formed the batts into rolls, spun the rolls into yarn on a spinning wheel, wove the yarn into cloth on a homemade loom, and made the cloth into clothing.

By 1879, when Heber was fifteen, he was regarded as old enough to accompany his father to Dry Canyon, southeast of Hyrum, to get logs. Both Heber and Simeon took a team and wagon, and after loading the wagons they started for the mill at Paradise to have the logs sawed into lumber.

The Allens joined with several hundred others from Cache Valley who were employed by subcontractors to grade the Utah & Northern Railroad as it stretched north from

Ogden to Montana. By 1880 Simeon and Boletta were working on a construction project in Ryan's Canyon, near Dillon, Montana—Simeon doing teamwork and Boletta serving as camp cook.

When the Utah & Northern was completed in 1882, Simeon and son Heber, who was now seventeen, undertook a subcontract to do the grading in the vicinity of the Cramer Stagecoach Station in Hellgate Canyon, along the route of the Northern Pacific. They worked some twenty-eight miles east of Missoula, Montana, approximately four hundred miles north of their Cache Valley home, to which they returned with their teams for the winter.[3]

The winters in Cache Valley weren't entirely profitless. Each winter Heber attended the Brigham Young College in Logan, where he eventually earned a teaching certificate. He also received good instruction in bookkeeping, training which suited him well in subsequent years.

In 1883 Simeon and Heber contracted to grade part of the Canadian Pacific Railroad—the stretch in southeastern Alberta between Medicine Hat and Calgary.[4]

Impressed with the country, and perhaps with the girls, Heber, now nineteen, remained in Canada for the winter, serving as a cowboy on the famous Cochrane Ranch, one of the large early day cattle outfits established by the noted eastern Canadian, Senator Matthew H. Cochrane. The next two years were spent in Cache Valley, farming with his father. They rented land and planted one hundred acres to wheat, raising twenty-seven hundred bushels—more than anyone else in the Hyrum area.

In 1886 Simeon and a colleague from Logan, Orson Smith, contracted to build nineteen miles of railroad grade north of Helena, Montana. This was one of the spurs which were strengthening the position of James J. Hill's Great Northern empire. Heber's training at Brigham Young College served him well when, at the start of the work, Simeon's bookkeeper quit and Heber was able to take over. They did about $120,000 worth of work that season—all apparently handled well by Heber. Simeon usually paid $125 a month

plus board to his bookkeeper, but he paid Heber only forty
dollars a month and board—the same wage received by
Heber's companions of the same age driving teams on the
scraper. They had two rock camps and ten or fifteen grading
outfits of teams. Simeon made five thousand dollars net from
this contract.

While they were still at their camp at Prickly Pear
Canyon, south of Wolf Creek, Montana, they were visited by
Charles O. Card, Bishop Isaac Zundell, and James W. Hend-
ricks, all of Cache Valley, who were just returning from an
expedition to explore southern Alberta as a potential site for
the establishment of a Mormon community. They had gone by
train to Spokane, Washington, then by pack horse across the
international boundary into Okanagan Valley of British
Columbia. There an old plainsman advised them to go east of
the Rocky Mountains to the great buffalo grounds. At Kam-
loops they entrained for Calgary on the Canadian Pacific
Railway's main line, which Simeon and Heber had helped to
build. In Calgary, then a small frontier settlement where a fort
had been built by the Northwest Mounted Police in 1875, they
purchased a team, a light wagon, and a plow, and explored the
country south of Calgary to the international boundary, pay-
ing special attention to the region bordering Lee's Creek. They
drove their team and wagon to Wolfe Creek, then known as
Carterville.

The next year Simeon and others built thirteen miles of
grade from Drummond toward Phillipsburg, Montana. When
that was finished, Simeon contracted to repair the grade from
Helena to Great Falls—a distance of about ninety miles—the
high water in the spring having damaged the grade in many
places. Supplies were hauled from Helena, and Heber, who
again kept the books and served as camp commissary, did
most of the buying. The workers made good money on these
contracts—up to twenty-five dollars per day per team.

In 1888 Heber planned to go to Salt Lake City to enroll at
the University of Utah. He remained there only the winter
quarter, however, because in April Simeon asked him to again
join his construction outfit. By then the railroad company had

moved Simeon's outfit from Great Falls to Spokane, Washington, at which point Simeon was given a contract to grade the line west of Spokane. Spokane was just in its infancy, and Heber and Simeon were among those who saw the first two locomotives driven over the new steel into the town.

When the earth-grading contract was finished, Simeon and Heber returned to Helena, and Heber decided to return to Utah to teach school. But instead, Heber responded to Simeon's request to escort his (Simeon's) plural wife and her five children, by ox team and wagon, to Canada, where they might escape prosecution for polygamy under the Edmunds and Edmunds-Tucker acts. They drove to a new settlement established by Charles O. Card in Alberta, 250 miles north of Helena. Arriving at what came to be called Cardston in November 1888, Heber soon met Amy Leonard, daughter of Truman Leonard of Farmington, Utah, who had likewise taken part of his plural family there. Heber and Amy were married the following April—the first wedding in the new settlement.

In Cardston, Heber became the schoolteacher, with pupils ranging from eight to thirty-five. Following the usual Utah custom, school was held for ten weeks—part of December, January, and February. Then in March they began plowing and seeding. During the ten weeks Heber was paid fifty dollars, which he was obliged to take in carpenter's work, wheat, potatoes, and other produce.

Simeon, meanwhile, homesteaded land near the new settlement of Mountain View and raised livestock. He and others also established the Cardston Mercantile and Manufacturing Company. After several years Simeon disposed of this interest and returned to Utah, where he died as the result of an accident in 1901. He was only sixty-two. (Boletta died thirty-six years later at the age of ninety-two.)

By the fall of 1889, less than a year after the Cardston store was established, Heber and Amy were asked to manage it on a commission basis. They did well with the enterprise and earned, during their first sixteen months, some two thousand dollars. They had proved to be too successful. The owners rescinded the commission agreement and put Heber and Amy on a flat salary of eighty dollars per month, thereby reducing their combined income by about a third.

After three years the dissatisfied Heber, who by now was also postmaster, left Cardston Mercantile to open a competitive store. He had saved eighteen hundred dollars and borrowed one thousand dollars from his father. Fully supportive, Amy agreed to operate the household on thirty dollars per month and the proceeds from the milk of four cows if Heber would do the milking. They opened for business in August 1893 and did well, buying most of their goods wholesale in Winnipeg.

Heber soon acquired his father's interest in the store and continued to expand it. In 1898 the Alberta Railway and Irrigation Company entered into a contract with The Church of Jesus Christ of Latter-day Saints, which was endeavoring to provide new land for settlers, to build an irrigation canal from the intake on the St. Mary River southeast of Cardston to what was to become Stirling and Magrath. Anxious to participate, Heber entered into a partnership to build a roller flour mill with a capacity of seventy-five barrels per day.

In 1902 Heber, now thirty-seven and making ten thousand dollars a year from his store and other enterprises, was called to replace Charles Card as president of Alberta Stake. When the stake was divided the next year to create Taylor Stake, Heber was made president of the new stake. For that purpose he left Cardston and took up residence in Raymond, the center of the Taylor Stake. He remained there as stake president for thirty-two years.

From the beginning of Utah's settlement, Brigham Young and his apostles had picked out men of enterprise to serve as bishops. They were usually entrepreneurs for their growing communities. Heber Allen fell into that tradition of grass roots or community entrepreneurship. After his move to Raymond he acquired control of the Raymond Mercantile Company while retaining his business, H. S. Allen and Company, in Cardston. In 1911 he sold out his Cardston store and transferred his interests there to agriculture. He developed a farm and ranch property called the Grandview Farm, where he engaged in mixed farming, raising hogs, cattle, purebred Percheron horses, and sheep, as well as grain crops. Grandview was a farm showplace in southern Alberta.

The years 1904 and 1905 were dry, and where careless farming was practiced, poor crops resulted. Many of the settlers declared that one could not make a living in the country by farming. Confident of Alberta's future, Heber told them they were wrong, and that he would buy a farm and prove it. So he bought a farm, made a good return on it, published and advertised his report, and managed to persuade the people to remain.

Heber was instrumental in establishing a high school in Raymond, called Knight Academy, of which he was president for many years. He was a school trustee at Cardston, member of the town council, and later member of the town council at Raymond. He was a trustee of Southern Irrigation District, director of Raymond Opera House Company, director and vice-president of Ellison Milling and Elevator Company, director of Canadian Sugar Factories, Ltd., and a founder of the Canadian Cooperative Wool Growers Association.

Heber Allen died in 1944, at the age of seventy-nine. Amy, in addition to rearing a large family, served for many years as president of the LDS Primary Association in Alberta.

* * *

The village of Uinta, immediately below the mouth of Weber Canyon five miles south of Ogden, was first settled in 1850 and was variously called East Weber, Easton, Deseret, and finally Uinta. The settlers, who engaged in irrigated agriculture and stockraising, established the usual pioneer enterprises—a molasses mill, sawmill, bridge and road system, and irrigation canals. Among the early settlers was a twenty-one-year-old native of London, Edmund Wattis, whose parents, having been converted to Mormonism, migrated with their children to Nauvoo, Illinois, in the 1840s, and on to Utah in 1849. Shortly after their move to Uinta, Edmund married

Mary Jane Corey.[5] Mary Jane was the daughter of Mormon immigrants who had come to Utah in 1851 (when Mary Jane was sixteen) and had also located in Uinta. Mary Jane had four brothers who came to play an important role in western development: George L., Charles J., Amos B., and Warren W. Corey. They and Mary Jane were also half brothers and sister to J. E. Spaulding, whose father had come west with Brigham Young, had been one of the first settlers in Uinta, and had served as an early branch president of that village. Two of the Corey boys married Spaulding girls and J. E. married a Corey girl, so there was a close family affinity. Edmund and Jane's seven children were reared in close proximity to many uncles, aunts, and cousins.

The Coreys and Wattises and their neighbors engaged in hardscrabble agriculture in a region that was a "tough proposition"—alkali soil, swarms of hungry grasshoppers, and lack of adequate water in late summer. Nevertheless, they sought to make a go of it, and several of the men served a term as branch president, bishop, or in other religious and village offices. One of their neighbors was Samuel Dye, the grandfather of Bernard DeVoto, and about whom DeVoto wrote in *Harper's Monthly Magazine* in 1933 under the title, "Jonathan Dyer: Frontiersman."[6]

In 1867 great things began to happen to the hard working but poverty-stricken residents of the village. Surveyors began marking out the route for the Union Pacific Railroad which would go through Weber Canyon, pass through the village, and eventually connect at Promontory Summit with the Central Pacific coming east from San Francisco. The chief contractor for the grading work in Utah was Brigham Young, who subcontracted the work out to teams of Mormon farmers and mechanics living near the line. Among those who obtained remuneration for this work of hauling ties and dirt and doing rockwork were the Coreys and Wattises. All working residents were "well paid in cash." When the road was completed to Uinta (then called Easton) in March 1869, a railroad station called "Deseret" was established. The village suddenly became the terminus for freight and passenger traffic heading south from the rail station to Salt Lake City and beyond. The little village, which had only twenty families in 1866 after a grasshopper infestation destroyed nearly all vegetation, was now alive with more than a thousand Irish tracklayers, Gentile freighters, and prostitutes. Many jerry-built stores and shops were opened—grocery stores, dry goods stores, candy stores, tobacco stores, meat markets, barber shops, saloons, billiard halls, restaurants, and "hotels." While the new "excitement" was not unambiguously welcomed, the children, many for the first time, now had shoes and rock candy and the women could buy mirrors and calico.

The Coreys pooled their resources and opened a store under the name Corey Brothers. Their business, operated as a family partnership, included hauling their goods to the teams constructing the railroad, and freighting from the new railroad to points in Nevada, Idaho, Montana, and Utah.

However, by the spring of 1871, when the Utah Central Railroad from Ogden to Salt Lake City was completed and placed in operation, the boom days of Easton, now called Uinta, were over. Nearly all the newcomers moved out and Uinta became once more a small agricultural community of less than three hundred persons who lived by irrigated agriculture and stockraising. In 1881 the Coreys moved their store to Ogden. By the turn of the century there was hardly more to Uinta than the meetinghouse/schoolhouse, a single remaining store, and the post office.

But the railroad left an important heritage. The Coreys, the Wattises, and other men and boys in the village had learned something about construction and merchandising. They had operated a successful merchandising outlet and had helped grade the Utah Central to Salt Lake City. They also worked on the Utah & Northern line up into Idaho and Montana. In 1881 they took a major contract to work on the Oregon Short Line from Granger, Wyoming, to Huntington, Oregon, a distance of 550 miles.[7] And, like their Cache Valley counterparts, they then, as a family corporation, took contracts to work on the construction of the Northern Pacific, Great Northern, and Canadian Pacific railroads. Crews of up to five hundred were employed under the supervision of the four Corey brothers, George L., Charles J., Amos B., and Warren W., their half brother J. E. Spaulding, and their nephews Edmund O., William H., and Warren L. Wattis. The Coreys and Wattises went on to obtain construction contracts with still other roads: Chicago & Northwestern, Burlington & Missouri, Colorado Midland, and Rio Grande Western. Leaving their Weber Valley homes in the spring, they did not return until bad weather closed them down in late fall.[8]

A January 1885 report in the *Salt Lake Tribune* describes their work at that time for the Canadian Pacific:

> They shipped their teams and tools to the northern terminus of the Utah and Northern, and drove some 700 miles northwest to the line of the road, since which they have pushed work with from 350 to 500 men with teams throughout the summer and are employing 200 men this winter. . . . Their work this winter is on a difficult tunnel, and four miles of heavy cuts, on a contract amounting to about $200,000. The tunnel is through hardpan, requiring to be timbered all the way, and is located on the Kicking Horse River, in British Columbia, fifteen miles west of the Columbia River.[9]

By this time they had assigned George L. Corey to run the store in Ogden, and the rest worked on construction. The store, which outfitted the firm, was itself a source of profit.

> They ship flour, feed and produce by the carload. . . . They import poultry, produce etc. from both East and West. . . . One member of the firm spends his time mostly on the road, traveling through Utah, Idaho, Montana, Nevada, and Wyoming, in which Territories they are gaining a large trade. . . . They [the Coreys and Wattises] may properly be termed a race of railroad builders, as they have probably built more miles of railroad during the past six years than any other firm engaged in the business.[10]

In addition to their work in constructing branch line railroads and reconstructing the line of the original railroads to improve grades and curves, they also undertook some sizable canal contracts. One of these was in Wyoming, where the engineer was Dr. Elwood Mead, who later became an internationally famous irrigation authority.[11]

To indicate the increasing role of the maturing Wattis boys in the outfit, in 1887 the partnership was named Corey Brothers & Company.

Corey Brothers, as mentioned earlier, was not alone. Dozens of other Mormon camps, with men from as far north as Weston, Idaho, to as far south as Willard, Utah, were engaged in filling such contracts. A contemporary non-Mormon observer suggested reasons for the Mormon success:

> They bid so close on grading jobs that no other contractor could compete with them, and they worked together like true brothers and sisters. [I] visited one of their grading camps and was amazed to see the order and cleanliness that was maintained under the most difficult conditions . . . the men were particular to wash and to comb their hair before each meal. The Mormon women did the cooking and waited on table. What was more, the grading was always completed within the time limits stipulated in the contract and was all done in a most satisfactory manner.[12]

Because of the modest conditions under which the workers had been reared, their costs of upkeep were not high. Many slept on the ground with some hay for a mattress on which they spread blankets. Tents were universal, with an occasional shack of crude lumber or sheet iron to house the blacksmith shop or some valuable equipment. Their recreation or amusement came primarily from a laborer who could play a mouth organ or a fiddle. Card games were common.[13]

In 1893 Corey Brothers & Company accepted a contract to build a railroad line up the Lewis and Clark River from Astoria to Portland, Oregon. In this year there was a general business depression, and the company financing the railroad was unable to meet its obligations. Because the Coreys and Wattises were unable to sustain the attendant financial loss, entrepreneurs from the Ogden area rallied to their support. David Eccles and his associates Thomas Dee, Matthew Browning, and others helped out. In this way David Eccles became involved in the company as a creditor. Ultimately, in 1900, the company was reorganized as the Utah Construction Company, with a total capitalization of two hundred thousand dollars. Ownership was now lodged with David Eccles (one-third of the stock), Thomas Dee and James Pingree of Ogden (one-third), and the Wattis brothers (one-third). The Coreys were moved into less critical positions.

After several good years under the management of William H. Wattis, Utah Construction was in a position to bid on the largest railroad contract ever let west of Chicago—construction of the seven hundred mile Western Pacific line from Salt Lake City to Oroville, California. The building of the railroad occupied five years and required the company to maintain a working force of more than six thousand men and several thousand teams. The company initiated construction from both ends—one group from Salt Lake City heading west, under the direction of Andrew H. Christensen; and one heading east from Oroville, under the direction of William H. Wattis. The nature of the work of the two camps was very different. The Utah end was mainly desert—no towns, no supplies, very little water. A few miles near Wendover, Utah, could not even be graded because there was nothing but salt beds and no dirt to make a grade. Salt water was just under the dry crust and under that was mud with no stability for holding up a load. The problem was solved, as Lester Corey has explained, "by laying miles of lumber planks on the salt, on which the railroad track was built. Many trainloads of earth and gravel were then hauled from miles away for the roadbed. This continued until there was sufficient stability to hold up the locomotives."[14]

The other crew graded from Oroville up the Feather River to the eastern slope of the Sierra Nevada. The Feather River

Canyon was at that time an immense gorge that was considered almost impassable—a narrow defile with steep rocky slopes so precipitous that there was not room for the roadbed without deep cuts. The roadbed had to be supported partly or altogether upon high masonry walls built up from a solid foundation. It included five long tunnels.[15] Along the entire route were forty-three tunnels and forty steel bridges with a combined length of more than ten miles. When the project was completed—in the face of the intervention of a severe depression, two major floods, and a fire that destroyed San Francisco—it was hailed as one of the great engineering marvels of modern times.

In 1912 Utah Construction acquired the Vineyard Land and Livestock Company, the largest ranch and livestock enterprise in Nevada, with three million acres of grazing land. This enterprise was helpful in supplying construction crews with teams and food.

In the 1920s and 1930s, under the leadership of the Wattises, Coreys, and Eccleses, Utah Construction undertook such projects as the Bear River Canal system and the American Falls, Deadwood, Guernsey, and Hetchy-Hetchy dams. With this experience the company was in a position to serve as the nucleus for the Six Company consortium that built the $49 million Boulder (Hoover) Dam.[16] Later, the same group built such large projects as the Grand Coulee Dam and the Bonneville system. Utah Construction had become one of the largest construction companies in the world—an achievement colossal enough to warm the heart of any village groceryman.

William H. Wattis, as general manager of the company, achieved fame, both locally and nationally. In addition to being head of Utah Construction and Vineyard Land & Stock Company, he was a director and member of the executive committee of the Amalgamated Sugar Company, vice-president and director of the Dee Memorial Hospital (now the McKay-Dee Hospital Center), Republican candidate for Governor of Utah in 1928 (when Democrat George H. Dern was elected), director of the United States Chamber of Commerce, vice-president of the Associated General Contractors of America, and founder of the Ogden Union Stockyards Company. He died of cancer in 1931, at the age of seventy-one.

Three years later, his older brother and associate, Edmund Orson Wattis, who had succeeded William H. as president of Six Companies, died at age seventy-eight.[17]

* * *

Because of its remote location and limited usable land resources, the Wasatch Front in Utah partook of the nature of an island economy: an ever-burgeoning population (due to immigration and the high birth rate) strode forth to work and return or to colonize. As with ancient Greece, Phoenicia, Venice, Genoa, Great Britain, and Japan, Utah could produce within its own borders only a portion of its income. The rest was earned by Jasons who went out in search of Golden Fleeces. Some of them—the Allens, the Coreys, the Wattises, and hundreds of others that could be named—performed positive services for their families and villages by going forth as Argonauts to obtain work and income. Their earnings brought cash into the communities from which they took temporary and ultimately permanent leave—cash that made possible family purchases of agricultural implements, Oregon lumber to build better homes, and machinery for the operation of local shops and factories. They also contributed to the welfare of other communities. They built railroads, supplied goods to miners, opened up forests, and developed irrigation systems. Where there was desert, where there was wilderness, where there was need of development, in Canada, Mexico, or the American West, intrepid Mormon pioneer-adventurers were present. Along with other westerners they helped to make the western desert blossom and the wilderness become a suitable place for civilized habitation.

NOTES

I wish to express appreciation to Chris Rigby Arrington, George Daines, and Davis Bitton for help in connection with this paper.

1. Richard Sherlock, "Mormon Migration and Settlement After 1875," *Journal of Mormon History* 2 (1975):53-68.

2. The information on the Allens has been gleaned from Kate Carter, ed., *Treasures of Pioneer History,* 6 vols. (Salt Lake City: Daughters of Utah Pioneers, 1952-1957), 5:64-65; Alvin Allen, *Ira Allen: Founder of Hyrum* (Hyrum, Utah: privately published, 1948?); "Hyrum Woman Packed Interesting Life History into Her 92 Years," *Logan Herald Journal,* March 5, 1937; Frank Steele, ed., "Heber Simeon Allen: His Life and Works," typescript in possession of the writer and at the Glenbow Foundation, Memorial Park, Calgary Alberta; and "Biography of Heber Simeon Allen," a manuscript of about 120 letter-size notebook pages in the handwriting of Elizabeth Skidmore Hardy Allen, second wife of Heber Allen, in the possession of Amy Allen Pulsipher, Salt Lake City, Utah. The latter appears to be an exact copy of a diary and "history" in the handwriting of Heber Allen himself, the original of which is in possession of a Heber Allen descendant who chooses to remain anonymous.

3. Grading was accomplished with horse-drawn, slip-and-tongue scrapers. These scrapers were later modified into what were called fresnos—horse-drawn scoops, operated by one man, used to move dirt short distances.

4. Other Cache Valley "boys" also worked on the Canadian Pacific. For example, see "Railroading in Canada," in Carter, *Treasures of Pioneer History,* 2:47-48, and following pages.

5. On Uinta, see *Tullidge's Quarterly Magazine* (Salt Lake City) 2:638-40; Milton R. Hunter, *Beneath Ben Lomond's Peak* (Ogden: Daughters of Utah Pioneers, 1949), 166-74. On the Coreys, see Leonard J. Arrington, "Utah Construction Company," in *David Eccles: Pioneer Western Industrialist* (Logan, Utah: Utah State University Press, 1975), 251-54; "Corey Bros. & Co.," in *Utah: Her Cities, Towns, and Resources* (Chicago: Manly & Litteral, 1891), 158-59; Royal Eccles interview with W. H. Wattis, September 1929, typescript in possession of the writer.

6. Bernard DeVoto, "Jonathan Dyer, Frontiersman: A Paragraph in the History of the West," *Harper's Monthly Magazine* 167 (September 1933): 491-501.

7. See especially Nelson Trottman, *History of the Union Pacific: A Financial and Economic Survey* (New York: Ronald Press, 1923), 180-82; *Deseret News*, May 26 and September 11, 1881; James H. Kyner, *End of Track* (Lincoln, Nebr.: Bison Books, 1960).

8. Lester S. Corey, "Utah Construction & Mining Co.—An Historical Narrative," typescript in possession of the writer, 3.

9. *Salt Lake Tribune*, January 1, 1885.

10. Ibid., January 1, 1887.

11. Corey, "Utah Construction & Mining Co.," 4.

12. Stewart Holbrook, *The Story of American Railroads* (New York: MacMillan, 1948), 192.

13. Corey, "Utah Construction & Mining Co.," 11-13.

14. Ibid., 14-15.

15. A description of some of the engineering problems is given in an article in the *Salt Lake Tribune*, August 22, 1910.

16. Other companies were Bechtel & Kaiser, McDonald & Kahn, J. P. Shea, Morrison-Knudsen, and Pacific Bridge.

17. Actually, William H. Wattis's immediate successor as president of Six Companies was W. A. Bechtel of San Francisco, but Bechtel died in August 1933 and was succeeded by Edmund Orson.

9

Vengeance vs. the Law: The Lynching of Sam Joe Harvey in Salt Lake City

Larry R. Gerlach

On August 25, 1883, Sam Joe Harvey was lynched after he killed Andrew Hill Burt, the Salt Lake City chief of police and city marshal. Although this is the only lynching recorded in the history of Salt Lake City, Dr. Larry R. Gerlach, Professor of History at the University of Utah, argues that it provides a chance for an in-depth study of the causes of mob violence and general community response to such violence. Based primarily on the extensive reports and commentary on the event in the three city newspapers at the time, Dr. Gerlach describes the events leading up to the lynching, the lynching itself, and the rather raucous debate over who was to blame for the incident. Dr. Gerlach points out that Salt Lake City learned a sobering lesson from the lynching experience: "A thin line separates civility from savegery, and whenever normally decent, law-abiding people decline the obligations of citizenship and dictates of conscience, the line becomes close to being obliterated." They learned "that the hallmark of a civilized society is the rule of law, not justice."

"One of the most horrible and thrilling tragedies ever enacted in this part of the country, took place on the public streets of this city between one and two o'clock this afternoon, and never have we beheld such tremendous excitement as was caused by it." Thus the August 25, 1883, edition of the *Deseret*

Evening News began its account of a murder-lynching in Salt Lake City that was truly one of the most extraordinary episodes of mob violence in the annals of the American West.

* * *

Apart from survival in a novel and sometimes hostile environment, Americans who streamed across the western portion of the United States during the latter half of the nineteenth century faced numerous human problems, chief among them the maintenance of law and order. Because the growth of population routinely outstripped the establishment of effective governmental institutions, community stability on the early frontier depended largely on voluntary compliance with both cultural norms and statutory laws. With governmental authority an ephemeral commodity in many nascent settlements, transgressors of the law frequently found themselves facing popular tribunals as vigilance committees often provided the transition to duly constituted courts. Sometimes the passing of the frontier preceded the transition from gun to gavel: some citizens remained quick to take the law into their own hands, occasionally to advance special interests, but more typically to counter perceived inadequacies in law enforcement and judicial administration. Consequently, two uniquely American modes of summary justice loomed large in the West: vigilantism, the unauthorized assumption of police powers by a self-appointed *posse comitatus*, and lynching, the illegal execution, usually by hanging, of persons known or suspected to be guilty of crimes.[1]

Judge Lynch and his henchmen maintained a busy circuit in the trans-Mississippi West in the years following the Civil War. During the last two decades of the "frontier era" alone (1882 to 1903), at least 934 persons received hempen justice in Western states.[2] Utah lagged considerably behind its neighbors in practicing lynch law, probably because of the theo-democratic influence of the Mormon Church and the concentration of people in agrarian villages instead of in mining camps or across grassy rangelands.[3] Nonetheless, at least twelve "necktie parties" were held in Utah Territory from 1869 to 1886; "lariat law" claimed seven victims before Sam Joe Harvey received short shrift at the end of a long rope.[4]

The illegal execution of Sam Joe Harvey, the lone lynching in Salt Lake City, is historically significant as a case study of mob violence. Whereas information concerning most lynchings is so sketchy as to permit little more than reconstructing an outline of the execution itself, the historical record concerning the Harvey lynching is unusually fulsome partly because the urban affair provided sensational copy for the city's three daily papers and partly because it sparked a newspaper war which fanned the fire of religious antagonism and called into question the conduct and integrity of municipal officials. Because of extensive public commentary, an examination of the lynching of Sam Joe Harvey affords an in-depth look not only at the causes of mob violence but also the responses of a community to a visit from Judge Lynch.[5]

* * *

Founded in 1847 as a gathering place for members of the Church of Jesus Christ of Latter-day Saints, Salt Lake City a generation later bore little resemblance to the Mormon village envisioned by Brigham Young.[6] In 1883 the city by the Great Salt Lake was a booming town of some twenty-five thousand persons, the capital of Utah Territory as well as the hub of a religious empire that extended throughout the Great Basin and into Southern California and Northern Mexico. Located on the Hastings Cutoff linking the Oregon and California trails and joined to the Union Pacific and the Denver & Rio Grande railroads, Salt Lake City was a hustling, bustling, commercial center whose sizable itinerant population included migrants and railroad laborers, cowboys and miners, freighters and soldiers, and a full complement of social misfits ranging from prostitutes to cardsharks. Compounding the usual socioeconomic tensions in a burgeoning frontier town was pervasive antagonism between the Mormon majority and the growing non-Mormon population that colored virtually every aspect of life in the community. Despite the staid social mantle of Mormonism, Salt Lake was a rough-and-tumble town; residents of the woolly if not wild western community were accustomed to tumultuous, sometimes violent, goings-on. But even the most hardened among them were shocked by the events surrounding the lynching of Sam Joe Harvey.

The principal in the tragic cause celebre was William H. ("Joe" or "Sam Joe") Harvey, an itinerant Negro bootblack in his mid-thirties.[7] Two days after the lynching, A. S. Johnson, an elderly black man who claimed to be Harvey's half-brother, told the coroner that the victim was actually Joseph Samuels of Farmington, Louisiana. According to Johnson, "Samuels," or "Harvey" as he was generally known, had had a troubled past. After serving a tour of duty with the Army—where a proclivity for fighting earned him the nickname "U.S."—he headed West like so many other ex-soldiers to seek his fortune. A tall, athletic-looking fellow, Harvey had a history of moving on—wanderings no doubt prompted by a "somewhat cranky" disposition and an apparent eagerness to use the .44 caliber revolver that was his constant companion. For several years he had lived in Pueblo, Colorado, but following a shoot-out there he had recently fled first to Cheyenne, and then west to Green River, Evanston, and Salt Lake.

Upon arriving in Salt Lake City in early August 1883, Harvey set up a shoeshine stand in front of Michael Heinau's barbershop at 234 South Main. Three weeks later he headed north to Ogden, presumably to seek employment on the railroad. The journey was short-lived. It is not clear whether Harvey lost his money en route to gamblers or robbers, only that he had been put off the train and had returned to Salt Lake City the morning of August 25 broke and in dire need of employment.

The other *dramatis persona* was Captain Andrew Hill Burt, fifty-five, head of the Salt Lake City police department.[8] Born in Dunfermline, Fifeshire, Scotland, on October 20, 1828, Burt along with his entire family was baptized into the LDS Church by a missionary in May 1848. He immigrated with his parents in the fall of 1849 to the United States and worked in the coal mines near St. Louis before journeying to Salt Lake City in September 1851. A zealous convert, Burt served his church in a variety of capacities. He was a laborer in the church quarry, a colonizer of southern Utah missions, a soldier in the Echo Canyon and Black Hawk wars, and since 1877, the bishop of the 21st Ward in Salt Lake City. Joining the Salt Lake police force in 1858, Burt quickly distinguished himself as a peace officer. Three years later he was named chief of police and in 1876 also became the town's first city marshal. In August 1883 the veteran lawman directed a force of eight paid men, including his son, Alexander, and "a number of special officers."[9]

Widely respected as an indomitable and incorruptible peace officer who had "the courage of a lion," Burt was one of the most renowned western lawmen of his day. He was fearless to the extreme, exhibiting a rather peculiar brand of courage as his special badge of valor. Although he repeatedly admonished his officers to be prepared for any emergency and to take special pains to guard against personal injury, he personally never carried a weapon other than a walking cane. During his long career he countless times broke up fights, took guns and knives away from men, and strode into "the midst of desperadoes with bullets flying thick around him" without ever receiving the slightest injury. Such "indifference almost amounting to recklessness regarding his own personal safety" stemmed from two factors. The first was his imposing physical strength and awesome temper: "terrible when aroused to action," Burt simply overpowered men. The second was an almost fanatical belief in himself as an instrument of God: before embarking upon potentially hazardous duties, he invariably prayed for divine protection. Andrew Burt, in short, considered himself invincible.

The events that led such starkly contrasting personages to a tragic crossing of paths began early in the morning of August 25 when Sam Joe Harvey began panhandling for money to buy food.[10] He was tired, hungry, and in a belligerent mood. When Fred Coulter, who operated the shoeshine stand in front of the Wasatch Building, refused to give him a quarter, Harvey angrily retorted: "You won't give me the money? Then I'll get even with you." Others who declined his solicitations also received threats to "get even."[11]

After finally obtaining a dollar from Heinau, Harvey proceeded to Frances H. Grice's restaurant located adjacent to the Old Salt Lake House at 153 South Main. For several years, Grice, himself a black man, had operated the cafe which catered to the social as well as culinary needs of Salt Lake's small black population. As Harvey ate, he told Grice of his monetary miseries and expressed fear that he would "freeze to death" come winter unless he secured employment. Grice advised him that while there was no work at the restaurant he should check back later about the possibility of working on his farm.

The restaurant was full of diners when Harvey returned shortly before one o'clock. Grice offered Harvey two dollars a day for performing general farm labor, but instead of accepting the offer, Harvey inquired about the location of the farm. When Grice replied that it didn't matter because he would provide transportation to and from the site, Harvey pointedly pressed the issue and, upon learning that the farm was located twelve miles from town, flew into a rage. He "belched out a lot of profanity" and declared that he would not travel such a distance. Now angered himself by the abusive tirade and the boisterous behavior that disrupted his noonday business, Grice curtly withdrew the job offer and ordered Harvey to leave. When Harvey continued his harangue, the proprietor rushed from behind the lunch counter, grabbed him by the coat lapels, and pushed him toward the door. Thereupon Harvey drew his pistol and threatened Grice. Potential disaster was averted when a terror-stricken Mrs. Grice began "shouting and stamping her feet in a vigorous manner" as if to chase away a marauding animal. Taken aback by her shrieks and flailings, Harvey put away his gun and ran through the kitchen and out into the back alley where he fled to Second South Street.[12]

An agitated Sam Joe Harvey rushed down Second South and around the corner to Thomas Carter's hunting and fishing emporium at 137 South Main. He had been at Carter's earlier that morning admiring a .45 Springfield repeating rifle, and he now hurriedly purchased the weapon along with two packages of cartridges for twenty dollars. Telling the storekeeper that he was heading for the country and that his wagon was about to depart, Harvey rushed from the store.[13] (Harvey's haste and the fact that he had suddenly acquired a substantial amount of money suggests that he may have committed a robbery within the last hour or two and feared arrest.)

Meanwhile, Marshal Andrew Burt sat in police head-quarters in the city hall chatting with Charles H. Wilcken, police officer and city water master. Their conversation was interrupted shortly after one o'clock by the jangle of the telephone. Upon learning from Grice about his confrontation with the gun-wielding Harvey, Burt and Wilcken bolted out the door and headed for the restaurant. They made their way on foot west on First South and then south along Main Street as fast as the noon-hour jumble of wagons, horses, and pedestrians would permit. After hearing the details of the incident from Grice, the three men set out in search of Harvey.

As the trio approached the northeast corner of Main and Second South, they spotted Harvey standing in front of A. C. Smith's drug store. Burt stepped boldly forward to make the arrest. Cornered, Harvey instinctively tightened his trigger finger. "Are you an officer?" he snarled. As the lawman replied affirmatively, Harvey raised his rifle. A single shot roared from the Springfield. Burt recoiled backward as the bullet ripped through his left arm just above the elbow, entered his chest just above the left nipple, passed through the cardiovascular cavity, and finally lodged in his right arm. He let out a groan, staggered momentarily, and then stumbled into Smith's drug store. As the alarmed clerks and patrons rushed toward him, Andrew Burt reeled behind the prescription case; his trusty cane slipped from his hand and he slumped to the floor. Moments later, he was dead.

At first, bystanders were unaware of Burt's condition, for Charlie Wilcken had become the center of attention. Almost simultaneously with the retort of the rifle, the water master sprang upon Harvey, wrenched the rifle from his grasp, and wrestled him to the ground. Amid screams of fright, the crowd dissolved—some going for help, but most fleeing for safety— leaving Wilcken to grapple with the assailant. During the ensuing struggle Harvey drew a pistol from his hip pocket and shot Wilcken through the left arm between the elbow and shoulder. As Harvey pressed the gun against the water master's side for a second shot, a passerby, Enoch Able, grabbed the revolver and threw it aside. Another witness, Samuel Benjamin, then rushed forward, picked up the rifle and revolver, and took them across the street into M. H. Lipman's mercantile. With the weapons secured, Wilcken, aided by Able and Homer J. Stone, succeeded in pinning the defenseless Harvey on his back near the drainage ditch that formed the gutter of the street. Momentarily police officers William Hilton and Thomas F. Thomas appeared on the scene and took Harvey into custody.[14]

A large crowd of agitated citizens, raising "deafening yells" and demanding that Harvey be "strung up and lynched," escorted the peace officers and their captive the slightly more than two blocks to the City Hall. Angry as it was over the shoot-out and the wounding of the popular Wilcken, the crowd was held in check because it was not yet generally known that Marshal Burt had been fatally wounded; in fact, many people thought Wilcken was the lone victim of the shooting.

Upon arriving at City Hall, a thoroughly frightened Sam Joe Harvey was ushered into police headquarters. Only policemen and reporters for the *Tribune, Chronicle,* and *Herald* were allowed in the building. A search of the prisoner found, in addition to sundry personal items, a large number of rifle and pistol shells as well as some $165.80 in gold, silver, and greenbacks. (Possession of such a large amount of money immediately raised the suspicion that Harvey had recently stolen the money.)[15]

During the search, the door to the marshal's office burst open and a man rushed into the room shouting: "Marshal Burt is dying." At that, one of the officers yelled at Harvey:

"Goddamn you, if Marshal Burt dies, you shall die before tomorrow morning." The lawman then struck Harvey between the eyes, knocking him to the floor. The attack proved contagious. Almost en masse the police guard leaped upon the prisoner, pummeling and kicking him. Repeatedly Harvey was knocked to the floor, picked up, and struck down again. He was also beaten over the head with billy clubs, brass knuckles, and shackles. He was hurled about the room so violently that on one occasion his head struck a washstand, causing a nasty gash on his forehead. Although the furious assault lasted but a few seconds, the battered and bloody Harvey, according to the *Tribune* reporter, "presented a fearful sight." Finally, an officer said: "Let us take him to jail."[16]

Meanwhile, the throng outside the City Hall grew steadily larger and more agitated. When word arrived that Burt lay dying, the crowd surged from the First South Street entrance to the building around to the First East (now State) Street side of the yard and then streamed through the grounds past the stables to the west door of the jail. Thinking Harvey already inside, the members of what was now becoming a mob excitedly peered through the barred windows hoping to catch a glimpse of the assassin.

With the attention of the crowd thus diverted, four officers tried surreptitiously to drag the "apparently benumbed" Harvey across the alleyway that separated the City Hall from the jail and slip him through the middle door of the prison. But it was impossible to avoid detection altogether, and at the sight of the prisoner cries of "hang the son of a bitch!" and "like expressions" filled the air.[17] No sooner had the door been slammed shut than the reporters, who had been denied access to the jail, heard the sound of a blow being struck, then "a fall like that of a felled ox," and finally a voice saying, "That will fix him; he won't need any mob."[18]

The mob, of course, thought otherwise. Drawn by the commotion, the multitude pressed forward to the middle door of the jail. As the clamor of the crowd began to crescendo, a man came running up shouting: "Marshal Burt is dead. Bring him out." News of Burt's death spread like wildfire through the

milling mass of humanity; "expressions of rage and vindic-
tiveness on the part of the populace assumed almost the
conditions of a paroxysm," as the air filled with a bloodthirsty
chorus: "Bring him out! Lynch him!"

The tumult and shouting abated somewhat when the jail
door suddenly swung open and three of the officers emerged.
Officer William Salmon, pistol in hand, ordered the crowd to
keep back. Apparently Salmon's real motive was to hold the
crowd at bay until the remaining officer could fetch Harvey
from his cell, for within moments the jail door opened a second
time and "the half-insensible wretch" was pushed out head-
long, tumbling to the ground at the officers' feet. Amid piercing
cries of vengeance, the lawmen walked away, leaving Harvey
helpless before the enraged multitude which, according to one
estimate, "numbered fully 2,000 persons."[19]

The murderous mob instantly fell upon Harvey and, with
yells and curses, savagely pounded, kicked, and stomped him
until his face was "a mass of blood and bruises." Harness straps
were removed from teams of horses standing in front of the
City Hall, but several men scurried about looking for the more
traditional ropes. Harvey's vain attempt to escape, coupled
with the surging of the mob, carried him eastward some fifty
feet from the jail door before he fell prostrate. Though near
exhaustion, Harvey struggled desperately to keep the noose
from being placed over his head. But, no match for his self-
appointed executioners, he soon sported a deadly hempen
necktie. Members of the mob seized the free end of the rope
and dragged their victim more than one hundred feet across
the yard into a stable at the west end of the jail. Quickly the
rope was tossed over a roof beam; "willing hands" eagerly
"strung up the writhing wretch." When Harvey's body was
completely suspended, the loose end of the rope was secured to
a post. "Amid cheers and jeers of the congregated multitude,"
the body of Sam Joe Harvey was left "swinging in the air."[20]

The instinct for self-preservation prompted Harvey to
fight for his life until the end. As soon as his feet left the
ground, he raised his arms above his head, clutching the rope
in order to relieve the pressure upon his neck. But an equally

determined lyncher scurried atop a nearby carriage and kicked first one hand and then the other until Harvey let go of the rope. Upon relaxing his grip, he "gasped paroxysmally, showed a slight tremor of muscular contraction; his arms dropped, and he was dead."[21] One citizen, a compulsive clock-watcher, remarked that exactly twenty-five minutes had passed between the shooting of Marshal Burt and the hanging of Sam Joe Harvey.[22]

The mob gazed grimly at its handiwork. It was not a pretty sight. As the *Herald* correspondent described the scene:

> The spectacle presented by the suspended body of the negro was one that will not soon be forgotten by those who saw it. His neck was stretched to twice its natural length; his head dropped towards the left shoulder; his mouth was forced open by muscular contractions; his face was a perfect jelly with bruises and cuts, and was covered all over with blood, which streamed down upon his clothing and dyed it deeply in the crimson tide. . . . It was a horrifying sight, one upon which none but the most hardy could look upon and afterwards sleep quietly and without disturbing dreams.[23]

"Thus," as the *Deseret News* put it, "was summary vengeance wreaked on the red-handed murderer."[24]

But the savage manifestation of vengeance did not satisfy the bloodlust of some men. Many felt Harvey's crime "so heinous and unprovoked and its results so disastrous" that death alone was "not satisfactory." Some in the infuriated throng wanted to drag the corpse through the streets of the city. One of the lynchers yelled: "Let's take him down and hang him outside where everybody can see him." But another member of the necktie party counseled against such action: "Never mind; he's comfortable enough where he is."[25] But as future events would show, Sam Joe Harvey was dead but he was not yet at rest.

Not everyone, of course, shared the mob's enthusiasm for

blood atonement or for taking the law into their own hands. Such a person was William H. Sells, a lumber dealer, who happened to be riding past city hall in his buggy while the lynching was in progress. Unaware that Harvey had already been lynched, Sells and a companion entered the jail yard and strongly warned against "any unlawful measures" in an effort to "avert another crime." The lynchers, thinking Sells was reprimanding them, became incensed. Several drew pistols against him and made it clear that they were "at bloody business" and were "not particularly averse to prosecuting the work further." Calmer heads, fearful of another lynching, urged Sells, "who was pretty roughly handled for a time," to leave; finally Officer Salmon took him to the jail where he remained in protective custody under lock and key for several hours until things quieted down. Not a few persons present believed that Salmon's action saved Sells's life. Several other men were also threatened with mobbing or lynching for expressing opposition to the illegal execution.

While the lynching was taking place in the jail yard, another chapter in the tragic tale was beginning to unfold at Smith's drug store. As news of Burt's shooting circulated through the city, an "immense" crowd gathered at the druggist's to monitor the marshal's condition. By the time Dr. J. M. Benedict completed his postmortem examination and officially declared the peace officer dead, the crowd had become noticeably agitated. And when Burt's sheet-covered body was carried from the store, the grief-stricken crowd became transformed into a frenzied lynch mob. The homicidal proposal of one man—"I say hang; who goes with me?"—met with "almost universal" assent.[26]

With shouts of vengeance, a sizable portion of the crowd broke and rushed toward the jail. As the crowd surged along the streets its numbers were "swelled by hundreds" more curious and vengeful citizens. Upon arriving at the jail yard and finding that Harvey had already been lynched, the crowd sent up a chorus of three cheers. Within minutes the throng had swelled into "the thousands" as men, women, and children from all over the city swarmed to the scene to see the morbid curiosity. In the opinion of the *Tribune* reporter, "a more excited crowd was never seen in this city than the one there represented."[27]

What happened next defies rational explanation. A *Deseret News* reporter, who had "never before so vividly realized the terrible frenzy of an unreasoning crowd of enraged people," thought "the revolting spectacle presented by Harvey's corpse, the face of which was horrible and repulsive beyond description," coupled with the "memory of his awful crime seemed to lash the feelings of the mob into renewed fury."[28] The "sickening sight" surely conveyed the message that vengeance had been achieved—that through physical and emotional torture Sam Joe Harvey had paid the ultimate price for his perfidy.

And yet—whether actuated by an unrequited desire for retribution or the irrational frenzy of bloodlust—a portion of the crowd suddenly rushed toward the corpse, cut the rope, and dragged the body through the alley and along State Street "rending the air with angry shouts as they went." The sight of an already mutilated corpse bouncing along the dirt road accompanied by a hallooing herd "hooting and yelling like mad" presented a horrifying spectacle of wanton barbarism.

After the body had been dragged a short distance down the street, Mayor William Jennings, accompanied by "several prominent citizens," arrived on the scene of "willful barbarity." Upon viewing the spectacle a gentleman accompanying the mayor immediately exclaimed: "This is barbarous, let us put a stop to this." Jennings agreed, but replied: "I can do nothing without the police, and none of them are here." But when his companion replied, "Damn it, let us try," the mayor, accompanied by U.S. Marshal E. A. Ireland, set out in pursuit of the crowd, calling upon them to stop. Somehow, his voice was heard above the din and the maddened throng obeyed the mayor's command. He then addressed the mob, "reasoning with them in such a manner as to allay the storm which had been up to that time raging." He also backed up his words with action. When it appeared that another attempt might be made to drag the body, Jennings went to the loose end of the rope, raised his heavy cane, and vowed to "brain" the first man to approach the corpse. His forthright action had the effect of quieting the mob and restoring order. With its fury spent and the object of its hatred laying mutilated in the street, the mob dispersed. Shaken by the spectacle, Mayor Jennings ordered Harvey's corpse taken to the city jail and locked up for safekeeping.[29]

While townspeople privately rehashed the events of what the *Herald* termed "the bloodiest and most exciting" day in Salt Lake history, municipal officials moved quickly to conclude the legal ramifications of the murder-lynching. At four o'clock a formal inquest closed the file on Sam Joe Harvey: a coroner's jury (John Groesbeck, Joseph Jennings, and W. W. Riter) impaneled by Coroner George J. Taylor declared that "W. H. Harvey . . . died in some sheds southeast of City Hall . . . by being hanged with a rope by an angry and excited multitude who seemed inspired by a feeling of vengeance for his assassination of Marshal Andrew Burt." Taylor then took the body to an unidentified location for immediate burial. Early that evening the coroner held another inquest, this time over the body of Andrew Burt. Jurors Jessie W. Fox, Robert Patrick, and William Naylor ruled that the marshal had died "at 10 minutes past 1, from the effects of a gunshot fired from the rifle in the hands of William H. Harvey."[30]

At eight o'clock that night the Salt Lake City Council met in a special session. Ironically, the "shocking affair" that led Mayor Jennings to convene the council was not the lynching of Sam Joe Harvey. Although the councilmen "strongly deprecated" the violent nature of the Harvey lynching and were "sorry the law could not take its course," they all agreed that "the miserable being" who killed Burt deserved "that justice which could only come by death." Because Burt, who had for more than two decades served the city as "an energetic and fearless officer," had been tragically "cut down" while in the active discharge of his official duty by a "ruffian assassin," the mayor proposed the city arrange and pay for funeral and burial ceremonies for the slain lawman. After reviewing the late marshal's record of public service in the most laudatory

manner, the council unanimously adopted a resolution expressing condolences to Burt's widow and children and appointing a committee to coordinate funeral and burial plans with the
family.[31]

Last rites for Andrew Burt were conducted on Tuesday,
August 28. At 8:30 A.M. the body was conveyed from the Burt
residence in the 21st Ward to the cavernous tabernacle adjacent to the rising temple, where it lay in state for an hour prior
to the commencement of funeral services at ten o'clock. Most
stores in the central area of the city complied with Major
Jenning's unofficial request to close from nine until noon in
order that friends might attend the funeral.[32] The outpouring
of bereavement was extraordinary. A "steady stream of humanity" passed by the casket during the viewing period, and by the
time services began mourners filled the main tabernacle's floor
and most of the balcony.

The congregation, reported to be "among the largest ever
assembled in this city," witnessed nothing less than an elaborate
state funeral. Seated on the dais were magistrates representing
city, county, and territorial government along with members
of the LDS Church hierarchy. The Mormon Tabernacle Choir
sang and ranking church leaders, including President John
Taylor, offered prayers and eulogies. At the conclusion of the
lengthy service, a funeral cortege consisting of some seventy-
six vehicles, three bands, and countless citizens on foot—"a
funeral procession that has seldom been equalled in extent of
proportions in the history of the community"—wended its way
to the city cemetery for interment ceremonies.[33]

* * *

Shock waves from the tragic events of August 25 continued to reverberate after Andrew H. Burt and William H.
Harvey had been laid to rest. The sensational murder-lynching
long remained the lingering talk of the town in Salt Lake City
and elsewhere in the territory. When an eyewitness brought
word of the dual tragedy to Provo, Mary Mount Tanner noted
that "it caused so much excitement we could think of nothing

else."[34] Reports of the incident were published in Ogden, where the editor of the newspaper strongly condemned the lynching, and in Park City, where some residents were infected by the fever of mob justice.[35] The August 25 edition of the *Park City Mining Record* carried stories of both the recent murder of miner Matt Brennan and the lynching of Harvey. That night a mob of masked avengers forcibly removed John (Black Jack) Murphy, the alleged murderer, from the Coalville jail, returned him to Park City, and hanged him from a telegraph pole.[36] The contagion for homicidal vengeance apparently also spread to Spring Hill Station on the Utah & Northern Railroad, where John Fletcher reportedly was lynched after killing an engineer.[37] Of primary importance, however, is how residents of Salt Lake City responded to the assassination of the chief of police and the subsequent manifestation of lynch law.

The cold-blooded murder of Andrew Burt left Salt Lakers grief stricken. The outpouring of sentiment makes it clear that Burt had been regarded as a pillar of both the secular and sectarian communities because of his long and distinguished service as a police officer and as a Mormon bishop. (Veneration of the fallen lawman was such that he immediately became part of folk legend: the circulation of stories that Burt had had a detailed premonition of the murder made his death appear to be an expression of divine will.)[38] The city councilmen voiced the sentiments of the entire community when, the night of Burt's funeral, they went on record deploring "the cruel, atrocious act that has deprived the corporation of a true and valiant officer, the community of an honest and upright citizen, the Church of a zealous and faithful official member, and a large family of a kind, generous, loving husband and father."[39]

So great was the esteem for Burt and so great the shock of his murder that the city council took unprecedented action not only in underwriting the funeral ($254.88), but also in providing financial assistance to his survivors. For reasons of legality and practicality, the council on September 6 turned down the offer of police officers to perform voluntarily Burt's duties as chief of police, jailor, market master, and inspector of provisions so that the compensation could still be paid to his family. But in appointing William G. Phillips as the new chief of police, the councilmen directed that the Burt family keep for the duration of its term the contract for providing meals for prisoners at fifteen cents per meal.[40] In addition, Mayor Jennings appointed a three-member committee to consider the possibility of contributing public funds to the estate of the deceased. The committee's report was considered and on September 25 the council voted to award the Burt family $2,000 because of "the peculiar circumstances" attending the marshal's death "while actively engaged in the discharge of his official duty."[41] The action of the city council, one of the earliest known instances of public compensation to the victims of crimes in Utah if not western history, was applauded as "substantial proof of the public recognition of his worth to his family surviving."[42]

While the murder of Andrew Burt drew the community together, the lynching of Sam Joe Harvey left it divided. Because lynch law was not unknown to Utah, the hanging of Harvey was a premeditated if impassioned act. For days following the double tragedy, residents discussed publicly as well as privately the circumstances and meaning of the mob execution.

At first glance the lynching seems readily comprehensible, even ordinary in its occurrence, because Harvey was the personification of Judge Lynch's victim. First, Harvey had committed a serious offense against society. National lynching figures are emphatic: homicide, especially the killing of a police officer or community leader, was the most frequent cause of lynching.[43] Because Andrew Burt was venerated both as a lawman and as a churchman, the motivation for revenge was especially strong. Second, Harvey was a drifter. Lynching records show that the poor and those without important kinship ties were usually considered by vigilantes to be less worthy of due process than persons of status or position in the community. Third, Harvey was black. Lynching statistics, including those from Utah, make it clear that a member of a racial minority was far more likely to be a victim of lynch law than a Caucasian.[44] Although there is nothing to indicate that color played a primary role in the Harvey lynching, race was undoubtedly a contributing factor in that it was always easier for the white majority to rationalize the illegal execution of a nonwhite.[45] Last, Harvey was guilty. It was a foregone conclusion that Harvey, having gunned down Burt in broad daylight in front of dozens of witnesses, would ultimately forfeit his own life.

Although the commission of a heinous crime by an itinerant Negro and the desire for vengeance by an outraged citizenry constitute the primary explanations of the lynching, the highly charged sociopolitical atmosphere pervading the community may have contributed to the shocking display of mob violence. It is not coincidental, I think, that a city noted for an unusual degree of community law and order experienced its lone lynching just as deep-seated religious tensions reached a peak. Perhaps the extraordinary temper of the times helps explain why a sizable number of law-abiding Salt Lakers temporarily went berserk first by lynching a man in a particularly brutal fashion and then by dragging the corpse through the streets. Moreover, the occasion of a historical event is often recapitulated in its aftermath: the Harvey affair is unique among lynchings in the West, and elsewhere in the country, in the degree to which it became an object of religous-based political controversy among community leaders and in the press.[46]

That the murder-lynching could not be discussed without reference to religious animosities is evident from comments made during Burt's funeral by Joseph F. Smith, a member of the First Presidency of the LDS Church. Speaking of the hazardous duties of lawmen, he declared that Mormon policemen had the most dangerous job of all because Salt Lake City was "the rendezvous of the off-scourings of the earth" who came to town "imbued with the idea that a 'Mormon' has no rights that an American citizen is bound to respect and consequently that to shoot down a 'Mormon' even though he may be an officer of the law in the discharge of his duty, would be applauded by the world and that a man in so doing would gain honor and credit." Ostensibly such specious remarks were intended to perpetuate the mystique of Mormon martyrdom by linking Burt's murder to nearly a half-century of persecutions suffered by the Saints. But instead his statement, printed in the *Deseret Evening News*, further divided the community along Mormon and non-Mormon lines.[47]

Smith's intemperate remarks fueled the religiously based journalistic war that broke out on August 26 when the *Salt Lake Daily Tribune* published an editorial criticizing the performance of the police before, during, and after the lynching. The paper leveled three charges at the police: that officers brutally beat their prisoner while searching him in the City Hall and after placing him in jail; that the armed lawmen deliberately turned Harvey over to the murderous mob to be lynched despite the fact that "the crowd was of that kind which three resolute policemen could have held at bay without difficulty"; and that the police took no steps to prevent either the illegal execution or the dragging of the corpse through the streets. "We do not believe," the editorial concluded, "that there has been a parallel to the case in American history. Mobs have hung men repeatedly, but never before that we remember of have the policemen who had the prisoner in charge, first beaten him into half sensibility and then turned him over to the mob." Because the lynching was "accomplished through the direct assistance of the officers who are the sworn conservators of the peace," the *Tribune* called for the suspension of the lawmen involved pending a full investigation of the lynching by city officials.

Although the *Tribune* emphasized that "this is not a question between Mormon and Gentile" but one "in which the good name of the city government is at stake," its call for an investigation of the police touched off a religious tempest. At a time when spiritual passions ran high, criticism of Mormons was often interpreted as criticism of Mormonism and, except for Harvey, all of the principals in the affair—Burt, Wilcken, Mayor Jennings, the city council, and the entire police force— were LDS. Moreover, the *Tribune's* gratuitous observation that the lynching had occurred "in the shadow of the temple of the Saints" was a pointed reminder of the bitterly anti-Mormon editorial policy maintained by the self-proclaimed oracle of Gentile Utah.

Predictably, that afternoon the *Deseret Evening News*, owned and operated by the Church, editorially countered the *Tribune*'s allegations. The *News* contended that Harvey had been struck "only once" by a policeman after the prisoner had made "violent resistance" to the search; that the persons who beat him in the courtyard and jail were not officers; that Harvey had not been handed over to the mob but instead had "darted out of the door like a cat into a crowd" in "a vain endeavor to escape"; and that the men who lynched him and dragged his body through the streets were not lawmen.

There was a hollow ring in the *News*'s rebuttal. All evidence indicates that Harvey was indeed severely beaten while in police custody, and it is highly doubtful that a frightened black man would either violently resist search by angry white lawmen or voluntarily bolt from the presumed safety of a jail into the midst of a howling lynch mob. And if the police did not literally hand him over to the lynchers and actively participate in the hanging, the fact remains that a group of armed policemen failed to protect their prisoner and stop an illegal execution. (There is no record of anyone having been taken from protective custody and lynched in the United States in the face of determined opposition from law enforcement officers—less because of the show of force than because of an ingrained desire to submit to legal authority.) There is only one satisfactory explanation for the failure of Salt Lake City police to prevent a midday lynching in the heart of town less than a hundred yards from police headquarters: they did not try.

In addition to defending the police, the *News* sought to discredit the *Tribune* by delivering one of the nastiest diatribes to disgrace the long and shameful journalistic sniping between the two papers. Taking exception to the charge that the lynching was a "Mormon outrage" (the *Tribune* never said it was), the *News* characterized its rival as "the organ of prostitutes, the apologist for the blackguard and the drunkard, the defamer of women, the slanderer of the dead, the cesspool into which the obscenity, blasphemy and purient gossip of roughs and loafers and smutty-minded men of the baser sort flows naturally." In fact, the *News* argued, the murder-lynching was "but the natural result of the influence and teachings" of the *Tribune* which "encouraged the criminal element to resist the officers of the law." The *News* even went so far as to obliquely threaten the "low-lived scribes" of the *Tribune* if they did not "go a little slow" in the matter. Feigning amazement that the *Tribune* had "not long ago been abated as a nuisance," the *News* warned that "people, however law abiding, will bear but to a certain limit and beyond that there is no accounting for what they will do, or how they may be seized with impulses like that which urged the mob forward on Saturday."

As suggested by the *Deseret News's* diatribe against the *Tribune*, the inability of the press to put aside religious animosities diverted attention from the question of police culpability. For a week Salt Lake's Fourth Estate was more concerned with parrying religious ripostes than with probing the facts of the lynching. After its initial wild attack on the *Tribune*, the *Deseret News* adopted a subdued posture while the Mormon-owned *Herald*, which at first had been critical of the lynching, commenced a strident attack against its morning rival very similar in language and tone to that of the *News*. Charging the "craven slanderers" and "prejudiced and scoundrelly persons" who published the *Tribune* of siding with "gamblers, prostitutes, cutthroats, peace disturbers, garroters and desperadoes" against the police, the *Herald* agreed that Burt's murder was "a natural outgrowth" of the *Tribune's* "interminable abuse of the police force."[48]

The *Tribune* retaliated in kind, directing its counterattack primarily against the "thorough bigot" who published the *Deseret News*. According to the *Tribune*, the threats of intimidation by the *News*, which made it impossible for witnesses of the lynching to tell their story "without danger to life or limb," and the failure of Mayor Jennings and the city council to investigate the execution stemmed from the "system of terrorism" and "bond of secrecy" that pervaded the "Mormon-ruled territory." The Mormon establishment, contended the *Tribune*, was content to dismiss charges of police complicity in the lynching as "another Gentile lie" just as it had done with the Mountain Meadows Massacre of 1857 and "a score of other deeds of murder and outrage . . . for which no one has ever been brought to account."[49]

Amid such bombast and blustering, the *Tribune* kept up its call for a formal investigation of the lynching. Terming it a "public disaster" for a lawman to be "gunned down by an outlaw," the paper conceded that it would "not have been in our heart to make much of an outcry" if nothing more had followed Burt's assassination than "the sudden rage of the populace resulting in the lynching of the gross offender." But, because the police used "unnecessary and cruel violence" against Harvey and turned him over to lynchers, "a full, fair, and open investigation" was "the only proper thing to do." According to the *Tribune*, Mayor Jennings's failure to at least suspend the officers involved "simply shows that he has no conception of the majesty and dignity of the law."[50]

The real casualty in the sorry affair was, of course, the "majesty and dignity" of the law. Realizing as much, LDS Church President John Taylor spoke at Burt's funeral not to eulogize the slain officer but to expound upon the themes of humanity and law and order. He decried the reckless disregard for human life that seemed to be "spreading and growing" in the territory and sternly admonished those who "let their passions control them." That Harvey was guilty of murder was no excuse for the lynching, he argued, because it was mandatory "for us living in a land that professes, at least, to be governed by law, equity and justice, to await the decision of the proper tribunals."[51]

But like the editorials of the non-Mormon *Tribune*, the rebuke by President Taylor fell on deaf ears. Although the identities of the men responsible for the lynching were common knowledge, no investigation was ever held and thus no one was ever held accountable for the public murder. Salt Lake City commissioners would do no more than state that they "strongly deprecated" the lynching and were "sorry the law could not take its course and be vindicated."[52] Intransigence by civil authorities alone, of course, does not explain why no effort was made to bring the murderers of Sam Joe Harvey to trial. The entire community was responsible for the miscarriage of due process.

The problem was not that Salt Lakers lacked a sense of justice or commitment to legal process and institutions. The *Tribune* was not alone in condemning Judge Lynch's handiwork. The *Deseret News* declared itself "against mob law in any shape," while the *Herald* even more strongly asserted that "this lawlessness, these lynchings, these popular uprisings must not only be frowned upon, but suppressed absolutely." Asserting that Utah was "populated by a civilized, law-abiding community whose reputation for peace and quiet is not behind that of any people on the face of the globe," the *Herald* emphatically vowed that "a few men must not be permitted to destroy that reputation, by turning communities into howling, senseless, uncontrollable mobs."[53]

Justice was frustrated in the Harvey lynching in part because the press, instead of serving as the voice of community conscience, was by act of omission and commission a party to the travesty of justice. Antilynching editorials essentially paid only lip service to law and order by discussing abstractions such as the qualities of a civilized people and the desirability of law and order instead of examining the specific violation of due process then haunting the community. Moreover, by engaging in religious wrangling instead of rebuking the lynchers, the press diverted attention from substantive questions regarding the lynching. The *Tribune* subordinated its responsible call for an investigation to its irresponsible charges of a Mormon "cover-up" while the *Deseret News* and the *Herald* facilely dismissed the *Tribune*'s serious allegations as a political effort to make "anti-Mormon capital" of the lynching and thus embarrass both the Church and the Mormon-dominated city administration. (There was an element of truth in both positions: the *Tribune* clearly desired to use the lynching to discredit Mormon hegemony in the city and territory, and the Mormon press was equally bold in trying to avoid negative publicity for the community and government officials.)

Perhaps the major reason why justice was not served is that most residents condoned the illegal execution. The morning after the hanging, the *Herald* voiced the Jeckyll-and-Hyde attitude so typical following a lynching: "We doubt if there is an intelligent, thoughtful citizen of Salt Lake who does not regret the tragic occurrence at the City Jail on Saturday afternoon, and yet is there a person who when he in sincerity asks his own heart if he would have it otherwise, can obtain a wholly affirmative response?"[54] The *Deseret News* agreed that "the general sentiment is opposed to mob violence, but universally acquiescent in the justice of the death dealt out to the assassin."[55] The only aspect of the lynching to be condemned was the dragging of the corpse through the streets. As the *Herald* noted, "the moral effects of such a spectacle are not healthful. . . . The murderer deserved death, but, as this is the extreme penalty in any case, we owe it to our humanity and civilization to at least go no further . . . we no longer satisfy justice or gratify any healthful disposition by resorting to or permitting willful barbarity."[56]

Of particular interest is the way the community attempted to rationalize and justify the lynching. Because of the resultant newspaper war, the Salt Lake press was filled with extensive explanations for the mob execution. Although newspaper opinion does not always reflect public sentiment, it is likely that the variety of views voiced by the Fourth Estate mirrored basic popular perceptions of the tragedy.

The lynching was almost universally excused because of the conviction that Sam Joe Harvey got what he deserved. The *Deseret News* applauded the "summary vengeance wreaked on the red-handed" assassin because of his "awful crime."[57] The *Tribune* agreed that Harvey "richly deserved to die."[58] More vengeful, the *Herald* declared that Harvey, "nothing more or less than a wild beast in human form," deserved to be mangled and strung up "like the dog he was."[59] (To reinforce the idea that Harvey was the kind of man "who could easily and readily be spared from any community," the *Deseret News* printed the rumor that Harvey had been responsible for the Brennan murder in Park City and that he shot Burt to avoid arrest for that crime.)[60] In short, Salt Lakers agreed that Sam Joe Harvey was a "bad hombre" who had gotten his just reward and that once he was gone "the best that can be done is to say nothing about him."[61]

In a more legalistic vein, the lynching was justified on the grounds of popular sovereignty—an ironic argument inasmuch as anti-Mormons had appealed to the same "higher law" to justify depredations against the Saints in Missouri and Illinois.[62] Beginning with the premise that "mob law" was sometimes "a necessity," the *Herald* noted that the lynching of Harvey "certainly was justifiable." It then pointed out that the lynch mob consisted not only of both Mormons and non-Mormons but also of "all classes" of society—"people who are seen every day on Main Street, and merchants, shopkeepers, clerks, etc. . . . good men and bad, the young and old, the infidel and the churchman, the quiet man and the rowdy, the better and the pure elements of the community." Thus the *Herald* could "readily excuse the perpetration of an immediate execution without due process of law when the offense is so flagrant and the incidents so tragical, because what a whole community sanctions and approves is in one sense law itself."[63] The *Deseret News* also emphasized that there was "not the slightest doubt" that Harvey was the assassin and that the lynch mob was motivated by "a common feeling of implacable anger and revenge, not unmixed with a sentiment of stern justice."[64] The lynching was, then, a rational action undertaken by citizens who purposefully took the law into their own hands.

Paradoxically, the lynching was also justified in terms of the irrational. The *Herald* argued that the mob, "incited by an apparently irresistible and general impulse," was "impelled forward and forced to act by an influence or power that has never been explained or defined." Men, who in their "sober, quiet moments" would wonder how they could have participated in "that awful tragedy" found themselves "powerless to restrain themselves. . . . They knew what they were doing and why they were doing it; but they did not for the moment know that they had been transformed into barbarians." To emphasize the point, the *Herald* found the Park City lynching of Murphy deplorable because it was a "cool and deliberate act, having none of the redeeming elements that in a measure excused the Salt Lake business."[65]

The conscious and subconscious elements of lynch-mob psychology were joined by the circumstances surrounding the murder of Marshal Burt. What, after all, could be expected when an esteemed lawman was "shot down in cold blood by a brutal negro, years of whose life were not worth seconds of that of his victim?" For the mob to have behaved differently would have required "much greater self-control on the part of the people of Salt Lake City than the members of this ordinary community possess." All things considered, the *Herald* contended, if one reflected "honestly and intelligently" upon the circumstances of the lynching, one could not believe the affair "could have been different." In fact, opined the paper, should the same situation occur again, "the result would again be what it has been this time."[66]

The effect of such rationalizing was to absolve the lynchers of both moral and legal guilt for their misdeeds. Because they were merely victims of circumstance, the press could deplore the lynching and yet be unable to "denounce and rave against the mad avengers who acted with such terrible promptness, determination and effect." After all, members of the mob were "incensed beyond the point of endurance and did not try to give their judgment full exercise; in this they acted as human nature generally prompts under such circumstances, and cannot be greatly blamed." All things considered, asked the *Herald*, could those who participated in the "awful and lawless demonstration" be censured "even by the cool-headed and cautious?" Its answer was "no."[67]

Then, too, the Harvey lynching revived the old canards about the ineffectiveness of the judicial system and the inefficiency of law enforcement. The judicial process may have been "slow and uncertain," but to argue that "full justice" was "the exception rather than the rule" was incorrect. And for the

Deseret News to justify the lynching because "just as likely as not the assassin would never be brought to justice" was irresponsible journalism. Still, many Salt Lakers were exasperated by the seemingly ineffectual court system and especially by the numerous delays in the then ongoing murder trial of Fred Hopt (also known as Welcome), and cries of "Now for Welcome" were heard at the Harvey lynching.[68] Nonetheless, it is doubtful that any of the lynchers acted because of the belief that an illegal execution was the only way to see justice served. Similarly, it may have been advisable, as the *Herald* argued, to "increase if not double" the city's police force, but there is no historical correlation between the size of the constabulary and the imposition of lynch law.[69] Inadequacies in the enforcement and administration of the law, whether real or imagined, are ultimately excuses for, not causes of, lawlessness.

Given the concerted effort to justify the lynching, it is not surprising that the affair was eventually interpreted as a positive development. At least the *Herald* on August 28 took solace in that the "bloody doings" of the past week were "full of hints, suggestions and instructions to everybody." The "instructions" were to the courts as the lynchers presumably served notice to the legal establishment that the judicial process, which had "limped, halted and stumbled," had better be "spurred up to a speedier gait and a more certain footing" lest swift and sure extralegal executions become commonplace. The "hints" were to the "lawless elements in the community" of the fate that awaited them should they persist in antisocial behavior. The "suggestions" were to the people at large—that lynchings have no place in a law-abiding community. "There has been a carnival of crime," the editorial concluded: "The lessons have all been taught, and now let us heed them, and by a return to the past conduct, ways and methods, wipe out whatever stain the past few days have put on the fair fame of Utah."

Ultimately, the Harvey lynching was viewed as an aberration. Despite the murderous mockery of justice, Salt Lakers still regarded themselves as law-abiding residents of a city whose peaceful reputation "stood out in striking contrast" with the "wild, semi-barbarous" towns of the West.[70] On September 2 the *Herald* pronounced the affair over: "A whole week gone and no lynching to record. Utah has suddenly returned to her good and quiet ways, as she departed from them." Though not soon forgotten, the agitation caused by the murder-lynching had passed and Salt Lakers returned to business as usual.[71]

The public debate ground to a halt as Salt Lakers determined to put the sorry episode behind them. The lynching had disgraced the city, and to pursue an investigation would only bring further embarrassment to prominent citizens, heighten religious tensions, and prolong the collective guilt of the community. After all, as contemporary historian Edward Tullidge observed, the "profound regret" that gripped the town after the lynching was not due to "condemnation of the public wrath" but rather to the fact that "a lynch law precedent had occurred in the history of our city."[72]

The detailed postmortem of the lynching conducted by the press revealed the basic causes of the mob execution—the desire for vengeance, a spirit of vigilantism, and the impetus of mob psychology. Given the circumstances of Andrew Burt's assassination, the imposition of lynch law by a maddened throng is understandable if inexcusable.

The public execution of Sam Joe Harvey was a tragedy not because a Salt Lake City mob lynched a murderer but because so many good people behaved so badly. The lynchers deserve primary condemnation for premeditated murder, but censure is also due the police for dereliction of duty, the city magistrates for refusing to investigate the lynching and bring the executioners to trial, and the press for excusing the lynchers and raising a religious red herring that diverted attention from the crime. However, the greatest blame belongs to the citizens of Salt Lake City who either acted as accomplices to the lynching or acquiesced in the cover-up. A thin line separates civility from savagery, and whenever normally decent, law-abiding people decline the obligations of citizenship and dictates of conscience, the line becomes dangerously close to being obliterated.

Still, the tragic affair taught Salt Lake residents an important lesson. Calls for a lynching would be raised sporadically into the twentieth century, but never again would even the semblance of a lynch mob form in the city. The visit from Judge Lynch, bloody and brutal, had made manifest the sobering truth that the hallmark of a civilized society is the rule of law, not justice.

NOTES

1. Vigilantism dates from the colonial period of American history; Lynch Law, which originally referred to the flogging of Virginia loyalists during the Revolution by Judge Charles Lynch, came to denote illegal hanging instead of corporal punishment by the middle of the nineteenth century. General studies of lynching and vigilantism include Richard Maxwell Brown, *Strains of Violence: Historical Studies of American Violence and Vigilantism* (New York: Oxford University Press, 1975); Robert Brent Toplin, *Unchallenged Violence: An American Ordeal* (Westport, Conn.: Greenwood Press, 1975); Thomas F. Parker, ed., *Violence in the United States*, 2 vols. (New York: Facts on File, 1974); Hugh Davis Graham and Ted Robert Gurr, eds., *Violence in America: Historical and Comparative Perspectives* (Washington, D.C.: U.S. Government Printing Office, 1969); John W. Caughey, *Their Majesties the Mob* (Chicago: University of Chicago Press, 1960); Wayne Gard, *Frontier Justice* (Norman: University of Oklahoma Press, 1949); and Hubert Howe Bancroft, *Popular Tribunals*, 2 vols (San Francisco: A. L. Bancroft, 1887). Specialized studies of lynching include Jessie Daniel Ames, *The Changing Character of Lynching* (Atlanta: Commission on Interracial Cooperation, 1942); Arthur F. Raper, *The Tragedy of Lynching* (Chapel Hill: University of North Carolina Press, 1933); James Harmon Chadbourn, *Lynching and the Law* (Chapel Hill: University of North Carolina Press, 1933); Walter White, *Rope & Faggot: A Biography of Judge Lynch* (New York: Alfred A. Knopf, 1929); National Association for the Advancement of Colored People, *Thirty Years of Lynching in the United States, 1889-1918* (New York: NAACP, 1919); and James Elbert Cutler, *Lynch-Law: An Investigation into the History of Lynching in the United States* (New York: Longmans, Green and Co., 1905).

2. Cutler, *Lynch-Law*, 179-80. Lynchings in Arkansas (200) and Louisiana (285) have been excluded because those "trans-Mississippi" states are culturally and historically southern instead of western. Figures for Iowa (16), Minnesota (6), and Missouri (91) have also been deleted on the grounds that they had passed the "frontier" stage of development by the end of the Civil War. Systematic efforts to record lynching statistics began in 1882; modern studies of lynchings at the local level invariably reveal not only that the figures customarily given for the 1880s and 1890s are low but also that the 1870s produced more lynchings than either of the later two decades.

3. In the intermountain region only Nevada posted fewer lynchings than Utah. Lynching figures for the area for 1882-1903 are as follows: Montana (85), Colorado (64), Wyoming (37), New Mexico (34), Arizona (28), Idaho (19), Nevada (5). Cutler, *Lynch-Law*, 180. Similarly, only Utah and Oregon failed to produce organized vigilantism. Brown, *Strains of Violence*, 101-3 and Appendix 3.

4. The following persons were lynched in Utah Territory:

Three unidentified men at Wasatch Station during the winter of
   1868-69
A man identified only as "a damned nigger" in Uintah, June 29, 1869
Charles A. Benson in Logan, February 18, 1873
Ah Sing in Corrine, April 13, 1874
Thomas Forrest in St. George, October 5, 1880
William H. (Sam Joe) Harvey in Salt Lake City, August 25, 1883
John (Black Jack) Murphy in Park City, August 26, 1883
John Fletcher at Spring Hill Station, August 26(?), 1883
George Segal in Ogden, April 20, 1884
Joseph Fisher in Eureka, July 6, 1886

In addition, William Thorrington was lynched on June 14, 1858, in Carson Valley, then Utah Territory but later part of Nevada; the lynching of Robert Marshall in Price on June 16, 1925, was the last victim claimed by Judge Lynch in Utah.

5. Despite its sensationalism and impact on the community, the Harvey lynching has been largely ignored by historians. Contemporary historians Edward W. Tullidge, *The History of Salt Lake City and Its Founders* (Salt Lake City: Edward W. Tullidge Publisher, 1886), 894-95, and Andrew Jenson, *Church Chronology: A Record of Important Events Connected to the History of the Church of Jesus Christ of Latter-day Saints, and the Territory of Utah* (Salt Lake City: Deseret News, 1886), 108, briefly note the

lynching. Orson F. Whitney, *History of Utah*, 4 vols. (Salt Lake City: George Q. Cannon and Sons, 1892-1904), 3:256, in a paragraph full of inaccuracies, mentions the hanging of "a negro desperado named Joseph Samuels." The *Souvenir History of the Salt Lake City Fire and Police Department* (Salt Lake City: Deseret News Press, 1901), 93, notes the murder of Burt and the hanging of his assassin. References to the lynching in modern histories are contained in Richard D. Poll, ed., *Utah's History* (Provo: Brigham Young University Press, 1978), where Richard O. Ulibarri, in "Utah's Unassimilated Minorities," 634, mentions the lynching of "Sam J. Hariney in Salt Lake City in 1885" (*sic*), and Thomas G. Alexander and James B. Allen, *Mormons and Gentiles: A History of Salt Lake City* (Boulder, Colorado: Pruett Publ. Co., 1984), 119-22, which using information from this article, covers the incident and its aftermath briefly but accurately. Albert F. Phillips incorrectly asserts in a chronicle of capital crimes in Utah that the Harvey hanging was "the first lynching that had occurred in Utah," *Salt Lake Telegram*, March 14, 1926; Jack Thomas describes the murder-lynching in a series on Salt Lake City police martyrs, *Salt Lake Telegram*, November 24, 1933. A concise account marked by literary license is Jerry Springer, "Twenty-five Minute Justice," *True West* 20 (February 1973):44.

6. Information about the nineteenth-century community can be gleaned from Tullidge, *History of Salt Lake City*; Poll, *Utah's History*; and Leonard J. Arrington, *Great Basin Kingdom: An Economic History of the Latter-day Saints, 1830-1900* (Cambridge: Harvard University Press, 1958). See also the profusely illustrated book by John S. McCormick, *Salt Lake City, the Gathering Place: An Illustrated History* (Woodland Hills: Windsor Publications, 1980). Thomas G. Alexander's and James B. Allen's *Mormons and Gentiles: A History of Salt Lake City* (Boulder Colorado: Pruett Press, 1984) appeared after this article was written.

7. For biographical information on Harvey, see the *Salt Lake Daily Herald*, August 26, 1883, and the *Deseret Evening News*, August 27, 1883.

8. For biographical information on Burt, see the *Deseret Evening News*, August 25 and 27, 1883, and the *Salt Lake Daily Herald*, August 26, 1883.

9. *Souvenir History of the Salt Lake City Fire and Police Department*, 85.

10. The account of events pertaining to the Burt murder and Harvey lynching is based upon extensive reports published in the

Deseret Evening News, August 25-27, 1883, the *Salt Lake Daily Herald,* and the *Salt Lake Daily Tribune,* August 26, 1883. To avoid an unnecessary multiplication of footnotes, no citations will be given unless substantive information is found exclusively in one newspaper.

11. *Salt Lake Daily Tribune,* August 26, 1883.

12. *Salt Lake Daily Herald,* August 26, 1883.

13. Ibid.

14. Ibid.

15. Ibid.

16. Newspapers at the time gave a general account of the physical abuse; a more detailed report appeared three years later in the *Salt Lake Daily Tribune,* July 15, 1886. The specifics and severity of the beating are uncertain, but all sources confirm that Harvey was beaten.

17. *Salt Lake Daily Herald,* August 26, 1883.

18. *Salt Lake Daily Tribune,* July 15, 1886.

19. Detailed accounts of the lynching appeared in the *Salt Lake Daily Herald* and *Salt Lake Daily Tribune* on August 26, 1883; the *Deseret Evening News,* not published on Sundays, printed only a general account of the hanging in its August 25, 1883 issue.

20. *Deseret Evening News,* August 25, 1883; *Salt Lake Daily Herald,* August 26, 1883.

21. *Salt Lake Daily Herald,* August 26, 1883.

22. *Salt Lake Daily Tribune,* August 26, 1883.

23. *Salt Lake Daily Herald,* August 26, 1883.

24. *Deseret Evening News,* August 25, 1883.

25. *Salt Lake Daily Herald,* August 26, 1883.

26. *Salt Lake Daily Tribune,* August 26, 1883.

27. Ibid.

28. *Deseret Evening News*, August 25, 1883.

29. In addition to the descriptions of the incident published in the newspapers August 25-26, 1883, see the eyewitness accounts reported in the *Salt Lake Daily Tribune*, September 5, 1883.

30. The official coroner's jury reports were published in the *Salt Lake Daily Tribune*, August 28, 1883. Burial records note simply that Burt was "killed" and that Harvey's death was due to "homicide." As for the location of Harvey's grave, the record states: "Grave obliterated in street." It is likely that he was buried in what is now Center Street near Burt's grave located in Plot A, Section 1, of the Salt Lake City Cemetery. Interment Records, 11552-11553, Sexton's Office, Salt Lake City Cemetery.

31. Council Record, Book 1, pp. 730-32, Salt Lake City Recorder's Office, City and County Building, Salt Lake City (hereafter referred to as Council Record). The Council's resolution was published in the *Salt Lake Daily Herald*, August 27, 1883. Members of the funeral arrangements committee were aldermen Robert Patrick and Alonzo H. Raleigh, councilor Daniel H. Wells, police officers Brigham Y. Hampton and William G. Phillips, and townsmen George M. Ottinger and John R. Winder.

32. Jennings announced that it would be "a gratification to himself and the members of the City Council" if businesses would close during the funeral. *Deseret Evening News*, August 27, 1883.

33. The program of service and order of procession appeared in the *Deseret Evening News*, August 27, 1883, and the *Salt Lake Daily Herald*, August 28, 1883. The *Deseret Evening News*, August 28, 1883, devoted almost a full page to the funeral. Other than noting that services for Burt were scheduled for the day, the *Salt Lake Daily Tribune*, August 28, 1883, ignored the funeral. Burt's grave is marked by a monument "erected by friends of the deceased" and bearing the inscription: "While in the discharge of his duty as City Marshall [sic] he met death at the hands of a desperado."

34. Mary Mount Tanner Diary, August 25, 1883, John Tanner Papers, Western Americana Division, J. Willard Marriott Library, University of Utah, Salt Lake City.

35. *Ogden Daily Herald,* August 25-26, 1883. Six months later, the *Herald* was obliged to report a lynching in its own community.

See Larry R. Gerlach, "Ogden's 'Horrible Tragedy': The Lynching of George Segal," *Utah Historical Quarterly* 49 (Spring 1981):157-72.

36. For the Murphy lynching, see the *Deseret Evening News*, August 27, 1883; the *Park Mining Record*, August 25, September 1 and 8, 1883; the *Salt Lake Daily Herald*, August 25 and 28, 1883; and the *Salt Lake Daily Tribune*, August 28, 1883. See also William M. McPhee, *The Trail of the Leprechaun: Early History of a Utah Mining Camp* (Hicksville, N.Y.: Exposition Press, 1977), 57-59, 134-35.

37. *Deseret Evening News*, August 27, 1883; *Salt Lake Daily Herald*, August 28, 1883.

38. Allegedly, Burt had a dream in the night two or three days before his murder that he related to several people including Charles Wilcken. According to someone who reportedly heard the story firsthand, Burt related his vision as follows:

> I thought there was a disturbance somewhere on the street, and went out to see about it. On the way to Main Street, Charlie Wilcken caught up with me and went along. We went to Cunnington's corner [2nd and Main] when a big black nigger came at me to shoot me. Charlie made a jump to save me but didn't succeed, and when the fellow shot a sensation passed through me, giving me a shock which woke me up.

Deseret Evening News, August 27, 1883. It should be noted that "premonitions" of tragedies are staples of Mormon folklore. See, for example, the extensive file of "Premonitions" in the Mormon Collection, Austin Fife Folklore Archive, Utah State University, Logan, Utah.

39. Council Record, Book 1, 734-35.

40. Ibid., 739-40.

41. Ibid., 741, 745-46, 758-59. Other than general references to "family," neither the Council nor the press made specific mention of wife and children. The reason, apparently, is that Andrew Burt was a polygamist married to Ann Olivia Box (1832-1920) and to Mary Ann Lucas (1849-1940). Given the tensions surrounding the antipolygamy crusade of the times, it is understandable that no mention was made of the fact that Burt, a public official, was a polygamist.

42. *Deseret Evening News*, September 7, 1883.

43. At least 4,743 persons were lynched in the United States from 1882 to 1968; 3,445 of them were black. The most comprehensive tabulation of lynchings is the typescript "Lynching Records" maintained by the librarians of the Tuskegee Institute, Tuskegee, Alabama.

44. Five of the nine lynching victims in Utah whose race is known are nonwhite—three blacks, one Chinese, and one Japanese. All those claimed by Judge Lynch in Utah were either itinerants or newcomers except for Charles Benson, the incorrigible "black sheep" of a prominent Logan family.

45. Other than descriptive references such as the "colored assassin" and the "negro assailant," the press took no particular notice of Harvey's race and printed none of the racial slurs and epithets that usually accompanied a racially motivated lynching. The negative racial attitudes so prevalent in White America at the time were generally evident in Utah, but with only eighty-six black residents, racism in Salt Lake City was more rhetorical than pragmatic. See Ronald G. Coleman, "A History of Blacks in Utah, 1825-1910" (Ph.D. diss., University of Utah, 1980).

46. Chronic tension between the Mormon defenders of Zion and the non-Mormon challengers of the Kingdom increased dramatically in the 1870s with the coming of the railroads, the expansion of metal mining, and the onset of a federal antipolygamy crusade. Religious rivalry reached new heights in 1882 with the passage of the Edmunds bill, which made unlawful cohabitation a felony, barred professing as well as practicing polygamists from voting or holding public office, and created a federal Utah Commission to supervise territorial elections. Paranoia pervaded both Mormon and non-Mormon camps, secular issues routinely became sectarian squabbles as the fires of bigotry were fanned by a local press given to slander, hyperbole, and religious partisanship. For tensions between Mormons and non-Mormons, see Arrington, *Great Basin Kingdom*; Gustive O. Larson, *The "Americanization" of Utah for Statehood* (San Marino, Calif: Henry E. Huntington Library, 1971); and Robert J. Dwyer, *The Gentile Comes to Utah: A Study in Religious and Social Conflict, 1862-1890* (Washington, D.C.: Catholic University of America Press, 1941). For territorial journalism, see J. Cecil Alter, *Early Utah Journalism: A Half Century of Forensic Warfare. . . .* (Salt Lake City, Utah State Historical Society, 1938); Wendell O. Ashton, *Voice in the West: Biography of a Pioneer Newspaper* (New York: Duell, Sloan & Pearce, 1950); O. N. Malmquist, *The Salt Lake Tribune, the First*

100 Years (Salt Lake City: Utah State Historical Society, 1971); and Monte B. McLaws, *Spokesman for the Kingdom: Early Mormon Journalism and the Deseret News, 1830-1898* (Provo: Brigham Young University Press, 1977).

47. *Deseret Evening News*, August 28, 1883.

48. *Salt Lake Daily Herald*, August 28, 1883. The *Herald* published a strongly worded denunciation of the lynching on August 26, 1883, before the *Tribune's* allegations were known.

49. *Salt Lake Daily Tribune*, August 29, 31, 1883.

50. Ibid., August 28-31, 1883.

51. *Deseret Evening News*, August 28, 1883.

52. Council Record, Book 1, 730. On only two occasions, the lynchings of Joseph Fisher in 1886 and Robert Marshall in 1925, was legal action taken against those responsible for an illegal execution.

53. *Deseret Evening News*, August 27, 1883; *Salt Lake Daily Herald*, August 28, 1883.

54. *Salt Lake Daily Herald*, August 26, 1883.

55. *Deseret Evening News*, August 27, 1883. Salt Lakers were not alone in approving of the lynching. A resident of Provo noted that after the local paper, the *Enquirer*, reported the "bad news" of Burt's death and the "good news" of the lynching, he did not hear "one single person condemn the doings of the Salt Lake 'mob' as the coroner's jury called it." *Salt Lake Daily Herald*, August 30, 1883.

56. *Salt Lake Daily Herald*, August 26, 1883.

57. *Deseret Evening News*, August 25, 27, 1883.

58. *Salt Lake Daily Tribune*, August 26, 1883.

59. *Salt Lake Daily Herald*, August 26, 1883.

60. *Deseret Evening News*, September 3, 1883.

61. *Salt Lake Daily Herald*, August 28, 1883.

62. Ibid., August 26, 28, 1883.

63. *Deseret Evening News*, August 27, 1883.

64. *Salt Lake Daily Herald*, August 28, 1883.

65. The appeal to popular sovereignty as grounds for actual or threatened violence against Mormons in New York, Ohio, Missouri, and Illinois reached its zenith in the acquittal of the men accused of murdering Church leader Joseph Smith: "For the Mormons, the Carthage trial epitomized the deficiencies of popular sovereignty as higher law." Dallin H. Oaks and Marvin S. Hill, *Carthage Conspiracy: The Trial of the Accused Assassins of Joseph Smith* (Urbana: University of Illinois Press, 1975), 214.

66. *Salt Lake Daily Herald*, August 26, 28, 1883.

67. Ibid., August 26, 1883.

68. *Deseret Evening News*, August 27, 1883. See also Kimberly Stuckenschneider Hanger, "The Frederick Hopt Murder Case: A Darker Side of Utah Territory," Senior Thesis, Department of History: University of Utah, 1983.

69. *Salt Lake Daily Herald*, August 29, 1883.

70. *Deseret Evening News*, August 27, 1883; *Salt Lake Daily Herald*, August 26, 28, 1883.

71. The bitterness generated by the newspaper controversy was so great that the Salt Lake press rehashed the Harvey lynching three years later following the lynching of Joseph Fisher in Eureka. See *Salt Lake Daily Tribune*, July 10, 13, 15 and 17, 1886; *Salt Lake Daily Herald*, July 11 and 14, 1886.

72. Tullidge, *History of Salt Lake City*, 894.